Psychol... Level Year 1 and AS

The Mini Companion

Mike Cardwell • Rosalind Geillis
Alison Wadeley

OXFORD
UNIVERSITY PRESS

OXFORD
UNIVERSITY PRESS

Great Clarendon Street, Oxford, OX2 6DP, United Kingdom

Oxford University Press is a department of the University of Oxford.
It furthers the University's objective of excellence in research, scholarship,
and education by publishing worldwide. Oxford is a registered trade mark of
Oxford University Press in the UK and in certain other countries

British Library Cataloguing in Publication Data
Data available

978-0-19-837528-9

1 3 5 7 9 10 8 6 4 2

Paper used in the production of this book is a natural, recyclable product
made from wood grown in sustainable forests.
The manufacturing process conforms to the environmental regulations of the
country of origin.

Printed in Great Britain by Bell and Bain Ltd., Glasgow

Acknowledgements

Editorial management and page layout: GreenGate Publishing Services
Cover photographer: Chris Cardwell
Cover image of cat: courtesy of Chris Cardwell

Links to third party websites are provided by Oxford in good faith and for
information only. Oxford disclaims any responsibility for the materials
contained in any third party website referenced in this work.

MIX
Paper from
responsible sources
FSC® C007785
www.fsc.org

Contents

Introduction

About this book

This *'Mini' Companion* is an abridged version of our main Year 1 and AS book – *Psychology A Level Year 1 and AS: The Complete Companion Student Book*. Like the main textbook, the contents of *this* book are also mapped exactly onto the AQA AS and A Level (Year 1) specifications. However, we have stripped down the content to leave only the essential material necessary for your exam. This *Mini Companion* is not meant to replace the main book, but to give you an additional resource that you can carry around with you – ideal for revision on the go!

This book is divided into seven chapters that match the topics in the specification. As with the main textbook, we have integrated Year 1 A Level and AS material into the same text. There are two main differences between the Year 1 A Level and AS material. First, A Level students need some extra evaluative content because their extending writing questions are worth 16 marks (whereas the AS equivalent is 12 marks). Second, some topics are for A Level only; we have indicated on the page where this is the case. You will be guided through the book so you know which material is appropriate for AS and which is only for A Level.

Most topics are covered on one page, the equivalent to a double page spread in the main textbook. For example, the pages below show coverage of two topics from developmental psychology – attachment.

FOURTH EDITION

for AQA

Psychology A Level Year 1 and AS

The Complete Companion Student Book

Mike Cardwell • Cara Flanagan   OXFORD

The **AO1** descriptive content for each topic is distilled down into just 200 words or so.

Key terms for each topic are explained for greater understanding.

Each page contains an **AO2** 'Apply it' feature in the form of a scenario, question and answer.

The **AO3** evaluative content is in the form of five (or occasionally six) points, each of the appropriate depth for 'effective' exam answers.

For AS students, three of these **AO3** evaluative points should be enough to answer a 12-mark extended writing question.

Our *Mini Companion* cat, **BB**, makes an appearance at various places in the book. She is a Bengal cross, and lives in Bristol.

On the opening page of each chapter we have included the **specification** entry for that section, so you can keep an eye on what you have to know.

We have used that specification material to construct **revision lists** that you can complete as you move from a basic understanding of a topic (column 1) to complete mastery of it (column 3).

Research methods topics are broken down into easy to understand segments.

The AO2 '**Apply it**' feature that appears on research methods pages gives you the opportunity to practice exam type questions relating to each topic.

And we provide **answers** to these questions!

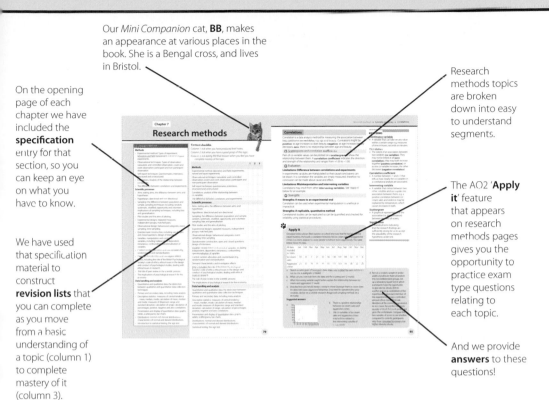

If a topic is only for Year 1 A Level, the banner at the top of the page will be striped (as here) rather than the solid banner at the top of spreads that are common to AS and Year 1 A Level. A Level material will also be marked **A LEVEL ONLY ZONE.**

We have included two extra **AO3** evaluative points for A Level students, as five points would be more appropriate for a 16-mark extended writing question.

The examinations

 The AS exams

How many papers? There are two AS papers, each lasting one-and-a-half hours.

What sort of questions? A mixture of multiple choice, short answer and extended writing questions. In both papers, all the questions will be compulsory.

How many marks? The total mark for each paper will be 72 marks.

Assessment objectives: All three sections assess AO1 (description), AO2 (application) and AO3 (evaluation).

Paper 1 (7181/1)

Introductory topics in psychology

This exam paper is divided into three sections, each worth 24 marks.

Section A Social psychology: Social Influence

Section B Cognitive psychology: Memory

Section C Developmental psychology: Attachment

Weighting of objectives: Paper 1 has approximate weightings of the different objectives of AO1 (40%), AO2 (25%) and AO3 (35%), although these can vary slightly.

Paper 2 (7181/2)

Psychology in context

This exam paper is divided into three sections, each worth 24 marks.

Section A Approaches in psychology

Section B Psychopathology

Section C Research methods

Weighting of objectives: Paper 2 has approximate weightings of the different objectives of AO1 (30%), AO2 (40%) and AO3 (30%), although these can vary slightly.

 The A Level exam

How many papers? There are three A Level papers, each lasting two hours. Two of these papers are based on the content in this book. The third (Issues and options in psychology) will be covered in our A Level Year 2 Mini Companion. There are some aspects of Paper 2 (i.e. selected topics in Research Methods) that will also be covered in the Year 2 book.

What sort of questions? A mixture of multiple choice, short answer and extended writing questions. In Paper 1 and Paper 2, all the questions will be compulsory.

How many marks? The total mark for each paper will be 96 marks.

Assessment objectives: All three sections assess AO1 (description), AO2 (application) and AO3 (evaluation).

What do these contribute to the overall A Level? Paper 1 and Paper 2 (covered in this book) are each worth 33.3% of your overall A Level mark. The remaining 33.3% are for Paper 3 (covered in the Year 2 book).

Paper 1 (7182/1)

Introductory topics in psychology

This exam paper is divided into four sections, each worth 24 marks.

Section A Social psychology: Social Influence

Section B Cognitive psychology: Memory

Section C Developmental psychology: Attachment

Section D Psychopathology

Weighting of objectives: Paper 1 has approximate weightings of the different objectives of AO1 (35%), AO2 (25%) and AO3 (40%), although these can vary slightly.

Paper 2 (7182/2)

Psychology in context

This exam paper is divided into three sections, Approaches and Biopsychology are each worth 24 marks and Research Methods is worth 48 marks.

Section A Approaches in psychology

Section B Biopsychology

Section C Research methods

Weighting of objectives: Paper 2 has approximate weightings of the different objectives of AO1 (25%), AO2 (50%) and AO3 (25%), although these can vary slightly.

Improving exam performance

◯ Practical considerations

What does the question require? Questions make very specific requests, and examiners have marks available only for these specific requirements. Time spent reading questions carefully is time well spent, and it will stop you setting off on an answer that is not actually dealing with the question set.

Time management is vital. Many students waste time by writing too much for questions that don't require it, and waste marks by not writing enough for questions that do. The marks that are available for each question (as well as the space available) inform you about how much you should write.

Plan your answers. One way of increasing your effectiveness on extended writing questions is to plan your answer. For example, a straightforward 'Outline and evaluate …' question would have 6 marks allocated for AO1 and 6 (10 for A Level) marks for AO3. If we applied the mathematical proportions assigned to AO1 and AO3 content to the number of words in a good essay (about 360 words or 480 words for A Level), then we have 180 words of AO1 and 180 words (300 for A Level) of AO3. This amounts to six AO1 points @ 30 words each and 3 AO3 points (5 for A Level) @ 60 words each.

◯ AO1 Description

Questions linked to this objective will be testing your ability to identify, outline, describe or explain (although this last term may also imply some evaluation). They are a chance to show off your knowledge of a particular area, with the different terms usually being associated with different numbers of marks available. Hence, 'Identify' tends to be used for 1 mark questions, 'Outline' and 'Explain' for slightly higher tariff questions and 'Describe' for the highest tariff AO1 questions (usually 6 marks). This is not a hard and fast rule, but it helps to recognise what you are being asked to do and to respond accordingly.

Higher AO1 marks tend to be given for more detailed answers. There are a number of ways you can add detail to your answer, for example:

- **Add some more information** about the concept, theory, study, etc. This means including some of the finer details rather than giving a fairly superficial representation of the content.
- **Giving an example** of the concept, or a study that illustrates some aspect of the theory.

For example, in response to the question 'Outline one explanation of why people obey authority'.

People are more likely to obey when they are in the agentic state, i.e. acting as an 'agent' for somebody in authority (not very detailed). Ordinarily people are in an autonomous state and take responsibility for their own actions but when in an agentic state they believe responsibility for anything they do lies with the authority figure (more information). For example, a soldier ordered to kill would not feel the guilt they would feel if they acted in the autonomous state, therefore would be more likely to obey (an appropriate example).

◯ AO2 Application

AO2 questions assess your ability to *apply* your knowledge in some way. This is your chance to show evidence of your knowledge of a particular topic but within a specific scenario, i.e. *in context* rather than at a theoretical level. These are particularly prominent on Paper 2, where the majority of the marks awarded on 'Research methods' are for AO2 because of the need for answers to be within the specific context of the stimulus material. Elsewhere these questions may assess your ability to explain a particular behaviour, your maths or research methods skills in the context of a particular topic or your ability to incorporate some specific stimulus material into your response to an extended writing question. There are two things you *must* do in an application question:

- **Show evidence of the underlying psychology** relevant to the stimulus material (i.e. what theory, explanation or study might explain the behaviour outlined in the stimulus material).
- **Link this explicitly and effectively** to the context of the stimulus material.

◯ AO3 Evaluation

Although AO3 is labelled as 'evaluation', this is not restricted to pointing out the limitations of a particular theory, explanation or study. It can include *strengths* (e.g. showing research support for something or that it applies across different cultures) and *limitations* (e.g. pointing out that there are gender differences which reduces its universal application or that it lacks research support). AO3 can also include *applications* (which show its value through its application in therapy, more general application or just in terms of increasing our understanding of an area). We have included a variety of different types of AO3 in this book. Effective evaluation involves a lot more than just identifying a critical point, it means *doing something* with that critical point. For example, the PEEL technique has four stages:

(P) Point – state the critical point

(E) Evidence – what is the evidence for this point?

(E) Elaboration – adding detail to the critical point being made or giving an example.

(L) Link back – e.g. showing what this critical point means for whatever is being evaluated.

For example:

*Many of Milgram's participants didn't believe the shocks were real (**P**). Despite the fact the learner cried in pain, the experimenter in Milgram's studies remained unconcerned (**E**). This might have led to participants not believing any real harm would come to the learner (**E**). This means that the research may lack internal validity (**L**).*

Types of exam question

Question type	Example	Advice
Simple selection/ recognition	Which **two** of the following are types of conformity? **A** Agentic state **B** Compliance **C** Group size; **D** Identification **E** Unanimity. *(2 marks)*	Questions such as these should be straightforward enough, so the trick is making sure you have selected the right answer to gain maximum marks. If you aren't sure which answer is the right one, try crossing through those that are obviously wrong, thus narrowing down your options.
Description questions (Describe, Outline, Identify, Name)	Name **three** stages in the development of attachments identified by Schaffer. *(3 marks)* Identify and outline **two** techniques that may be used in a cognitive interview. *(4 marks)* Outline the fight or flight response, including the role of adrenaline. *(6 marks)*	These AO1 description questions can come in lots of different forms, but will never be worth more than 6 marks for any one part of a question. To judge how much to write in response to a question, simply look at the number of marks available, allow about 25 words per mark. If the sole command word is 'Name' or 'Identify', there is no need to develop a 25-word per mark response, simply identifying or naming is enough.
Differences/Distinguish between	Distinguish between obsessions and compulsions. *(2 marks)* Identify **two** differences between insecure-resistant and insecure-avoidant attachment. *(2 marks)*	Students often ignore the instruction to 'distinguish between' or 'identify differences' and simply outline the two terms or concepts named in the question. This is not what is required, and would not gain credit. The word 'whereas' is a good linking word to illustrate a difference between two things.
Applying knowledge	Two students were having the following conversation: **Amy:** It's really embarrassing. I keep forgetting my art teacher's new married name and still call her Miss Short instead. I think she is getting really annoyed with me. **Dylan:** I am going to have the opposite problem I think. I really can't remember the name of my maths teacher and she is due back from maternity leave next week. My mind goes blank and I can only remember the name of the teacher that has been covering for her. Using your knowledge of interference as an explanation of forgetting, explain why Amy and Dylan cannot easily recall their teachers' names. *(4 marks)*	In these (AO2) questions, you will be provided with a scenario (the question 'stem') and asked to use your psychological knowledge to provide an informed answer. You must make sure that your answer contains not only appropriate psychological **content**, but that this is set explicitly within the **context** outlined in the question stem. In the first example on the left, some students would ignore the question stem and simply provide a description of insights from interference theory. Other students might ignore the underlying psychology completely and simply engage with the material in the stem in some other way. Neither approach is appropriate, and would result in a disappointingly low mark. We have included a number of 'Apply your knowledge' features throughout the book so you can practise your skills in this area. The scenarios in these features tend to be lengthier than in actual exam questions, but the skill in answering them is the same.
Research methods questions	You will be given a description of a study and then a number of short questions such as: (i) Write a suitable hypothesis for this study. *(3 marks)* (ii) Identify the experimental design used in this study and outline one advantage of this experimental design. *(3 marks)* (iii) Name a measure of dispersion the psychologist could use. *(1 mark)* (iii) At the end of the study the psychologist debriefed each participant. Write a debriefing that the psychologist could read out to the participants in Condition A. *(6 marks)*	Most research methods questions are set within the context of a hypothetical research study. This means that your answers must also be set within the context of that study. If you don't set your answers within the specific context of the study, you cannot receive full marks. Most research methods questions have a fairly low tariff (i.e. 1, 2 or 3 marks), although, as with the last question, they can be worth as much as 6 marks. We have included a number of sample questions in the research methods chapter. The more you practise these, the better you will become at them, and with mastery comes increased confidence.

Question type	Example	Advice
Maths questions	Calculate the mean time taken for the cat to escape from the puzzle box. Show your calculations. *(2 marks)* ▼ *Table 1: The median accuracy score for the standard interview and the cognitive interview.* Sketch an appropriate graphical display to show the median accuracy scores in Table 1. *(6 marks)*	'Maths' questions can appear anywhere on the paper, and can assess your ability to carry out simple calculations, construct graphs and interpret data. For example, in the first question, a correct answer *and* appropriate working are necessary for maximum marks. Six marks may seem a lot for the second question, but 1 mark is given for each of six aspects of the requested graph, e.g. displaying the data as a bar chart, correct plotting of the bars, labeling axes correctly, having an informative title etc.
Evaluation questions	Briefly evaluate learning theory as an explanation of attachment. *(4 marks)* Explain **one** strength and **one** limitation of the cognitive approach in psychology. *(6 marks)* Discuss **two** limitations of the biological approach in psychology. *(6 marks)*	Evaluation can be 'general' as in the first question on the left, or specific as in the second. For the latter question, marks will only be given for that specific content. Miss part of it out and you miss out on marks; put more than one strength or limitation and it won't be creditworthy. You must elaborate your evaluative points for maximum marks.
Mixed description and evaluation questions	Briefly outline and evaluate the authoritarian personality as an explanation of obedience to authority. *(4 marks)* Briefly outline and evaluate **one** explanation for forgetting. *(6 marks)*	The command words (e.g. outline, evaluate) will tell you that description *and* evaluation are required. As a rule of thumb, in questions like these you should divide your AO1 and AO3 content equally.
Extended writing questions	Describe and evaluate **two** studies of social influence. *(12 marks AS/16 marks A Level)* Describe and evaluate the working memory model of memory. *(12 marks AS/16 marks A Level)*	As a rough guide, you should write 30 words per mark so for a 12-mark answer, 360 words would be appropriate and 480 words for a 16-mark answer. Three well-developed AO3 points are usually sufficient for a 12-mark question, and five for a 16-mark answer.
Extended writing questions with specific instructions	Discuss Bowlby's maternal deprivation theory. Refer to evidence in your answer. *(12 marks AS/16 marks A Level)* Matt is dismissive of Charlie's choice of music because Charlie just seems to download the same tracks as all his friends because he doesn't want to be the odd one out when it comes to musical taste. Charlie reminds Matt that when they went travelling in Italy last summer Matt had suggested they should have their train tickets stamped in a yellow machine because everyone else was doing it before boarding the train. Discuss **two** explanations for conformity. Refer to Matt and Charlie in your answer. *(12 marks AS/16 marks A Level)*	Some extended writing questions have an extra specific instruction, as in the two examples on the left. The first simply asks you to include evidence (i.e. research evidence as AO3) in your answer. You might well have been going to do this anyway, but now it is required. It doesn't mean that all your AO3 has to be 'evidence', but perhaps a couple of research studies that either support or challenge Bowlby's theory would suffice. The second example includes an AO2 (application) component (i.e. explaining Matt and Charlie's specific types of conformity). For a 12-mark question, 2 of the marks would be allocated to AO2, in a 16-mark question 4 marks would be allocated to AO2.

Table 1: The median accuracy score for the standard interview and the cognitive interview.

	Standard interview	Cognitive interview
Median	10	15

The way your exams are marked

Questions and mark schemes

Examiners first read through your answer, noting down your performance on the different qualities being assessed. They then apply the mark scheme by comparing what you have written with the written descriptors of the different levels in the mark scheme.

To arrive at a mark, the examiner will start at the lowest mark band to see if the answer meets or exceeds the descriptor for that band. If it does, they move up to the next level, decide if it meets or exceeds the criteria for this level, and so on, until they find a level that fits your answer in terms of the different qualities being assessed. This is not always as easy as it sounds as some criteria for the level may be present and some absent, so an examiner looks for the 'best fit' between an answer and a descriptor level. For example, in response to a 3-mark or 6-mark question, if an answer is mostly band 2 but has some characteristics of a band 3 answer, then it would receive a mark near the top of band 2. Likewise, if an answer is mostly band 2 but had some characteristics of a band 1 answer, then it would receive a mark nearer to the bottom of band 2.

AO1 Description

The table below represents how AQA distinguish between the different levels for a 3-mark or 6-mark question.

Description questions (AO1: 3-mark or 6-mark questions)					
Level	3-mark question	6-mark question	Knowledge	Organisation	Specialist terminology
3	3	5–6	Generally accurate and generally well detailed	Clear and coherent	Used effectively
2	2	3–4	Evident with some inaccuracies	Mostly clear and organised	Some appropriate use
1	1	1–2	Limited and lacks detail	Lacks clarity and organisation	Either absent or used inappropriately
	0	0	No relevant content		

Knowledge You would be expected to be accurate in a high-level answer. However, the requirement is only for you to be 'generally accurate'. Any inaccuracies should be relatively minor. What about names and dates? Well, they serve the function of adding detail to an answer, but are not necessary for an *accurate* answer.

Organisation Next, an examiner would assess whether your answer flows and whether your arguments are clear and presented in a logical manner. This is where planning pays off as you can impose a structure to your answer before you start writing. This is always more effective than just sticking stuff down as it occurs to you!

Specialist terminology Finally, they assess your use of the correct psychological terms (giving evidence that you have actually understood what you have read or been taught) rather than presenting material in lay terms.

AO2 Application

The table below represents how AQA distinguish between the different levels for 2-mark or 4-mark AO2 questions (the most common).

Application questions (AO2: 2-mark and 4-mark questions)						
Level	2-mark question	4-mark question	Knowledge	Application	Organisation	Specialist terminology
2	2	3–4	Knowledge of appropriate psychology is clear	Clear and appropriate	Generally coherent	Effective use of terminology
1	1	1–2	Knowledge of appropriate psychology is partial	Inaccurate or missing	Lacks clarity	Either absent or inappropriate
	0	0	No relevant content			

Knowledge All AO2 Application questions assess understanding of a particular concept. This may be a theory, explanation, study, or some other psychological concept. The examiner will be looking for the accuracy of your account of this concept and the appropriate amount of extra detail you add to your answer (this would obviously be less in a 2-mark question).

Application This refers to the 'application of the knowledge' that you have previously described. Is the concept you have chosen 'appropriate', i.e. does it make sense to use this knowledge to explain this particular scenario? How effective is your use of the knowledge, i.e. have you effectively fitted the concept around the scenario?

AO3 Evaluation

The table below represents how AQA distinguish between the different levels for 3-mark or 6-mark AO3 questions.

Evaluation questions (AO3: 3-mark or 6-mark questions)					
Level	3-mark question	6-mark question	Evaluation	Organisation	Specialist terminology
3	3	5–6	Clear and effective	Coherent and well organised	Used effectively
2	2	3–4	Mostly effective	Mostly clear and organised	Used appropriately
1	1	1–2	Lacks detail and/or explanation	Poorly organised	Either absent or used inappropriately
	0	0	No relevant content		

Effective evaluation (AO3) For a mark in level 3, evaluation needs to be *effective*, i.e. examiners will assess whether you have made the most of a critical point. A simple way is to *Identify the point* (e.g. that there is research support), *Justify the point* (e.g. provide the findings that back up your claim), *Elaborate the point* (e.g. linking back to the thing being evaluated).

How many AO3 points? There is no hard and fast rule about this. For a 3-mark question, one elaborated critical point could be enough, although you could also aim for two points with slightly less detail. For a 6-mark question, two elaborated points could be enough, but again you could aim for three points. However, many questions specify how many points they require (e.g. one critical point, or one strength and one limitation), so you need to read each question carefully.

AO2 Extended writing questions

Both AS and A Level papers contain extended writing questions. These allow you to develop a more in depth response to a particular question. They contain a mixture of AO1 and AO3 (and occasionally AO2) skills. These skills are not marked independently in an essay question, but rather the examiner will be looking for the level that best reflects your answer, whilst bearing in mind the relative weighting of the different skills (typically AO3 is more heavily weighted, so is more influential in determining the final mark).

Extended writing questions (12-mark and 16-mark questions)							
Level	12-mark question	16-mark question	Description	Evaluation	Organisation	Specialist terminology	Application
4	10–12	13–16	Accurate and generally well detailed	Thorough and effective	Clear and coherent	Used effectively	Appropriate and links made explicit
3	7–9	9–12	Evident although some occasional inaccuracies	Mostly effective	Mostly clear and organised	Mostly used effectively	Appropriate although links not always explicit
2	4–6	5–8	Mostly descriptive and lacking accuracy in places	Limited effectiveness	Lacks clarity and organisation in places	Used inappropriately on occasions	Only partially appropriate
1	1–3	1–4	Limited and many inaccuracies	Limited, poorly focused or absent	Poorly organised	Either absent or used inappropriately	Limited or absent
	0	0	No relevant content				

Effective revision

Get yourself motivated

People tend to do better when they are highly motivated. We have taught many mature students who all wished they had worked harder at school the first time around. You don't owe success to your teachers or your parents (although they would be delighted), you owe it to the person you will be ten years from now. Think what you would like to be doing in ten years, and what you need to get there, and let that thought prompt you into action now. It is always better to succeed at something you may not need later than to fail at something you will.

Work with your memory

In an exam it is harder to access information learned by rote. When someone feels anxious it is easier for them to recall knowledge they understand well. Just reading or writing out notes may do little to help you create enduring memories or to understand the content. However, if you do something with your knowledge it will increase your understanding and make it more likely that material is accessible when you need it. Psychologists call this 'deep processing' as opposed to the 'shallow processing' that takes place when you read something without really thinking about it. Constructing spider-diagrams or mind-maps of the material, or even explaining it to someone else, involves deep processing and makes material more memorable.

Become multi-sensory

Why stick to using just one of your senses when revising? Visual learners learn best by seeing what they are learning, so make the most of text, diagrams, graphs, etc. By contrast, auditory learners learn best by listening (and talking), taking in material using their sense of hearing. You may associate more with one of these styles than the other, but actually we can make use of both these types of learning styles. As well as reading your notes and looking at pictures and diagrams, try listening to your notes and talking about topics with other people, and even performing some of the material, e.g. by role-playing a study.

Short bursts are best

One of the problems with revision is that you can do too much of it (in one go, that is…). As you probably know all too well, your attention is prone to wander after a relatively short period of time. Research findings vary as to the optimum time to spend revising, but 30–45 minutes at a time appears to be the norm. What should you do when your attention begins to wander? As a rule, the greater the physiological change (i.e. going for a walk rather than surfing the internet), the more refreshed you will be when returning for your next 30–45 minute stint. There is another benefit to having frequent planned breaks – it increases the probability of subsequent recall.

Revisit regularly

Have you ever noticed that if you don't use an icon on your computer for a long time, the cunning little blighter hides it? Your computer seems to take the decision that as you are not using it regularly, it can't be that important, so neatly files it away somewhere. Your brain works in a similar way; knowledge that is not used regularly becomes less immediately accessible. The trick, therefore, is to review what you have learned at regular intervals. Each time you review material, it will take less time, and it will surely pay dividends later on!

Work with a friend

Although friends can be a distraction while you are trying to study, they can also be a very useful revision aid. Working together (what psychologists call 'collaborative learning') can aid understanding and make revision more interesting and more fun. Explaining something to someone else is a useful form of deep processing (see above), and by checking and discussing each other's answers to sample questions, you can practise your 'examiner skills' and therefore your understanding of what to put into an exam answer to earn the most marks.

Chapter 1

Social influence

4.1.1 Social influence

- Types of conformity: internalisation, identification and compliance. Explanations for conformity: informational social influence and normative social influence, and variables affecting conformity including group size, unanimity and task difficulty as investigated by Asch.
- Conformity to social roles as investigated by Zimbardo.
- Explanations for obedience: agentic state and legitimacy of authority, and situational variables affecting obedience including proximity, location and uniform, as investigated by Milgram.
- Dispositional explanation for obedience: the Authoritarian Personality.
- Explanations of resistance to social influence, including social support and locus of control.
- Minority influence including reference to consistency, commitment and flexibility.
- The role of social influence processes in social change.

Key terms (highlight each cell when you can define the term for 3 marks)

Types and explanations for conformity	Conformity to social roles	Explanations for obedience	The authoritarian personality	Resistance to social influence	Minority influence	Social change
Compliance	Social roles	Agentic state	Authoritarian Personality	Externality	Commitment	Social change
Conformity		Legitimate authority	Dispositional	Internality	Consistency	Social norms interventions
Identification		Obedience to authority	F scale	Locus of control	Flexibility	
Informational social influence			Right-wing authoritarianism	Social support	Minority influence	
Internalisation						
Normative social influence						

Content checklist

1. *In each 'describe, apply and evaluate' cell tick when you have produced brief notes.*
2. *Once you feel you have a good grasp of the topic add a second tick to the cell.*
3. *When you feel you have complete mastery of the topic and would be able to answer an exam question without the aid of notes highlight the cell.*

I am able to...	Describe	Apply	Evaluate
Types of conformity and explanations for conformity			
Variables affecting conformity			
Conformity to social roles			
Situational variables affecting obedience			
Explanations for obedience			
A dispositional explanation: the authoritarian personality			
Resistance to social influence			
Minority influence			
Social influence processes in social change			

KEY TERMS

Conformity
- A form of social influence that results from exposure to the majority position and leads to *compliance*.

Compliance
- Occurs when an individual accepts influence because they hope to achieve a favourable reaction from those around them.

Identification
- The extent to which an individual relates to a model or a group of people and feels that they are similar to them. Identification means that the individual is more likely to imitate the model's or the group's behaviour.

Informational social influence
- A form of influence, which is the result of a desire to be right – looking to others as a way of gaining evidence about reality.

Internalisation
- An individual accepts influence because the content of the attitude or behaviour proposed is consistent with their own value system.

Normative social influence
- An individual conforms with the expectations of the majority in order to gain approval or to avoid social disapproval.

Apply it

Scenario. Andy has just started his first job, working as a picker in a large distribution warehouse. He has a couple of good A Levels and wants to do well so he can progress into management. He watches the other workers carefully, taking his cue from them in how he collects and delivers the goods to the transport bay. At one point in the morning a klaxon sounds and the other workers stop what they are doing and leave the building. Andy follows them without hesitation.

What type of conformity is Andy displaying and why does he conform to the behaviour of the other workers? (4 marks)

Explanation. Andy is displaying internalisation. He conforms to the behaviour of the other workers because of informational social influence. Because he is new to the job, he accepts that the way that the other workers behave must be the appropriate way of carrying out the role of picker. When the klaxon sounds, the situation is ambiguous so he follows the other workers because they are more 'expert' than he is.

Types of conformity and explanations for conformity

Types of conformity

Compliance Individuals agree with the group to gain their approval or avoid their disapproval. This does not result in any change in the person's underlying attitude, only the views and behaviours they express in *public*.

Internalisation Individuals may go along with the group because of an acceptance of their views. This can lead to acceptance of the group's point of view both publicly *and* privately.

Identification In some instances, an individual might accept influence because they want to be associated with another person or group. By adopting the group's attitudes and behaviours, they feel more a part of it.

Explanations of conformity

Normative social influence This is to gain approval and acceptance and to avoid censure and disapproval and so is an example of compliance. People conform to the majority position in public but do not internalise it as it does not carry over into private settings nor endure over time.

Informational social influence This occurs when an individual accepts information from others as evidence about reality, and is more likely if the situation is ambiguous or where others are experts. The individual does not just comply in behaviour alone but also changes their attitude in line with the group position. This is an example of internalisation.

Evaluation

Difficulties in distinguishing between compliance and internalisation
The relationship between compliance and internalisation is complicated by how we define and measure public compliance and private acceptance. For example, it is assumed that a person who publicly agrees with a majority yet disagrees with them in private is demonstrating *compliance*. It is possible that acceptance has occurred in public yet dissipates later in private, because they have forgotten information given by the group or received new information.

Research support for normative influence
Linkenbach and Perkins (2003) found adolescents exposed to the message that the majority of their age peers did not smoke were subsequently less likely to take up smoking. Schultz *et al.* (2008) found that hotel guests exposed to the normative message that 75% of guests reused their towels each day reduced their own towel use by 25%. These studies support the claim that people shape their behaviour out of a desire to fit in with their reference group.

Research support for informational influence
Studies have demonstrated how exposure to other people's beliefs has an important influence on social stereotypes. For example, Wittenbrink and Henley (1996) found that participants exposed to negative information about African Americans (which they were led to believe was the view of the majority) later reported more negative beliefs about a black individual.

Normative influence may not be detected

Nolan *et al.* (2008) investigated whether people detected the influence of social norms on their energy conservation behaviour. People believed that the behaviour of neighbours had the *least* impact on their own energy conservation, yet results showed that it had the *strongest* impact. This suggests that people rely on beliefs about what *should* motivate their behaviour, and so under-detect the impact of normative influence.

Informational influence is moderated by type of task

For some judgements there are clear *non*social criteria for validation, which places this sort of judgement within the realm of *physical* reality. However, other judgements cannot be made using objective criteria because they are more subjective. Here, people rely on *social* consensus. As a result, majorities should exert greater influence on issues of *social* rather than *physical* reality, and this is precisely what research tends to show (Laughlin, 1999).

Variables affecting conformity

 Key study: Asch (1956)

Procedure Participants were seated around a table and asked to look at three lines of different lengths. They took turns to call out which of the three lines they thought was the same length as a 'standard' line with the real participant always answering second to last. On 12 of the 18 trials (the critical trials) confederates were instructed to give the same incorrect answer.

Findings On the 12 critical trials the average conformity rate was 33%. One quarter of the participants did not conform on any of the critical trials, half conformed on 6 or more, and 1 in 20 conformed on all 12. The majority of participants conformed to the incorrect answers because of compliance.

Standard line   Comparison lines

 Variables affecting conformity

Group size There was little conformity when the majority consisted of just one or two confederates. With a majority of three confederates, the proportion of conforming responses rose to about 30%. Further increases in majority size did not increase this level of conformity, indicating that the size of the majority is important but only up to a point.

The unanimity of the majority When the real participant was given the support of another real participant or a confederate who gave the right answers throughout, conformity levels dropped to 5.5%. When a confederate gave a different wrong answer, conformity rates dropped to 9%. Breaking the group's unanimous position was the major factor in conformity reduction.

Difficulty of the task Situational differences (task difficulty) and individual differences (self-efficacy) are both important in determining conformity. With more difficult tasks, the level of conformity increased (Asch, 1956). Lucas *et al.* (2006) found high self-efficacy participants remained more independent than low self-efficacy participants.

 Evaluation

Asch's research may be a 'child of its time'

Perrin and Spencer (1980) repeated Asch's study in the UK but found very little conformity. When they used youths on probation as participants and probation officers as the confederates, they found levels of conformity similar to those of Asch in the 1950s. Conformity is more likely if the perceived costs of *not* conforming are high (as was the case during the McCarthy era in the US).

Problems with determining the effect of group size

A limitation of research in conformity is that studies have used only a limited range of majority sizes. Bond (2005) points out that, apart from Asch's, no study has used a majority size greater than 9, and typically majority sizes have been much smaller. This means that very little is known about the effect of larger majority sizes on conformity levels.

Independent behaviour rather than conformity

In two-thirds of the critical trials, participants did not conform despite being faced with an overwhelming majority expressing a different view. Asch believed that rather than showing human beings to be overly conformist, this demonstrated a tendency for participants to show independent behaviour.

Unconvincing confederates

It would have been difficult for the confederates in Asch's study to act convincingly when giving the wrong answer, which would pose serious problems for the validity of the study. However, Mori and Arai (2010) overcame this problem by using special polarising filters and obtained similar results to Asch. This suggests that the confederates in the original study had acted convincingly.

Cultural differences in conformity

Research suggests that there are important cultural differences in conformity. Smith *et al.*'s (2006) meta-analysis found the average conformity rate for individualist cultures was about 25%, whereas for collectivist cultures it was much higher at 37%. Markus and Kitayama (1991) suggest that a higher level of conformity arises in collectivist cultures because it is viewed more favourably.

Apply it

Scenario. Sabrina has just finished studying conformity and would like to use what she has learned to demonstrate to her younger brother just how easy it is for people to go along with the crowd in group situations. Sabrina worries about him being too impressionable so feels this will be a valuable lesson for him. She wants to use an Asch-type task with a group of four friends who will act as the majority.

Using your knowledge of variables affecting conformity, explain how Sabrina could increase the likelihood of her brother conforming on the task. (4 marks)

Explanation. Asch found that group size influenced conformity, therefore Sabrina's four friends would represent a suitable majority size to make conformity more likely. Unanimity is also important in determining conformity so Sabrina would have to brief her friends that on the trials where they gave the wrong answer, they must all give the same wrong answer. Finally, as Asch found that conformity levels were higher with difficult as opposed to easy tasks, she could make the size discrepancy between the comparison lines and the standard lines smaller, so her brother would be more likely to conform to the judgement of the majority.

KEY TERM

Social roles

- These refer to the behaviours associated with a given social position or status.

Conformity to social roles

 Key study: The Stanford Prison Experiment Haney *et al.* (1973)

Procedure Zimbardo screened male student volunteers and the 24 most stable of these were randomly assigned to play **social roles** – either of 'prisoner' or 'guard'. The prisoners were given a prison uniform and assigned an ID number. Participants allocated the role of guard were given uniforms, clubs, whistles and wore reflective sunglasses. The study was planned to last two weeks.

Findings Over the first few days of the study the guards grew increasingly tyrannical and abusive towards the prisoners. Even when participants were unaware of being watched, they still conformed to their role of prisoner or guard. Five prisoners had to be released early because of their extreme reactions (e.g. crying, rage and acute anxiety). The study was finally terminated after just six days following the intervention of Christina Maslach.

Other research: The BBC Prison Study (Reicher and Haslam, 2006)

Procedure 15 male volunteers were randomly assigned to the role of guard or prisoner in a specially created 'prison'. Prisoners and guards were matched as closely as possible on key personality variables. The study was to run for 8 days.

Findings The key finding of this study was that participants did not conform automatically to their assigned role as had happened in the SPE. Prisoners increasingly identified as a group and challenged the authority of the guards, who had failed to identify with their role. This led to a shift of power within the group.

Evaluation

Conformity to roles is not automatic

Haslam and Reicher (2012) take issue with Zimbardo's conclusion that conformity to role-related scripts was the primary source of guard brutality in the SPE. Although Zimbardo gave his guards no *direct* orders he did give them a general sense of how he expected them to behave. This contradicts Zimbardo's claim that 'behavioural scripts associated with the roles of prisoner and guard were the *sole* source of guidance'.

The problem of demand characteristics

Banuazizi and Movahedi (1975) argued that the behaviour of the guards and prisoners was a response to demand characteristics in the experimental situation. They presented details of the SPE procedure to a large sample of students who had never heard of the study. They correctly guessed the purpose of the study and predicted that guards would act in a hostile, domineering way and prisoners in a passive way.

Were these studies ethical?

Zimbardo's study followed the guidelines of the Stanford University ethics committee that approved it. However, he acknowledged that the study should have been stopped earlier as many of the participants were experiencing distress. Reicher and Haslam's study used the same basic set-up as Zimbardo, but took greater steps to minimise the potential harm to their participants.

The SPE and its relevance to Abu Ghraib

The same conformity to social role effect evidenced in the SPE was also present in the Abu Ghraib military prison. Zimbardo believed the guards who committed the abuses were the victims of situational factors (e.g. lack of training, no accountability to higher authority) that made abuse more likely. Misuse of the power associated with the role of 'guard' led to the abuse of prisoners in both situations.

What did we learn from these studies?

Zimbardo's conclusion was that people descend into tyranny because they conform unthinkingly to the roles that authorities prescribe. Reicher and Haslam reject the claim that group behaviour is necessarily mindless and tyrannical. The results of the BBC prison study suggest that the way in which members of groups behave depends upon the norms and values associated with their specific social identity.

Apply it

Scenario. Rob's dad has just come back from a business meeting in Scotland. He flew there and back and is complaining about how he was treated during the security screening at his local airport. He describes the staff as 'rude' and 'power crazed' and wonders if they only employ rude and aggressive people.

Using your knowledge of research into conformity to social roles, explain why the security staff might be behaving in the way described by Rob's dad. (4 marks)

Explanation. Zimbardo's SPE found that male student volunteers quickly conformed to the role they associated with a prison guard, therefore it is likely that the people employed on security at the airport might have done the same. In the SPE, as they settled into their role the guards grew increasingly tyrannical and abusive towards the prisoners. This is consistent with the 'rude and aggressive' behaviour shown by the security staff as described by Rob's dad.

Situational variables affecting obedience

⬡ Key study: Milgram (1963)

Procedure Milgram recruited 40 participants at a time over a series of conditions, each varying one aspect of the situation to calculate its effect on **obedience to authority**. Participants drew lots (fixed) so a real participant was always the teacher and a confederate the learner. The teacher had to deliver shocks in 15 volt increments (up to 450 volts) whenever the learner made a mistake. In the voice feedback study, the learner was in a separate room.

Findings Prediction by different groups was that very few participants would use more than 150 volts and only 1 in 1,000 would continue to 450 volts. In fact 65% of the participants continued to the maximum shock level (450 volts). All participants continued to at least 300 volts, with only 5 withdrawing at that point.

⬡ Situational factors in obedience

Proximity When the teacher and the learner were seated in the same room (proximity study), the obedience levels dropped to 40% as the teacher could see and hear the consequences of their actions. In *touch proximity* study where there was direct physical contact with the learner, the obedience rate was only 30%. In *experimenter absent* study, the obedience rate dropped further to 21%.

Location Many participants admitted that they would not have given the shocks if the study had not been conducted in a laboratory at Yale University. However, when the study was repeated in a less prestigious location, obedience rate dropped only slightly to 48%.

The power of uniform Uniforms are easily recognisable and convey power and authority, which becomes symbolised in the uniform itself. Bushman (1988) found obedience rates were highest when a female confederate wore a uniform (72%) than when she dressed as a business executive (48%) or a beggar (52%).

⬡ Evaluation

Ethical issues

Baumrind (1964) claimed Milgram had little concern for the well-being of his participants. For example he had deceived his participants into believing it was a study on the effects of punishment on learning. This prevented them from making an informed decision about their participation. The right to withdraw had been compromised by the use of experimental 'prods'.

Internal validity: a lack of realism

Banuazizi and Movahedi (1975) argued the behaviour of the guards and prisoners was a response to demand characteristics in the experimental situation. They presented details of the SPE procedure to a large sample of students who had never heard of the study. They correctly guessed the purpose of the study and predicted that guards would act in a hostile, domineering way and prisoners in a passive way.

Individual differences: the influence of gender

Milgram is criticised for ignoring gender as an individual difference. However, Blass (1999) carried out a meta-analysis of nine studies that had used male *and* female participants. Eight of the nine found no gender differences, suggesting gender is not an important issue in determining obedience.

External validity: the obedience alibi

Mandel (1998) claims that conclusions about the determinants of obedience are not borne out by real-life events. A study of Reserve Police Battalion 101 showed that, despite the presence of many factors shown by Milgram to increase defiance (e.g. physical proximity), men carried out their orders without protest.

Historical validity: would the same thing happen today?

Blass (1999) carried out an analysis of replications of Milgram's study carried out between 1961 and 1985. He found no relationship between the date of publication and the obedience levels obtained. Likewise, Burger (2009) found almost identical levels of obedience to those found by Milgram 46 years earlier, demonstrating that Milgram's study has considerable historical validity.

KEY TERMS

Obedience to authority
- This refers to a type of social influence whereby somebody acts in response to a direct order from a figure with perceived authority.

Apply it

Scenario. Zak's parents have recently moved him from a prestigious public school, where he was a boarder, to a local comprehensive. In his public school, he was taught in small classes of about 7–8 students, so there was much more one-to-one contact with the teacher. In the comprehensive the classes are much larger, with very little one-to-one contact. His former teachers wore academic gowns; his new teachers dress more casually. Zak doesn't feel the same need to do as he is told in the new school, and for the first time in his school life he is in trouble for discipline problems.

Use your knowledge of the situational factors involved in obedience to explain why Zak is less obedient in his new school. (4 marks)

Explanation. In Milgram's 'experimenter absent' study, participants felt able to defy the authority figure. Similarly, in Zak's new school, the authority figure (the teacher) is not in such close proximity as in his previous school, therefore he finds it easier to defy them. Obedience was higher in the more prestigious settings, which explains why Zak is less obedient in his new (less prestigious) school. Research has shown that obedience rates are high when the authority is in uniform. In Zak's former school the teachers wore the 'uniform' of academic robes whereas in his new school the teachers are more casually dressed, so students might be less likely to obey them.

KEY TERMS

Agentic state
- A person sees himself or herself as an agent for carrying out another person's wishes.

Legitimacy of authority
- A person who is perceived to be in a position of social control within a situation.

Apply it

Scenario. Watching the TV news broadcast about UK airstrikes against Syria, Myles wonders what enables a pilot to release missiles and bombs in the knowledge that they cause such devastation to humans. He doesn't think he could obey such an order. Jean, his mother, who teaches psychology, explains about the agentic state and the legitimacy of authority, and why these would contribute to the pilots' decision.

Describe how Jean would explain the pilot's obedience using the agentic state and legitimate authority explanations. (6 marks)

Explanation. Because the pilot has received orders from someone else in the chain of command, he is in an agentic state. His actions are therefore virtually guilt-free, however harmful the consequences. Refusing to follow these commands would mean the pilot would be breaking the commitment that he made when he joined the British Armed Forces, i.e. to do his duty.

For a person to shift to the agentic state they must perceive the orders as coming from a legitimate authority. In this case it would be his commanding officer who fulfils that role and who has given the orders to fire. If an authority figure's commands are of a potentially harmful or destructive form, as would be the case when dropping bombs, then for them to be perceived as legitimate they must occur within some sort of institutional structure (i.e. the British Armed Services).

Explanations for obedience

The agentic state

An individual moves from an autonomous state, where they see themselves as responsible for their own actions into an **agentic state**, where they see themselves as an agent carrying out another person's wishes. As a result, the individual feels *no* responsibility for the actions the authority dictates.

Self-image and the agentic state People may adopt an agentic state in order to maintain a positive self-image. Actions performed under the agentic state are, from the participant's perspective, virtually guilt-free.

Binding factors In order to break off the experiment, the participant must breach the commitment that he made to the experimenter. The participant fears that if they break off they will appear arrogant and rude, which binds them into obedience.

Legitimacy of authority

For a person to shift to the agentic state they must perceive a **legitimate authority**, i.e. someone who is perceived to be in a position of social control within a situation. In Milgram's study, the participant enters the laboratory with an expectation that someone will be in charge. The experimenter, upon first presenting himself, fills this role for them.

The definition of the situation There is a tendency for people to accept definitions of a situation that are provided by a legitimate authority. Although it is the participant himself who performs the action he allows the authority figure to define its meaning.

Legitimate authority requires an institution If an authority figure's commands are of a potentially harmful or destructive form, then for them to be perceived as legitimate they must occur within some kind of institutional structure (e.g. a university, a laboratory).

Evaluation

The agentic state explanation and real-life obedience
The idea of rapidly shifting states fails to explain the very gradual and irreversible transition that Lifton (1986) found in his study of German doctors at Auschwitz. Staub (1989) suggests that rather than agentic shift being responsible for this transition, it is the experience of carrying out acts of evil over a long time that changes the way in which individuals think and behave.

Agentic state or just plain cruel?
One common belief is that Milgram had detected signs of cruelty among his participants, who had used the situation to express their sadistic impulses. This belief was supported by Zimbardo in the SPE, where within just a few days, the guards inflicted rapidly escalating cruelty on increasingly submissive prisoners despite the fact there was no obvious authority figure instructing them to do so.

The legitimate authority explanation and real-life obedience
Legitimacy can serve as justification to harm others. If people authorise another person to make judgements for them about what is appropriate conduct, they no longer feel that their own moral values are relevant to their conduct. As a consequence, when directed by a legitimate authority figure to engage in immoral actions, people are alarmingly willing to do so.

The agentic state as loss of personal control
Fennis and Aarts (2012) suggest that the reason for 'agentic shift' is a reduction in an individual's experience of personal control, i.e. where they feel 'less in control of' their actions, as would have been the case in the unfamiliar psychology laboratory. Under such circumstances people may show an increased acceptance of *external* sources of control to compensate for this.

Obedience in the cockpit – a test of legitimate authority
Tarnow (2000) provided support for the power of legitimate authority through a study of aviation accidents. As with Milgram's study, where the participant accepts the experimenter's definition of the situation, Tarnow found excessive dependence on the captain's authority and expertise. 'Lack of monitoring' errors were evident in 19 of the 37 accidents investigated.

The authoritarian personality

 The authoritarian personality and the F scale

This provides a **dispositional** explanation for why some individuals require little pressure in order to obey. High scores on the F scale is indicative of an **authoritarian personality**. Individuals with this type of personality obeyed authority and enforced strict adherence to social rules and hierarchies. Adorno *et al.* (1950) found that people who scored high on the **F scale** tended to be raised by parents with an authoritarian parenting style and a strong emphasis on obedience.

Right-wing authoritarianism (RWA)

Altemeyer (1981) identified three of the original personality variables that he referred to as **right-wing authoritarianism** (RWA).

- conventionalism (an adherence to conventional norms and values)
- authoritarian submission (aggressive feelings towards norm-breakers)
- authoritarian aggression (uncritical submission to legitimate authorities).

Key study: Elms and Milgram (1966)

Procedure Follow-up study of participants who had taken part in one of Milgram's experiments two months before. They selected 20 'obedient' (450 volts) participants and 20 'defiant' participants (who had refused at some point). Participants completed the F scale and were interviewed about their childhood and their attitudes to Milgram's experimenter and learner.

Findings The researchers found higher levels of authoritarianism among participants classified as obedient compared with those classified as defiant. Obedient participants reported being less close to their fathers during childhood, and saw the experimenter in Milgram's study as more admirable, and the learner as much less so.

Evaluation

Research evidence for the authoritarianism/obedience link

A problem for obedience studies is the participants' suspicions that the shocks might be fake. Dambrun and Vatiné (2010) overcame this by *informing* participants that the experiment was a simulation and that the shocks and were not real, but simulated. Despite this, participants responded as if the situation was real, and those who displayed higher levels of RWA were the ones who obeyed the most.

The social context is more important

Milgram did not believe the evidence for a dispositional basis to obedience was strong. He showed that variations in the social context of the study (e.g. proximity of the victim, location) were the main cause of differences in participants' levels of obedience, not variations in personality. Relying on an explanation of obedience based purely on authoritarianism lacks the flexibility to account for these variations.

Differences between authoritarian and obedient participants

Elms and Milgram found differences in the characteristics of the authoritarian personality and of obedient participants. Many of the fully obedient participants had a very good relationship with their parents, rather than the overly strict family environment associated with the authoritarian personality. This suggests authoritarianism is not the only cause of obedience.

Education may determine authoritarianism *and* obedience

Middendorp and Meloen (1990) found less-educated people are more authoritarian than the well educated. Participants with lower levels of education tended to be more obedient than those with higher levels. This suggests that instead of authoritarianism causing obedience, lack of education could be responsible for both authoritarianism *and* obedience.

Left-wing views are associated with lower levels of obedience

Altemeyer's idea of RWA suggests that people who define themselves as politically 'right wing' would be more likely to obey authority, but would people who define themselves as 'left-wing' would be *less* likely to obey? Bègue *et al.*, (2014) provide support for this. On a fake game show, participants who described themselves as 'left-wing' delivered shocks of lower intensity.

Apply it

Scenario. Having recently moved to the UK from a country where absolute obedience was demanded by the ruling regime, Amer and Raghda are concerned that their children should not grow up to be overly obedient. After reading about the authoritarian personality, they try to ensure that this does not develop in their own children.

Suggest two changes Amer and Raghda might make to their approach to child-rearing that would reduce the chance of their children developing an authoritarian personality. (2 marks)

Explanation. Because the authoritarian personality is associated with an authoritarian parenting style, Amer and Raghda could adopt a more child-centred 'authoritative' style. Because children acquire an authoritarian personality through learning and imitation, Amer and Raghda must make sure they do not model uncritical obedience in their own behaviour.

KEY TERMS

Externality
- Individuals who tend to believe that their behaviour and experience is caused by events outside their control.

Internality
- Individuals who tend to believe that they are responsible for their behaviour and experience rather than external forces.

Social support
- The perception that an individual has assistance available from other people, and that they are part of a supportive network.

Locus of control
- People differ in their beliefs about whether the outcomes of their actions are dependent on what they do (internal locus of control) or on events outside their personal control (external locus of control).

Apply it

Scenario. Parveen is just starting a course at an FE college in the Midlands, having attended a very strict all-girls school up until now. Her parents are concerned because she is easily influenced by those around her. They fear she will stray from the straight and narrow and will lose the strict values they have strived to instil in her. Parveen's best friend Hayat is also starting at the college at the same time.

Using your knowledge of the importance of social support, explain why Parveen will be better able to resist social influence with Hayat's presence. (4 Marks)

Explanation. Asch's research on conformity found that the presence of social support made it easier for an individual to resist conformity pressure from the majority. For example, Parveen may find herself in a situation with her new peer group where she is pressured to drink alcohol, as 'everybody else is drinking'. Having social support in the form of Hayat breaks the unanimous position of the group because Hayat also declines to drink. This makes Parveen feel more confident and better able to stand up to the majority.

Explanations of resistance to social influence

Social support

Resisting conformity Asch (1956) found the presence of **social support** enables an individual to resist conformity pressure from the majority. The introduction of an ally who appeared to resist the majority by giving the right answer caused conformity levels to drop sharply, from 33% to just 5.5%. Social support makes the individual feel more confident and better able to stand up to the majority.

Resisting obedience The obedient behaviour of others makes even a harmful action appear acceptable. However, their *disobedience* can change that perception. Individuals are better able to resist obedience if they have an ally who opposes the authority figure. Disobedient peers therefore act as role models on which the individual can model their own defiant behaviour.

Locus of control

The nature of locus of control A strong *internal* **locus of control** is associated with the belief that we can control events in our life. People high in **internality** rely less on the opinions of others, and are better able to resist social influence.

A strong *external* locus of control is associated with the belief that what happens is determined by external factors. People high in **externality** believe what happens is largely out of their control. They are more likely to accept the influence of others and take less personal responsibility for their actions.

Internality and resistance to social influence Research has uncovered characteristics that have relevance for resisting social influence, e.g. high internals are active seekers of information, and so are less likely to rely on the opinions of others, making them less vulnerable to social influence.

Evaluation

Social support: The importance of response order
Allen and Levine (1969) studied whether the response position of the person providing social support made any difference. Support was more effective in position 1 than in position 4. A correct first answer, in confirming the participant's own judgement, produces an initial commitment to the correct response even though other group members give a different answer.

Social support: Support may not have to be valid to be effective
Allen and Levine (1971) found that both *valid* and *invalid* social support (i.e. from a confederate with poor vision) were effective in reducing conformity. However, valid social support had much more impact, showing that an ally is helpful in resisting conformity, but more so if they offer valid social support.

Locus of control is related to normative but not informational influence
Spector (1983) found a significant correlation between locus of control and predisposition to normative influence, with externals more likely to conform than internals. However, he found no relationship for informational influence, with locus of control not appearing to be a significant factor.

Locus of control: People are all more external than they used to be
Twenge *et al.* (2004) found that young Americans increasingly believed their fate was determined more by external factors rather than their own actions. This increasing externality was a consequence of the alienation experienced by young people and the tendency to blame misfortunes on outside forces.

Social support in the real world: The Rosenstrasse protest
The Rosenstrasse protest is a stark illustration of Milgram's research in real-life. Milgram found the presence of disobedient peers gave the participant the confidence to defy the authority. The Rosenstrasse women felt confident to defy the authority of the Gestapo because they faced them together.

Research support: Locus of control
Avtgis (1998) carried out a meta-analysis of studies of the relationship between locus of control and conformity. Individuals who scored higher on *external* locus of control tend to be more easily influenced, and are more conforming than those who score higher on *internal* locus of control.

Minority influence

 Minority influence and behavioural style

Conversion to a minority position tends to be deeper and longer lasting because people have internalised the minority's point of view. To bring about conversion, minorities must adopt a particular behavioural style of being consistent, committed and flexible in their arguments.

Consistency If the minority adopt a consistent approach, others come to reassess the situation and consider the issue more carefully. Wood et al.'s (1994) meta-analysis found that consistent minorities were more influential.

Commitment This is important because it suggests certainty and confidence in the face of a hostile majority. If minority members demonstrate greater **commitment** it might persuade other group members to take them seriously .

Flexibility Mugny (1982) suggests **flexibility** is more effective at changing majority opinion than rigidity. A rigid minority risks being perceived as dogmatic, but a minority that is *too* flexible risks being seen as inconsistent.

 Key study: Moscovici et al. (1969)

Procedure Each group had four naïve participants and a minority of two confederates. They were shown a series of blue slides that varied only in intensity and were asked to judge the colour of each slide.

Consistent condition, confederates repeatedly called blue slides 'green'.

Inconsistent condition, confederates called the slides 'green' on two-thirds of trials, and 'blue' on the remaining one-third.

Control condition (no confederates), participants called all slides 'blue'.

Findings The consistent minority influenced the naïve participants to say 'green' on over 8% of the trials. The inconsistent minority exerted very little influence, and did not differ significantly from the control group.

 Evaluation

Research support for flexibility
Nemeth and Brilmayer (1987) provided support for the role of flexibility in a simulated jury situation. When a confederate put forward an alternative view and refused to change his position, this had no effect on other group members. However, a confederate who compromised did exert an influence, but only if they shifted *late* in negotiations (perceived as showing flexibility).

The real 'value' of minority influence
Nemeth (2010) argues that, as a result of exposure to a minority position, people consider more options and make better decisions. This view is supported by Van Dyne and Saavedra (1996), who found that workgroups had improved decision quality when exposed to a minority perspective.

Do we *really* process the minority's message more?
Mackie (1987) argues it is the *majority* who are more likely to create greater message processing. If the majority express a *different* belief to the one we hold, we consider it carefully to understand why this is the case. People tend not to waste time trying to process why a minority's message is different, so it tends to be less rather than more influential.

A 'tipping point' for commitment
Xie et al. (2011) discovered a 'tipping point' where the number of people holding a minority position is sufficient to change majority opinion. They used computer models of social networks, with individuals encountering individuals representing an alternative point of view. The percentage of committed opinion holders necessary to 'tip' the majority into accepting the minority position was just 10%.

Minority influence in name only
Nemeth (2010) claims it is difficult to convince people of the value of dissent. People accept the principle only on the surface, but they become irritated by a dissenting view that persists. This means that the opportunities for innovative thinking associated with **minority influence** are lost.

KEY TERMS
Commitment
- The degree to which members of a minority are dedicated to a position. The greater the perceived commitment, the greater the influence.

Consistency
- Minority influence is effective provided there is a stability in the expressed position over time and agreement among different members of the minority.

Flexibility
- A willingness to be flexible and to compromise rather than being rigid, inflexible and dogmatic when expressing a position.

Minority influence
- A form of social influence where members of the majority group change their beliefs or behaviours as a result of their exposure to a persuasive minority.

Apply it
Scenario. Rachel and Joe are touched by the news stories about migrants from the Middle East fleeing war and oppression and looking for a new life in Europe. They try to convince people to welcome migrants into their community, and to help financially in converting a row of disused terrace houses into homes for migrant families.

Using your knowledge of minority influence, explain how Rachel and Joe can convince members of their community to accept migrants and contribute to the renovation of the houses for their use. (4 marks)

Explanation. Rachel and Joe must put together their reasons why people in their town should help the migrants and must then present these arguments consistently. If they express their arguments in a consistent manner, people are likely to consider the issues more carefully. Consistency also suggests commitment to a cause. By showing they are willing to give up their time and energy to help migrants, even in the face of hostility from some members of the community, Rachel and Joe will be able to persuade others to take them seriously and to share their concern for the migrants.

Social change
- This occurs when a society or section of society adopts a new belief or way of behaving, which then becomes widely accepted as the norm.

Social norms interventions
- Attempt to correct misperceptions of the normative behaviour of peers in an attempt to change the risky behaviour of a target population.

Apply it

Scenario. The mayor of a city in the South-West is determined to persuade people to use their cars less and public transport more. He intends to set up a congestion charge for cars coming into the city centre and limit the parking to make people to use public transport instead. He knows this will be an unpopular message to the people of the city so seeks advice on how he can achieve this social change.

Using your knowledge of the social influence processes in social change, explain how the mayor can bring about this social change. (4 marks)

Explanation. He could use techniques based on minority influence. For example, he could draw attention to the issues (congestion, pollution, etc.), which produces a conflict in the minds of those who want to drive, but don't want congestion or pollution and do want a cleaner city. If the mayor sets an example by not using his own car, his arguments will be taken more seriously (augmentation principle). He could also change the current reliance on cars by using a social norms intervention, e.g. by informing citizens that the majority of people who live in the city expressed a willingness to make more use of public transport and use their cars less.

Social influence processes in social change

⬤ Social change through minority influence

If an individual is exposed to a persuasive argument under certain conditions, they may change their views to match those of the minority.

Stages of social change (e.g. the suffragettes)

1. **Drawing attention to an issue** which may then create a conflict in the minds of the majority e.g. suffragettes used different tactics to draw attention to the fact that women were denied the same voting rights as men.

2. **Cognitive conflict** The minority creates a conflict between what majority group members believe and the position advocated by the minority, e.g. between the status quo and the position advocated by the suffragettes.

3. **Consistency of position** Minorities are more influential when they express their arguments consistently e.g. the suffragettes were consistent in their views, regardless of the attitudes of those around them.

4. **The augmentation principle** Minorities who appear willing to suffer for their views are taken more seriously. Because the suffragettes were willing to risk imprisonment, their influence was *augmented*.

5. **The snowball effect** Minority influence spreads more widely until it reaches a 'tipping point', leading to wide-scale **social change**, e.g. universal suffrage was finally accepted by the majority of people in the UK.

⬤ Social change through majority influence

The social norms approach holds that if people perceive something to be the norm, they tend to alter their behaviour to fit that norm. The gap between the perceived and actual norm is a 'misperception', and correcting this misperception is the basis for **social norms interventions**.

An example: 'Most of us don't drink and drive' – Although just 20% of young adults reported having driven after drinking in the previous month, 92% believed that the majority of their peers had done so. Correcting this misperception led to the reduction in the frequency of drink-driving.

⬤ Evaluation

Social change through minority influence may be very gradual

As there is a tendency to conform to the majority position, in real-life, groups are more likely to maintain the status quo rather than engage in social change. Minority influence, therefore, is frequently more *latent* than direct (i.e. it creates the potential for change rather than actual social change).

Being perceived as 'deviant' limits the influence of minorities

The potential for minorities to influence social change is often limited because they are seen as 'deviant' by the majority. Their message would have little impact would have little impact because the focus of the majority's attention would be on the *source* of the message (the deviant minority) rather than the message itself.

Limitations of the social norms approach

Not all social norms interventions *have* led to social change. In an intervention aimed at student drinking, students did not report lower self-reported alcohol consumption as a result of the campaign, despite receiving normative information that corrected their misperceptions of drinking norms (DeJong *et al.*, 2009).

Social norms and the 'boomerang effect'

In social norms interventions, those whose behaviour is *more* desirable than the norm will also receive the message. Schultz *et al.* (2007) found evidence of a 'boomerang' effect in that although a social norms campaign was effective in getting heavy energy users to use less electricity, it also caused those who used less than the norm to *increase* their usage.

Overcoming the deviant minority problem: The Communist Manifesto

To persuade the majority to embrace their position, minorities must overcome the problem of being portrayed as deviants. Early communists made it clear that: *'We aren't the deviants, we are just like you – it's the bourgeoisie who are against us all'*. Their approach was eventually successful in bringing about social change with the Communist revolution.

Chapter 2

Memory

3.1.2 Memory

- The multi-store model of memory: sensory register, short-term and long-term memory. Features of each store: coding, capacity and duration.
- Types of long-term memory: episodic, semantic and procedural.
- The working memory model: central executive, phonological loop, visuo-spatial sketchpad and episodic buffer. Features of the model: coding and capacity.
- Explanations for forgetting: proactive and retroactive interference and retrieval failure due to the absence of cues.
- Factors affecting the accuracy of eyewitness testimony: misleading information, including leading questions and post-event discussion; anxiety.
- Improving the accuracy of eyewitness testimony, including the use of cognitive interview.

Key terms (highlight each cell when you can define the term for 3 marks)

The multi-store model	Types of long-term memory	The working memory model	Explanations for forgetting	Factors affecting the accuracy of eyewitness testimony	Improving the accuracy of eyewitness testimony
Sensory register	Episodic	Central executive	Proactive interference	Misleading information	Cognitive interview
Short-term memory	Semantic	Phonological loop	Retroactive interference	Leading questions	
Long-term memory	Procedural	Visuo-spatial sketchpad	Retrieval failure	Post-event discussion	
Coding		Episodic buffer		Anxiety	
Capacity					
Duration					

Content checklist

1. *In each 'describe, apply and evaluate' cell tick when you have produced brief notes.*
2. *Once you feel you have a good grasp of the topic add a second tick to the cell.*
3. *When you feel you have complete mastery of the topic and would be able to answer an exam question without the aid of notes highlight the cell.*

I am able to...	Describe	Apply	Evaluate
Multi-store model			
Features of STM (coding, capacity, duration)			
Features of LTM (coding, capacity, duration)			
Types of LTM – Episodic			
Types of LTM – Semantic			
Types of LTM – Procedural			
Working memory model (including coding and capacity)			
Explanations for forgetting – Proactive interference			
Explanations for forgetting – Retroactive interference			
Explanations for forgetting – Retrieval failure			
Accuracy of EWT – misleading information: leading questions			
Accuracy of EWT – misleading information: post-event discussion			
Accuracy of EWT – Anxiety			
Improving accuracy of EWT – Cognitive interview			

	STM	LTM
Capacity	Less than 7 chunks	Potentially unlimited
Coding	Acoustic (sound)	Semantic (meaning)
Duration	Measured in seconds and minutes	Measured in hours and days

KEY TERMS

Capacity
- A measure of how much can be held in memory. Measured in bits of information, such as the number of digits. STM has a limited capacity (it has been suggested 7±2 items) while LTM has a potentially infinite capacity.

Coding
- The way information is changed so that memory can be stored. Information entering the brain via the senses is stored in various forms. Information can be stored as visual codes (images), acoustic codes (sounds) or semantic codes (the meaning of experiences).

Duration
- A measure of how long a memory lasts before it is no longer available. LTM potentially lasts forever but STM has a short duration, meaning information is quickly lost unless it is repeated over and over again is a process called maintenance rehearsal.

Long-term memory (LTM)
- Memory for events that have happened in the past. This lasts anywhere from 2 minutes to 100 years. LTM has potentially unlimited duration and capacity and tends to be coded semantically.

Short-term memory (STM)
- Memory for immediate events. Measured in seconds and minutes rather than hours or days. Short-term memories, as the name suggests, last for a very short time and disappear unless rehearsed. STM also has a limited capacity and tends to be coded acoustically. This type of memory is sometimes referred to as working memory.

Capacity

The capacity of STM

Jacobs (1887) used the digit span technique to measure the **capacity** of **STM**. He found the average span for digits was 9.3 items and 7.3 for letters. Jacobs proposed more digits could be recalled as there are only 9 digits compared to 26 letters.

The magic number 7±2

After reviewing research, Miller (1956) concluded that the span of STM is seven plus or minus two items. When dots are flashed on a screen people are able to count seven dots but not many more. This is the same for musical notes, letters and words. Miller further proposed STM capacity can be enhanced by grouping sets of digits and letters into meaningful units known as 'chunks'.

Evaluation

The capacity of STM may be even more limited
Cowan's (2001) review of STM capacity studies suggests that capacity is more likely to be limited to about four chunks of information rather than 7±2 items. This is supported by research into the capacity for visual stimuli which found that four items was the limit (Vogel *et al.*, 2001).

The size of the chunk matters
The size of the chunk seems to affect how many chunks can be recalled. Simon (1974) found that people had a shorter memory span for eight word phrases (larger chunks) than for one-syllable words (smaller chunks).

Individual differences
Individual differences mean the capacity of STM varies between people. Jacobs found digit span (the ability to recall items in a list) increases with age; eight year olds could recall an average of 6.6 digits whereas for 19 year olds the mean recall was 8.6 digits.

Duration

The duration of STM

How? Peterson and Peterson (1959) devised a laboratory experiment to test 24 students over eight trials. Each trial consisted of the participant being given a consonant syllable and a three-digit number (e.g. THX 512). Participants recalled the consonant syllable after a retention interval during which they counted backwards from the three-digit number presented. Recall was tested over retention intervals of 3, 6, 9, 12, 15 and 18 seconds.

Showed? On average, participant recall of the consonant syllable was 90% correct over 3 seconds, 20% correct after 9 seconds and only 2% correct after 18 seconds. This suggests that when verbal rehearsal of the consonant syllable is prevented (by counting backwards) the **duration** of STM is very short.

The duration of LTM

How? In a natural experiment, Bahrick *et al.* (1975) tested over 400 people, aged 17–74 years, for their memory of classmates from when they were at school. A photo-recognition test required participants to identify high-school yearbook images of their classmates from 50 photos. In a free-recall test participants listed names of classmates in their graduating class.

Showed? In the photo-recognition task, participants tested within 15 years of graduating from high school showed 90% accuracy when identifying photos of their classmates. After 48 years this declined to about 70% accuracy. For free-recall of classmates' names participants were 60% accurate after 15 years whereas after 48 years recall accuracy fell to 30%.

Evaluation

Peterson and Peterson's testing was artificial

People don't normally want or need to remember meaningless consonants so the test did not reflect everyday memory activities. However, it could be said we do sometimes try to remember fairly meaningless items such as groups of numbers (phone number) or letters (post codes). Therefore, the study could hold some relevance to memory in everyday life.

STM results may be due to displacement not decay

The counting task may have displaced the memory of the syllable. Reitman (1974) used auditory tones instead of counting which prevents displacement (the tones don't interfere with verbal rehearsal) and found the duration of STM was longer. If the forgetting seen in the Petersons' study was due to displacement rather than decay the duration of STM was not measured.

LTMs may have been regularly rehearsed

In Bahrick et al.'s study participants may have kept in contact with their classmates and seen them over the years since graduation. This would explain the high levels of recall seen as they would be rehearsing the memory of their classmates every time they met, spoke to or thought about them.

Coding

 Coding in STM and LTM

How? In a laboratory experiment Baddeley (1966) gave participants lists of words that were acoustically similar (sounded the same, e.g. cat, cab, can) or dissimilar and lists of words that were semantically similar (meant the same, e.g. great, large, big) or dissimilar.

Showed? When testing STM, participants had difficulty remembering acoustically similar word lists but could recall semantically similar words. In **LTM**, participants became muddled when recalling semantically similar words but were able to recall acoustically similar word lists. This suggests that STM uses acoustic **coding** whereas LTM uses semantic coding.

 Evaluation

Baddeley may not have tested LTM

When testing STM, Baddeley asked participants to recall a word list immediately after hearing it. LTM was tested by recalling 20 minutes after hearing the word list. It is questionable as to whether this is a sufficient amount of time to test LTM.

STM may not be exclusively acoustic

Brandimonte et al. (1992) found that when participants were given a visual task (pictures) and prevented from using verbal rehearsal (saying la, la, la) they were still able to perform well on a visual recall task. Normally, we would translate the visual images into a verbal code in STM but saying la, la, la repeatedly prevented this, meaning participants used visual codes.

LTM may not be exclusively semantic

Frost (1972) showed that recall in LTM was related to visual as well as semantic categories. Nelson and Rothbart (1972) found evidence of acoustic coding in LTM. Therefore LTM does not seem restricted to semantic coding. As with STM the coding used varies according to circumstances.

Apply it

Scenario. Petra is making a cake. On reading the recipe she finds that she does not have many of the ingredients in her cupboard. She drives 20 minutes to her local supermarket but on arrival realises she cannot remember what she needed to buy to be able to make the cake.

Using your knowledge of STM why can't Petra remember the ingredients she needs to buy? (3 marks)

Explanation. The ingredients for the cake were held in her STM. However, when driving 20 minutes to the supermarket she did not rehearse the items and so the memory decayed as STM has a very limited duration. Furthermore, as she needed to remember a lot of ingredients this may be more than the capacity of STM (less than 7 items) and so all the items could not be recalled unless she found a way to chunk items together.

Multi-store model
- An explanation of memory based on three separate stores, and the processes that transfer information between these stores.

Sensory register
- Information collected by your eyes, ears, nose, fingers, etc. While the capacity of the sensory register is large, the duration is very brief (only holding information for less than half a second). The method of coding depends on the sense organ involved, e.g. visual for the eyes, acoustic for the ears.

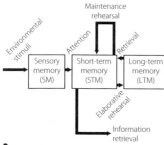

Apply it

Scenario. Sam suffered a serious head injury after falling from his bicycle. On recovering it quickly became clear his memory ability had been damaged. STM duration was greatly reduced. For example, he could not recall information his doctor had just told him or remember what he had for lunch as soon as he had eaten. His LTM showed some damage in that he could not remember his experiences at university but could recall factual knowledge such as capital cities.

To what extent does the case study of Sam support the multi-store model of memory? (4 marks)

Explanation. Sam's STM duration is much shorter than other adults and it seems he is unable to rehearse information to keep it in STM. This suggests he cannot form LTMs (he quickly forgets what he ate for lunch or advice from his doctor), supporting the multi-store model's suggestion that information moves from STM to LTM. However, as Sam can remember some types of LTM (semantic – facts) but not others (episodic – university life) it suggests the model's view of LTM is too simplistic because if LTM was single store, Sam shouldn't be able to access any LTMs.

The multi-store model of memory

First described by Atkinson and Shiffrin (1968) the model is called **multi-store** because it consists of three memory stores linked by processes that transfer information from one store to the next. Each store has unique characteristics: capacity, coding and duration.

- **Sensory register (store):** Information is held at each of the senses in a sensory register. The capacity of these registers is very large but if no attention is paid to the store information remains for only a few milliseconds, meaning the sensory registers have a very brief duration.
- **Attention (process):** Paying attention to one of the sensory stores transfers data to the STM.
- **Short-term memory (store):** STM has a **limited duration** – information will quickly decay if it isn't rehearsed. STM also has a **limited capacity** – information will be displaced by new information entering STM. Information is usually **coded acoustically**.
- **Maintenance rehearsal (process):** Repeating information held in the STM will create a LTM. The more information is rehearsed, the better it is remembered.
- **Long-term memory (store):** LTM is **potentially unlimited** in duration and capacity. Information is usually **coded semantically**.
- **Retrieval (process):** The process of getting information from LTM involves the information passing back through STM, making it available for use. Forgetting can occur if you cannot locate the memory in LTM or if the memory was never made permanent in the first place.

◉ Evaluation

Supporting evidence for separate stores
Laboratory studies into capacity, coding and duration support the existence of separate stores each with different characteristics (see pages 24). Brain imaging studies have also demonstrated differences in the stores. Beardsley (1997) found prefrontal cortex activity during tasks requiring STM but not for tasks where LTM was needed.

Case studies suggest different brain areas are involved
Scoville and Milner (1957) cite the case of HM. Following an operation to reduce severe epilepsy, in which the hippocampus was removed from both sides of the brain, HM could not form new LTMs although his memory for events before the surgery was intact.

The multi-store model is too simple
Research suggests STM is actually divided into a number of qualitatively different stores (see page 27) forming a working memory. Research has also shown there are different types of LTM, e.g. maintenance rehearsal can explain long-term storage of semantic memory (knowledge of the world) but does not explain the formation of episodic memories of events experienced (see page 28).

Forming LTM involves more than maintenance rehearsal
Craik and Lockhart (1972) argue the deeper the processing the more memorable the information becomes. 'Deep' processing is more complicated than just repeating information. Craik and Lockhart found **shallow processing** (considering the appearance of words) lead to poorer recall than **deep processing** (considering the meaning of words).

How separate are STM and LTM?
The suggestion than STM occurs before formation of LTM may be inaccurate. For example, in order to chunk the information AQABBC in STM, LTM is needed to give the chunks meaning (exam board, TV channel). Ruchkin *et al.* (2003) found brain activity was greater when participants recalled real words than when they recalled made-up words, indicating more than just STM was involved.

Working memory model

Baddeley and Hitch (1974) proposed the **working memory model** after arguing the STM was more than one single store. Instead, they described a working memory comprised of a number of different stores.

- **Central executive**: An attentional process to monitor incoming data from the senses and LTM. It determines how the **slave systems** are allocated to tasks. It has a very limited capacity – it cannot attend to too many things at once and is unable to store data. The slave systems also have limited capacity.
- **Phonological loop**: This slave system deals with auditory (sound) information and preserves its order. Subdivided into the **phonological store** (stores the words you hear – like an inner ear) and **articulatory process** (a verbal loop enabling you to repeat words (maintenance rehearsal) – like an inner voice).
- **Visuo-spatial sketchpad**: The slave system responsible for visual (what objects look like) and/or spatial information (the physical relationship between objects). Subdivided into the **visual cache**, storing information about visual items like colour and form, and an **inner scribe**, which deals with spatial relationships between objects.
- **Episodic buffer**: An extra storage system to hold information relating to both visual and acoustic information. It integrates information from the other stores and sends information to LTM. It also has a limited capacity.

 Evaluation

Dual task performance supports the existence of different stores
Hitch and Baddeley (1976) found that when participants were given a task involving the central executive (a true or false logic task) and a second task involving the central executive and articulatory loop (saying random numbers) their performance was slower on the logic task than when the second task just used the articulatory loop (saying la, la, la).

Evidence for the phonological loop and articulatory process
The phonological loop explains the word-length effect – the finding that people show greater recall for short words than for longer words. The phonological loop holds the amount of information that can be said in 2 seconds. Longer words cannot be rehearsed as well as shorter words and so recall performance suffers for words that take longer to articulate.

Evidence from brain-damaged patients
Shallice and Warrington's (1970) case study of KF supports the working memory model. Following a motor cycle accident KF showed much greater short-term memory forgetting for auditory information than visual information, suggesting visual and auditory information are dealt with by different memory stores.

The central executive is too vague
Eslinger and Damasio (1985) report the case of EVR who had a cerebral tumour removed. He performed well on reasoning tasks (suggesting an intact central executive) but had poor decision-making skills (suggesting central executive damage). It seems the central executive is more complex than the model proposes.

Evidence from brain-damaged patients is problematic
Firstly, the trauma of experiencing an injury may itself lead to a change in behaviour so that a person performs worse on certain tasks such as decision-making. Secondly, individuals may have other difficulties such as problems focusing attention and therefore underperform on certain tasks.

Apply it

Scenario. Mariam enjoys singing along to music while completing a still-life drawing for her art homework. However, she finds the same songs distracting when trying to listen to her friend explain events in a chapter of a novel they are studying in English class.

Use your understanding of the working memory model to explain Mariam's dual task performance. (4 marks)

Explanation. To complete her art homework Mariam is using her visuo-spatial sketchpad to consider the colour and form of objects (visual cache) and the relationships between the objects in the still-life composition (inner scribe). She is able to do this while singing to music as a different store, the phonological loop, is attending to this auditory information. However, the phonological store has a limited capacity so is unable to successfully perform two auditory tasks simultaneously (singing and listening to her friend explain events in the chapter).

KEY TERMS

Episodic memory
- Memory for personal events such as your favourite teacher from primary school. This type of LTM includes contextual details plus emotional tone.

Priming
- Automatic enhanced recognition of specific stimuli, e.g. exposure to word 'yellow' makes it more likely a person would say 'banana' when asked to name a fruit.

Procedural memory
- Memory for how to do things, e.g. riding a bike or how to tie shoelaces. These LTMs become automatic following repeated practice.

Semantic memory
- General knowledge about the world, e.g. knowing that London is the capital of England. Semantic memories can be concrete such as knowing that ice is made of water, or abstract such as mathematical knowledge.

Apply it

Scenario. A teacher decided to interview her A-level class about their studies and school life. One student, Emily, said 'I remember how stressed I felt when revising for my mock exams. I was moody at home and seemed to constantly argue with my parents'. Zac reported, 'I feel confident in my knowledge of different biological processes'. Katie explained, 'I need to practise writing for the exam. I tend to use my laptop for homework and know I type quicker than I can write'.

Identify the different types of LTM each student is discussing. (2 marks)

Explanation. Emily's comment is an example of episodic memory as she is recalling her own personal experience of sitting mock exams. Zac is focusing on his semantic memory of facts while Katie is discussing her procedural memory for typing compared to writing.

Different types of LTM

LTM is divided into **explicit** (or declarative) memory and **implicit** (or procedural) memory.
- Explicit memory: *'Knowing that'*. **Episodic** and **semantic memories** such as knowing different breeds of dog (semantic) and remembering your pet dog from childhood (episodic).
- Implicit: *'Knowing how'*. **Procedural memories** such as knowing how to drive a car.

◔ Episodic memory

Memories for episodes (an event or a group of events occurring as part of a larger sequence, e.g. memory of going to university). Episodic memories are concerned with **personal experiences** and have three elements: specific details of the event, the context and the emotion.

◔ Semantic memory

Memories for general knowledge about the world that is shared by everyone. For example, memories for the function of objects, as well as more abstract memories such as mathematics and language. Generally begin as episodic memories as we learn through personal experience but gradually lose their association with a specific event and transition into semantic memories.

◔ Procedural memory

Skills such as knowing how to ride a bike and swim. Through repetition and practice they become automatic. These memories are **implicit** – the skill can be performed with little awareness of the steps needed to carry it out.

⬡ Evaluation

Supporting evidence from brain scans
Different areas of the brain are active when different kinds of LTM are accessed. For example, when recalling personal events (episodic memory) activity is seen in the hippocampus and frontal lobe while procedural memories are associated with the cerebellum (control of fine motor skills) and the motor cortex.

Distinguishing procedural and declarative memories
The case of HM (see page 26) adds weight to the suggestion of different types of LTMs. After surgery HM could still form new procedural memories, e.g. he was able to learn mirror draw. However, he could not remember being taught this skill so had no episodic memory of the learning experience.

Episodic memories may not be a gateway to semantic memories
Hodges and Patterson (2007) found some Alzheimer's patients were able to form new episodic memories but not semantic memories. Irish *et al.* (2011) reported cases of Alzheimer's sufferers who had poor semantic memories but generally intact episodic memories. This suggests that episodic memories may be a gateway to semantic memory but it is possible for semantic memories to form separately.

Problems with evidence from patients with brain damage
Most studies involve living patients carrying out tasks to determine the extent of their memory function. However, damage to a particular area does not necessarily mean that area is responsible for that type of LTM – it may be acting as a relay station. Damage to the relay station would explain the memory problems observed.

Priming and a fourth kind of LTM
The perceptual-representation system (PRS) has been proposed as a fourth type of LTM relating to **priming**. Spiers *et al.*'s (2001) study of 147 amnesia sufferers found that their procedural memories and PRS were intact but their other two systems (the temporal system supports episodic and semantic memory) were not. This implies two kinds of implicit memory exist that were not affected by amnesia.

Description of interference theory

⬡ Retroactive interference

How? In Müller and Pilzecker's (1900) laboratory experiment, participants had 6 minutes to learn lists of nonsense syllables. Following a retention interval they were asked to recall the syllables.

Showed? They found recall was poorer when participants were given a task between learning the lists and recalling them. The task (describing three landscape paintings) caused **retroactive interference** (RI) because the painting task interfered with prior learning of the syllables.

⬡ Proactive interference

How? Underwood (1957) analysed studies in which participants' memory for numerous lists of words were tested after 24 hours.

Showed? If participants memorised 10 lists or more they remembered only about 20%. If they only learned just one list, recall was over 70%. Underwood concluded that when learning a series of lists, words in later lists are not learned as well as words encountered earlier on. This shows proactive interference as each list learned makes it harder to learn subsequent lists.

⬡ Similarity of test materials

How? In McGeoch and McDonald's (1931) study, participants were given a list of 10 adjectives (List A) to learn. In the 10 minutes between learning List A and recalling List A they were given a second list to learn (List B).

Showed? If words on List B were synonyms of the adjectives of List A then recall for List A was poor (12%). If List B was nonsense syllables less interference occurred (26% recall). The highest recall was seen when List B consisted of numbers (37% recall). These findings show interference is strongest when items to be remembered share common features.

⬡ Evaluation

Range of research evidence

Laboratory based research has demonstrated the effect of both retroactive and proactive interference (see Müller and Pilzecker, McGeoch and McDonald, and Underwood). While laboratory research could be criticised for using artificial lists of words or syllables (which could reduce participant motivation to learn the items), Baddeley and Hitch found evidence of interference in a real life setting (see Apply it box).

Real-world application to advertising

Danaher et al. (2008) found recall and recognition of an advertiser's message was reduced when participants were exposed to two advertisements for competing brands within a week. Multiple exposure to an advertisement on one day may reduce interference from competitors' advertisements by strengthening the memory trace.

Interference only explains some forgetting

It could be argued that interference is a relatively unimportant explanation of forgetting. For interference to occur the two memories need to be quite similar and so cannot explain all forgetting experienced. Anderson (2000) concluded that while interference does play a role in forgetting it remains unclear how much forgetting can be attributed to interference.

Interference may lead to temporary, rather than permanent, forgetting

Ceraso (1967) found that if recall (availability) was tested after 24 hours performance remained the same. However, if recognition of items (accessibility) was tested, memories showed spontaneous recovery. This suggests interference occurs because memories cannot be accessed, not because they have been lost.

Individual differences in effects of proactive interference

Participants with a greater working memory span were less susceptible to proactive interference when learning three word lists than participants with low working memory spans (Kane and Engle, 2000).

Apply it

Scenario. Baddeley and Hitch (1977) investigated rugby players' memory for teams they had played against during the rugby season. Some players played every game of the season while others, due to injury, missed some games. Players who participated in every game of the season showed poorer recall of opposing teams than injured players who had played fewest games.

Use your understanding of interference to explain the forgetting shown by the rugby players. (4 marks)

Explanation. The time interval for all players was the same (from the start to the end of the rugby season). If forgetting occurred because of decay then all players should have shown similar levels of forgetting. However, as the players who played more games forgot more teams, it suggests interference was the cause of forgetting because the more items (teams) they learned the poorer their recall shown. Memories of teams played later in the season may disrupt memory for teams played at the start of the season (retroactive interference) or memories for teams played at the start of the season hindered learning of new teams played as the season progressed (proactive interference).

Cues

- Things that serve as a reminder either forming a meaningful link to the items to be remembered, or may be environmental cues (a room) or related to mental state (being sad or drunk).

Retrieval failure

- Forgetting due to the absence of cues. The memory cannot be retrieved – it is available but not accessible. Successful retrieval relies on the presence of cues.

Apply it

Scenario. Psychology students asked participants to learn lists of words in either a classroom where lavender-scented candles were burning or the same classroom where no additional smell was added. The next day all participants were asked to recall the word in the same classroom while lavender-scented candles were burning. Participants who learned the lists in the presence of the lavender scent showed greater recall than those who learned the lists without smelling lavender.

How might the psychology students explain their findings in relation to retrieval failure? (3 marks)

Explanation. The lavender smell acted as a context-dependent cue for the participants who were initially exposed to the scent while learning the word lists – they encoded the cue at the time of learning the words. Participants who were not exposed to lavender when learning the word lists would not find lavender a useful cue in the retrieval phase as it was not present at the time of learning and so would not help them access those memories.

Description of retrieval failure

 ## The encoding specificity principle

Memory is most effective if information present at the time of encoding is also present at the time of retrieval. **Cues** at the learning and recall phases do not have to be identical but the closer the cues are the more retrieval is aided.

How? Tulving and Pearlstone (1966) gave participants 48 words belonging to 12 categories; each presented as category + word e.g. fruit-apple.

Showed? Participants in the free recall condition showed, on average, 40% recall. Participants in the cued-recall condition (given category headings such as 'fruit') recalled 60% of the words.

 ## Context-dependent forgetting

How? In Godden and Baddeley's (1975) study scuba divers learned a set of words either on land or underwater. They were later asked to recall these words in the same learning environment or a different environment.

Showed? Highest recall was seen when divers recalled words in the same environment as they learned them (e.g. learned underwater and recalled underwater, learned on land and recalled on land).

 ## State-dependent forgetting

How? Goodwin *et al.* (1969) asked male participants to remember lists of words when they were either drunk or sober. Participants in the drunk condition consumed enough alcohol to be three times over the UK drink driving limit. After 24 hours recall of the word list was tested.

Showed? Recall was highest when participants recalled in the same state as when they learned the words, e.g. learned and recalled while drunk.

 ## Evaluation

There is a lot of research support for the importance of cues

Evidence supporting this explanation of forgetting can be seen across a range of experiments: lab, field and natural as well as anecdotal evidence and so has relevance to everyday memory experiences.

Real-world applications

Smith (1979) showed that just thinking of the room in which the original learning took place (mental reinstatement) was as effective as actually being in the same room at the time of retrieval. Another real-world application is the use of retrieval cues in the cognitive interview (see page 33).

Retrieval failure is a more important explanation of forgetting

Tulving and Psotka (1971) asked participants to learned lists of 24 words divided into six categories. For each list participants wrote down as many words as they could remember (free recall). Participants were then presented with category names (such as trees, precious stones) and asked to recall words (cued recall). In the free recall condition the more lists the participants learned the poorer the recall – evidence of retroactive forgetting. However, cued recall was about 70% no matter how many lists had been learned.

Absence of cues cannot explain all forgetting

Most of the research into cues involves learning lists of words so findings might not apply to more complex learning, which is less easily triggered by single cues. The outshining hypothesis states a cue's effectiveness is reduced by the presence of better cues. Context effects are largely eliminated when learning meaningful material so while absence of retrieval cues can explain some everyday forgetting it cannot explain all forgetting.

The danger of circularity

The relationship between cues and retrieval is correlational rather than causal

Cues do not *cause* retrieval, they are just associated with retrieval. Baddeley (1997) suggests the encoding specificity principle is impossible to test because it is circular. The principle states if a cue leads to retrieval of a memory then the cue must have been encoded, if retrieval fails then the cue cannot have been encoded. But it is impossible to test whether an item has or hasn't been encoded in memory.

Accuracy of eyewitness testimony: Misleading information

Leading questions experiment 1

How? Loftus and Palmer's (1974) laboratory experiment tested the effect of exposure to a **leading question** on memory for traffic accidents. 45 participants watched seven film clips, answering a questionnaire after each film containing one critical question, 'About how fast were the cars going when they hit each other?' One group of participants received this question. The other four groups were given the verbs *smashed, collided, bumped* or *contacted* in the place of the word *hit*.

Shown? The group exposed to the verb 'smashed' gave the highest mean speed rating (40.8 mph). The 'contacted' group gave the lowest (31.8 mph). The verb used leads to a certain answer, i.e. *smashed* implies a fast speed.

Leading questions experiment 2

How? Loftus and Palmer (1974). Participants shown a 1-minute film clip of a car crash were asked about speed using the verb *hit* or *smashed*. A control group received no speed question. One week later they were asked, 'Did you see any broken glass?' (The correct answer was *no*.)

Shown? 16 participants in the *smashed* group recalled seeing broken glass compared to 7 in the hit group. Those who thought the car was travelling faster (as implied by the verb) might be more likely to think there would be broken glass.

Post-event discussion

Conformity effect

How? Gabbert *et al.* (2003) showed pairs of participants a different video of the same event, exposing each person to unique items. In one condition pairs discussed what they had witnessed before recalling individually.

Shown? 71% of witnesses who had discussed the event went on to mistakenly recall items they could have learned only from discussion with their partner.

Repeat interviewing

Each time a witness is interviewed, the interviewer's comments risk being incorporated into the witness' memory. The interviewer may unintentionally use leading questions which also have the potential of altering memories. This is a greater risk when interviewing child witnesses.

Evaluation

Misleading information can lead to false memories

College students, who had visited Disneyland as a child, evaluated adverts containing misinformation about Bugs Bunny (not a Disney character) or Ariel (modern Disney). Braun *et al.* (2002) found participants exposed to this misleading information were more likely to report meeting these characters than participants in a control group.

Real-world applications

Examples of exonerations of innocent people following DNA testing have confirmed research findings that the memories of eyewitnesses should be treated with caution to prevent wrongful convictions.

Laboratory experiments may not represent real-life experiences

Laboratory settings may not recreate the same level of importance and/ or emotions as real-life. When participants thought they were watching a real-life robbery and believed their statements would be used in a trial, their identification of the perpetrator was more accurate (Foster *et al.*, 1994).

Age differences in remembering sourced information

Schacter *et al.* (1991) found elderly people had more difficulty remembering the source of information than younger people, making their **EWTs** more vulnerable to inaccuracies.

Response bias rather than storage

Participants were given questions that were either consistent or inconsistent with a scene viewed. When later asked questions in a different order those exposed to inconsistent questions showed less accurate recall of the scene. However, when questions were asked in the same order, no difference in accuracy was seen (Bekerian and Bowers, 1983)

KEY TERMS

Eyewitness testimony (EWT)
- The evidence provided in court by a witness, with a view to identifying the perpetrator of the crime. The accuracy of witness recall may be affected during initial encoding, subsequent storage and eventual retrieval

Leading questions
- A question that suggests to the witness what answer is desired or leads the witness to the desired answer.

Misleading information
- Supplying the witness with information that may lead their memory of the crime to be altered and so reducing accuracy of recall.

Post-event discussion
- A conversation between co-witnesses or interviewer and witness after a crime has occurred. Details discussed may contaminate a witness' memories for the event.

Apply it

Scenario. Walking home from school Chris witnessed a car crash. When he got home he told his parents about the accident. They asked whether anyone was injured, how fast the cars were travelling when they smashed into each other and the extent of the damage to the cars. Next day at school Chris discussed the incident with other students who had witnessed the accident. His friend Tom saw the crash from the other side of the road. He said one of the drivers had cuts on his face and guessed he must have hit his head on the steering wheel.

Why should the police treat Chris' eyewitness testimony with caution? (3 marks)

Explanation. Chris has engaged in post-event discussion with his parents and friends, which may have exposed him to misleading information. For example, Tom's comments may distort Chris' memory so he believes he too could see the driver's injuries (even though this may not be possible from where Chris was standing). His parents' use of the verb 'smashed' might lead Chris to estimate a higher speed than the actual as well as more damage to the cars as 'smashed' suggests a more dramatic event.

KEY TERMS

Anxiety

- A nervous emotional state where we fear something unpleasant is about to occur. Physiological arousal such as increased heart rate and rapid breathing are experienced.

Weapon focus

- The anxiety experienced when the presence of a weapon distracts attention from other features of the event. This reduces the accuracy of identification of the perpetrator.

Apply it

Scenario. Train passengers travelling home after a football match witnessed a fight between rival supporters in one of the carriages. One of the supporters drew a knife and threatened a fan from the other team. Passengers who witnessed the incident were asked by police to look at a series of photographs to identify the supporters involved in the confrontation.

From your knowledge of the effects of anxiety, what advice can you give the police about whether they can expect passengers to correctly identify the fans? (4 marks)

Explanation. Findings from lab studies suggest accurate recall of the supporters' identities would be poorer due to the presence of the knife. The **weapon focus** effect predicts the passengers' attention would be focused on the knife to the detriment of other features of the scene, such as the faces of those involved in the fight. However, interviews with real-life victims of violent bank robberies found those who were directly threatened showed more accurate recall than bystanders, meaning some passengers may be able to correctly identify the fans, especially if they were directly threatened. Passengers' level of emotional sensitivity may mean some witnesses will be more accurate that others. Neurotic witnesses are expected to show poorer recall than those deemed more stable (less emotionally sensitive).

Accuracy of eyewitness testimony: Anxiety

Anxiety has a negative effect on memory

How? Johnson and Scott (1976) arranged for participants to be sitting in a waiting room while an argument was going on in the next room. In condition one a man ran through the waiting room carrying a greasy pen (low **anxiety**). In condition two the man was holding a bloody knife (high anxiety). Later, participants were asked to identify the man from a set of photographs.

Shown? Mean accuracy in identifying the man was 49% in condition one (pen), dropping to 33% accuracy in condition two (knife). Recordings of participants' eye movements showed the presence of the knife caused attention to be focused on the weapon rather than the man's face.

Anxiety has a positive effect on memory

How? Christianson and Hubinette (1993) interviewed 58 people 4–15 months after witnessing bank robberies. Witnesses were either bank tellers (high anxiety as directly threatened) or bystanders (lower anxiety).

Shown? All witnesses showed good memories of the event (better than 75% accurate recall). The bank tellers had the best recall, suggesting that high anxiety creates more enduring and accurate memories.

The Yerkes-Dodson effect

Deffenbacher (1983) found 10 of the studies reviewed showed higher levels of arousal increased eyewitness accuracy while 11 showed the opposite. The Yerkes-Dodson effect explains that when anxiety/arousal is moderate memory performance would be enhanced but when anxiety/arousal is too low or too extreme accuracy is reduced.

Evaluation

Real life versus laboratory studies

One strength of Christianson and Hubinette's research was that the effect of anxiety was studied in the context of a real crime. Laboratory studies may not create the levels of anxiety experienced by witnesses of actual crimes.

No simple conclusion

Christianson and Hubinette found higher levels of anxiety led to more accurate recall, but Deffenbacher found increased anxiety reduces accuracy in laboratory studies and real-life studies show an ever greater loss of accuracy. These contradictory findings may be explained by considering the level of violence experienced by witnesses. Halford and Milne (2005) found victims of violent crimes showed more accurate recall than witnesses of non-violent crimes.

Weapon focus may result from surprise rather than anxiety

In Pickel's study (1998) participants who saw a thief enter a hairdressers carrying a raw chicken (low threat, high surprise) or handgun (high threat, high surprise) were poorer at identifying the thief than those who saw the thief with scissors (high threat, low surprise) or a wallet (low threat, low surprise).

Level of emotional sensitivity may affect recall accuracy

Bothwell et al. (1987) found **'stable' personalities** (less emotionally sensitive) showed increasing levels of accuracy as stress increased whereas for **'neurotic' personalities** accuracy decreased as stress increased. The modest effect sizes seen in anxiety studies may be due to the averaging out the low accuracy and high accuracy scores from different personalities.

An alternative model to Yerkes-Dodson

Fazey and Hardy's (1988) suggests that, rather than a gradual decrease in performance as anxiety increases beyond an optimal level (the Yerkes-Dodson effect), sometimes a catastrophic decline in performance occurs due to increased mental anxiety. While the inverted U of the Yerkes-Dodson model explains the effect of physiological arousal, the **catastrophe theory** explains the effect of mental anxiety.

Improving the accuracy of eyewitness testimony:
The cognitive interview

 Description of the cognitive interview (CI)

Based on psychological principles concerning effective memory recall, Geiselman *et al.* (1984) developed four distinct components.

- **Mental reinstatement of original context**

  Mentally recreate the physical and psychological environment of the event.

  Aims to make memories more accessible by providing contextual and emotional cues to aid memory retrieval.

- **Report everything**

  Include every single detail of the event no matter how insignificant or irrelevant.

  Memories are interconnected so recall of one detail may cue memories of other details.

- **Change order**

  Take alternative pathways through the timeline, e.g. reverse the order of events.

  Recalling in a different order prevents pre-existing schema influencing what is recalled.

- **Change perspective**

  Recall the incident from multiple perspectives, e.g. imagine how events would have appeared to others at the scene.

  Considering what others may have seen disrupts the effect schemas have on recall.

 Evaluation

Research into the effectiveness of the CI

A meta-analysis of 53 studies found the CI generated on average 34% more correct information than standard interview techniques (Köhnken *et al.*, 1999). Effectiveness may be due to individual components of the CI technique. Milne and Bull (2002) found when asked to *report everything* and *mentally reinstate the event* recall was significantly higher compared to a control group and conditions where just one component was used.

Quantity versus quality

Köhnken *et al.* (1999) found an 81% increase in correct information compared to the standard interview. However, they also found a 61% increase of incorrect information. Police need to treat all information collected from CIs with caution as use of the technique does not guarantee accurate recall.

CI may be useful when interviewing older witnesses

Older witnesses may be overly cautious when reporting events so the CI's emphasis on the importance of mentioning any detail no matter how unimportant is useful. Mello and Fisher (1996) found the CI produced more information than the standard interview for recall of a film clip. This advantage was greatest for older participants (mean age 72 years) compared to younger participants (mean age 22 years).

Time constraints restrict the use of the CI

The CI takes longer to conduct than a standard interview and officers require special training, which also takes time to deliver. For these reasons police offers prefer to use deliberate strategies aimed at limiting an eyewitness' report to the minimum amount of information deemed necessary.

Difficulties in establishing effectiveness

The CI is difficult to research in the real world as police forces may choose to use different components of the technique. For example, the Thames Valley Police do not ask witnesses to consider the event from *another perspective* while other police forces only use *mentally reinstate the event* and *report everything* (Kebbell and Wagstaff, 1996).

Apply it

Scenario. Saul was shopping in his local supermarket when he saw another customer hiding items in their jacket. The customer then tried to leave the store but security guards gave chase and eventually caught the customer just before they reached the store exit, at which point both guard and customer tumbled to the ground. When police arrived the customer accused the security guard of deliberately throwing them to the ground. The guard, however, argued they both tripped. Police officers decide to interview Saul to gain a better understanding of the incident.

What advice would you give police who wish to interview Saul using the CI technique? (4 marks)

Explanation. Saul could consider events from another perspective. For example, what might shoppers nearer to the exit have seen? He could also change the order when recalling, such as starting from the moment the two fell to the ground and working backwards. These techniques aim to disrupt the effect schemas have on Saul's recall of the event. The CI technique has been shown to improve the amount of correct information recalled compared to the standard interview, but it can also decrease the quality of information. Research has shown incorrect information also increases. Therefore, Saul's recollections should be treated with caution and cross-referenced with other evidence.

Chapter 3

Attachment

3.1.3 Attachment

- Caregiver–infant interactions in humans: reciprocity and interactional synchrony. Stages of attachment identified by Schaffer. Multiple attachments and the role of the father.
- Animal studies of attachment: Lorenz and Harlow.
- Explanations of attachment: learning theory and Bowlby's monotropic theory. The concepts of critical period and internal working model.
- Ainsworth's Strange Situation. Types of attachment: secure, insecure-avoidant and insecure-resistant. Cultural variations in attachment, including van Ijzendoorn.
- Bowlby's theory of maternal deprivation. Romanian orphan studies: the effects of institutionalisation.
- The influence of early attachment on childhood and adult relationships, including the role of an internal working model.

Key terms (highlight each cell when you can define the term for 3 marks)

Caregiver–infant interactions and stages **(Schaffer)**	Animal studies **(Lorenz, Harlow)**	Explanations of attachment **(Learning theory, Bowlby)**	Types of attachment **(Ainsworth)**	Damaged attachments **(Bowlby, Romanian orphans)**	Influence of early attachments
Reciprocity	Imprinting	Monotropy	Secure	Maternal deprivation	Internal working model
Interactional synchrony		Critical period	Insecure-avoidant	Institutionalisation	
Multiple attachments		Internal working model	Insecure-resistant		

Content checklist

1. In each 'describe, apply and evaluate' cell tick when you have produced brief notes.
2. Once you feel you have a good grasp of the topic add a second tick to the cell.
3. When you feel you have complete mastery of the topic and would be able to answer an exam question without the aid of notes highlight the cell.

I am able to...	Describe	Apply	Evaluate
Caregiver–infant interactions: reciprocity and interactional synchrony			
Stages of attachment identified by Schaffer			
Multiple attachments and the role of the father			
Animal studies of attachment: Lorenz			
Animal studies of attachment: Harlow			
Explanations of attachment: Learning theory			
Explanations of attachment: Bowlby's monotropic theory			
Concepts of a critical period and an internal working model			
Ainsworth's Strange Situation			
Types of attachment: secure, insecure-avoidant, insecure-resistant			
Cultural variations in attachment including van Ijzendoorn			
Bowlby's theory of maternal deprivation			
Romanian orphan studies: the effects of institutionalisation			
The influence of early attachment on childhood and adult relationships, including the role of an internal working model			

Caregiver–infant interactions

 Reciprocity

Infants coordinate their actions with those of the **caregiver** to form a kind of conversation. Caregivers use the infant's signals to anticipate behaviour and respond accordingly. Caregiver sensitivity lays the foundation for later **attachment** between caregiver and infant.

 Interactional synchrony

How? Meltzoff and Moore (1977) carried out a controlled observation. An adult displayed three different facial expressions (tongue protrusion, mouth opening and lip protrusion) and one-hand gesture to see if the infant imitated. Observations were recorded and infant responses judged by independent observers.

Showed? Infants as young as 2 or 3 weeks old imitated specific gestures. In a later study, it was found 3-day-old infants showed the same **interactional synchrony**. The ability to mimic gestures at such a young age suggests that imitation behaviour is not learned but an innate ability.

 Real or pseudo-imitation

Piaget (1962) argues true imitation only develops at the end of the first year. Interactional synchrony is 'response training', e.g. when the infant copies the adult they are rewarded with a smile so the behaviour is repeated. This is pseudo-imitation: not consciously translating what they see into a matching movement.

However, Murray and Trevarthen (1985) support Meltzoff and Moore's view.

How? Two-month-old infants interacted with their mother via a video monitor in real time. A pre-recorded video tape of their mother was then played meaning the mother's facial and bodily gestures did not respond to those of the infant.

Showed? Infants showed real distress when their gestures did not elicit a meaningful response. This suggests the infant is an active partner in interaction rather than just displaying rewarded responses.

 Evaluation

Research explains how children begin to understand mental states

Meltzoff (2005) developed a 'like me' hypothesis of infant development: first, there is a connection between what an infant sees and imitation; second, infants associate their own acts and underlying mental states; third, infants project their own internal experiences onto others performing similar acts – leading to a **theory of mind**.

Behaviour may be an intentional response

Abravanel and DeYong (1991) exposed infants aged 5 weeks and 12 weeks to two object models who showed tongue protrusion and mouth opening/closing. Neither age imitated the models. However, 5 week olds did show partial tongue protrusions when this behaviour was modelled by an adult, showing that imitation behaviour is a specific response to other humans.

Problems with testing infant behaviour

Infants' mouths are in fairly constant motion and the expressions tested occur frequently, making it difficult to determine specific imitation from general facial activity. To increase internal validity of their data, Meltzoff and Moore used independent observers (who had no idea what the adult had portrayed) to judge the infants' gestures.

Failure to replicate research findings into intentional synchrony

Marian et al. (1996) replicated Murray and Trevarthen's study but found infants couldn't distinguish between real-life interactions and pre-recorded videos of their mother, suggesting infants are not actually responding to the adult. However, the problem may lie with the procedure rather than the imitation abilities of infants involved in the study.

Research suggests a relationship between synchrony and attachment

Isabella et al. (1989) found more strongly attached infant–caregiver pairs showed greater interactional synchrony. Infants who imitated a lot from birth had a better quality of relationship at 3 months (Heimann, 1989).

KEY TERMS

Attachment
- An emotional bond between two people that endures over time. A two-way process leading to behaviours such as clinging and proximity-seeking. Serves the function of protecting an infant.

Caregiver
- Any person who provides care for a child such as a parent, grandparent, sibling, childminder.

Interactional synchrony
- When interacting with each other people tend to mirror each other's facial and body movements. Emotions as well as behaviours can be imitated.

Reciprocity
- Where the actions of one partner elicit a response from the other partner. The responses are not necessarily similar, as in interactional synchrony

Apply it

Scenario. Jacob was studying mothers interacting with their babies. He reported, '**Infant–Mother X**: the mother sticks out her tongue. Her child imitates the action to an extent, partially protruding its tongue in response. The mother then quickly drops her lower jaw so her mouth opens wide. Again, the child copies. **Infant–Mother Y**: Infant Y shows distress through crying and holding its arms out towards the mother. The mother responds by picking the child up and holding him to her body. As she strokes her child's face the infant stops crying and smiles.'

Use your knowledge of caregiver interactions to determine which infant–caregiver pair is displaying reciprocity and which pair is showing interactional synchrony. (4 marks)

Explanation. Infant–Mother Y are showing **reciprocity**. This is because the actions of one elicit a response in the other. E.g. the child cries and the mother responds by offering comfort, leading to a second response (smiling) from the infant. It is like a conversation. Infant–Mother X are showing interactional synchrony. This is because the infant is mirroring the mother's facial gestures. E.g. the mother sticks out her tongue and the child copies the gesture.

Development of attachment

Schaffer's stages of attachment

How? Schaffer and Emerson (1964) studied 60 Glaswegian infants from mainly working-class homes. At the start of the study infants ranged from 5 to 23 weeks and were studied up to their first birthday. Mothers were visited every four weeks during which they reported their infant's response to separation in seven everyday situations, such as being left alone in a room or with other people. Intensity of protest and who the protest was directed at were recorded. Stranger anxiety was assessed through the infant's response to the interviewer.

Showed? Findings were used to construct a description of how attachment develops from stage 1 (indiscriminate), to stage 2 (beginnings of attachment) and stage 3 (discriminate), through to stage 4 (multiple attachments).

Stage 1 – Indiscriminate attachment: Birth to two months

Infants produce similar responses to inanimate and animate objects. Towards the end of this period they begin to show greater preference for social stimuli and tend to be more content when with people. Reciprocity and interactional synchrony help establish relationships with others.

Stage 2 – The beginnings of attachment: Around four months

Infants show general **sociability** (enjoyment of being with other people) preferring human company over inanimate objects. They are able to distinguish between familiar and unfamiliar people but do not show **stranger anxiety**: they can be easily comforted by anyone.

Stage 3 – Discriminate attachment: From seven months

Infants show separation anxiety (distinctly different protest when separated from their primary attachment figure). They show joy when reunited with that particular person and are most comforted by that person. Infants also show stranger anxiety during this period. Quality of the relationship determines attachment formation: mothers who responded quickly and sensitively to the infant's needs and offered the most interactions had intensely attached infants. Schaffer and Emerson found for 65% of the children the first specific attachment was the mother while 30% showed a joint attachment to the mother and one other person.

Stage 4: Multiple attachments

Soon after the primary attachment is formed, the infant develops a wider circle of multiple attachments. Schaffer and Emerson found that, within one month of first becoming attached, 29% of infants had multiple attachments. Within 6 months this had risen to 78% and by the age of one year most infants had developed multiple attachments, with one-third of infants forming five or more **secondary attachments**. Infants also showed separation anxiety in their secondary attachments to fathers, grandparents, siblings, etc.

Evaluation

Unreliable data

Schaffer and Emerson's data may be unreliable as it was based on mothers' reports of their infants. Mothers who are less sensitive to their infant's protests may be less likely to report them. This would create a **systematic bias** which would challenge the validity of the data.

Biased sample

The unique characteristics of the families included in the sample may have biased the sample. A working-class sample from the 1960s may not apply to other social groups in modern society. Today, more women work, meaning children are cared for outside the home. There has also been a rise in stay-at-home fathers in the past 25 years (Cohn *et al.*, 2014).

Apply it

Scenario. Danielle and Kristy were chatting about their children's development. 'I can't leave her with anyone at the moment,' Kristy explained. 'Every time my sister tries to hold her she screams and reaches out for me. When I hold her it's as if her whole face lights up.' Danielle mentioned she doesn't seem to have that difficulty with her son: 'He seems to enjoy being held by everyone. As long as he is having a cuddle or being fed he's happy in anyone's arms'.

Which stage of attachments, identified by Schaffer, do Kristy and Danielle's children seem to have reached? (4 marks)

Explanation. Kristy's child is at stage 3: discriminate attachment. She is displaying stranger anxiety by crying when held by others, such as her aunt. Kirsty seems to be her primary attachment figure as she shows joy when she is reunited with her. Danielle's child is probably younger than Kristy's child as he seems to be at stage 2: the beginnings of attachment. He has yet to form one specific attachment and so is happy to be comforted by anyone; he shows general sociability rather than stranger anxiety.

Are multiple attachments equivalent?

Bowlby (see page 40) believed the infant forms one special emotional relationship (monotropy), with secondary attachments forming an emotional safety net. For example, fathers may offer a special kind of care while sibling relationships teach negotiation skills. Rutter (1995), however, argues all attachment figures are equivalent. Attachments are integrated to form an infant's attachment type.

Cultural variations

The stage model might only apply to **individualistic cultures** (focused on the individual/immediate family's needs). Sagi *et al.* (1994) compared attachments in infants raised in a kibbutz with infants raised in family-based sleeping arrangements. Closeness of attachment with mothers was almost twice as common in family-based arrangements than the communal care of the kibbutz. In **collectivist cultures** (focused on needs of the group) multiple attachments may be more common.

Stage theories suggest development is rather inflexible

For example, Schaffer's stages suggests single attachments are gained before multiple attachments. The problem is that the stage theory becomes a standard by which families are judged as normal. In some situations and cultures multiple attachments may develop first – applying the stage theory risks labelling this as abnormal.

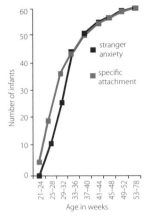

▲ *Schaffer and Emerson (1964) development of specific attachment and rates of stranger anxiety in 60 infants.*

 The role of the father

Schaffer and Emerson found fathers were more likely to be a joint first attachment figure (27%) than an infant's first attachment (3%). This may be because fathers spend less time with their infants. However, studies have shown little relationship between father accessibility and attachment.

Sensitivity to infant's needs

Fathers may lack the emotional sensitivity needed to form an intense attachment. Biologically, the female hormone oestrogen underlies caring behaviour, making women more orientated towards interpersonal goals than men. Socially, sex stereotypes may still affect male behaviour, e.g. being sensitive to the needs of others is seen as a feminine trait.

 Evaluation

Gender differences may not exist

While some research suggests men are less sensitive to infant cues compared to mothers others have found no gender differences. For example, Frodi *et al.* (1978) reported no differences in the physiological reactions of men and women when exposed to videos of infants crying.

Men do form secure attachments

Despite possible differences in sensitivity there is evidence that men do form secure attachments with their children, as in the case of single (male) parent families. Frank *et al.* (1977) found that in two-parent families where the father is the primary caregiver, the mother and father are joint primary attachment figures.

Fathers play an important role as secondary caregivers

Fathers play an important role as secondary caregivers. Fathers have consistently been found to be more playful, physically active and better at providing challenging situations. A lack of sensitivity may play a positive role in development as it fosters problem-solving by making greater communicative and cognitive demands on children (White and Woollett, 1992).

KEY TERMS

Contact comfort
- Physical contact with a caregiver that can provide physical and emotional comfort. For example, a crying baby held by its mother will calm down due to the feeling of safety physical contact provides.

Imprinting
- An innate readiness to develop a strong bond with the mother which takes place during a specific time in development, probably the first few hours after birth/hatching. If a bond is not formed at this time it probably will not happen in the future.

Apply it

Scenario. The following passage appeared in an article on a parenting website. 'Attachment formation is not dependent on feeding. The person who feeds the infant is not necessarily the person who will become the child's main source of comfort. Rather, it seems it is the degree of comfort a caregiver can offer that determines the successful formation of an emotional bond.'

Consider the extent to which attachment research supports the claims made by the passage shown above. (5 marks)

Explanation. Harlow's research into infant rhesus monkeys supports the claims made in the passage. Harlow found the infants spent the majority of time clinging to the cloth-covered mother, regardless of whether it provided food or not. They seemed to use the cloth mother as a safe base: running to it when startled and keeping in close proximity when playing with new toys. This suggests comfort rather than food was the basis of attachment formation as suggested by the website article. However, Harlow studied rhesus monkeys not human infants and therefore caution should be taken when generalising to humans. Although Schaffer and Emerson's research agreed with Harlow's as they found infants were not most attached to the person who fed them, rather it was the quality of the relationship that mattered (the comfort the caregiver offered).

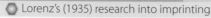

Lorenz's (1935) research into imprinting

How? Gosling eggs were left with their natural mother or placed in an incubator. When they hatched, the first thing the goslings saw was either their natural mother or Lorenz. When placed in the presence of either their mother or Lorenz, goslings who had imprinted on the mother followed her and those imprinted on Lorenz followed him.

Showed? The goslings who saw Lorenz first showed no recognition of their natural mother – they had **imprinted** on Lorenz. Imprinting is restricted to a **critical period**, if the gosling was not exposed to a moving object during this time imprinting did not occur. Lorenz found imprinting to humans does not occur in some animals, e.g. curlews.

Long-term effects. Lorenz (1952) noted that imprinting is irreversible and long lasting. It also had an effect on later mate preference (sexual imprinting), with animals choosing a mate similar to the object with which they were imprinted.

Harlow's (1959) research into contact comfort

How? Infant rhesus monkeys were placed in cages with two wire monkeys, one of which was covered in soft cloth. The amount of time the infants spent with each 'mother' was measured. A mechanical teddy bear was used to deliberately frighten the monkeys and their responses were recorded.

Showed? Most time was spent with the cloth-covered mother. Monkeys with a wire mother who gave milk spent a short time feeding then quickly returned to the cloth-covered mother. When afraid all infants clung to this soft mother and kept in close proximity when playing with new objects. Attachment developed through **contact comfort** rather than feeding as proposed by the learning theory (see page 39).

Long term effects. Motherless monkeys developed abnormally. They froze or fled when approached by other monkeys, did not show normal mating behaviour or cradle their own babies. Like, Lorenz, Harlow identified a critical period – time spend with peers before 3 months of age helped motherless monkeys recover, however, recovery was not seen in infants who spent more than 6 months alone.

Evaluation

Research support for imprinting in animals
Guiton (1966) found leghorn chicks imprinted on yellow rubber gloves used for feeding, and male chickens later tried to mate with the gloves. This implies animals are born with a predisposition to imprint on a moving object within a critical period and that early imprinting is linked to later reproductive behaviour.

Generalising animal studies to human behaviour
Much more human behaviour is governed by conscious decisions, but a number of studies have found observations of animal attachments are mirrored in studies of humans. For example, Schaffer and Emerson (see page 37) found feeding does not form the basis of attachment.

Imprinting is no longer seen as irreversible
Guiton (1966) found that by spending time with their own species, chickens who had initially tried to mate with the rubber gloves were able to engage in normal sexual behaviour. Imprinting is now thought of as a more 'plastic and forgiving mechanism' (Hoffman, 1996).

Confounding variables in Harlow's study
As the two heads of the wire monkeys were different it is possible that the infant monkeys preferred the cloth-covered mother as it had a more attractive head. Harlow's conclusion may lack internal validity.

Ethics of Harlow's study should be questioned
As the infant monkeys showed later difficulties forming relationships with other monkeys it could be said the study created lasting emotional harm. However, some may argue that the knowledge gained can be used to improve care for human (and primate) infants, making it more ethically acceptable.

Learning theory of attachment

All behaviour (including attachment) is learned rather than innate. Children are born 'blank slates' upon which experiences are written. Learning occurs through **classical** or **operant conditioning**.

Classical conditioning

- Before conditioning: food is the **unconditioned stimulus** (UCS) and pleasure is the **unconditioned response** (UCR).
- During conditioning: items present when feeding occurs become associated with food. This might include the mother, the chair in which she sits, even sounds. These items are called **neutral stimuli** (NS).
- After conditioning: consistent pairing of the mother (NS) with food (UCS) means the stimulus takes on the properties of the UCS. The mother has now become the **conditioned stimulus** (CS) and produces a **conditioned response** (CR), in this case pleasure.

Operant conditioning

- Hunger is a drive that motivates the infant to reduce the discomfort experienced when hungry
- Feeding reduces this drive, leading to pleasure. This is **positive reinforcement** – it is rewarding and so the behaviour is more likely to be repeated in future. Food becomes the **primary reinforcer** because it supplies the reward.
- The person who supplied the food is associated (through classical conditioning) with avoiding discomfort and so becomes the **secondary reinforcer** – they become a source of reward in their own right. Attachment occurs as the child seeks the person who supplies the reward.

Social learning theory

Children observe their parents' affectionate behaviour and imitate this (children **model** the behaviour of their role models). Parents also instruct their children about how to behave in relationships and reward appropriate attachment behaviour such as giving kisses and hugs.

Evaluation

Learning theory has some explanatory power

Association and reward do play a part in learning. However, food may not be the main reinforcer, rather the attention and responsiveness from a caregiver are important rewards not considered by **learning theory**. Infants may also imitate responsiveness and so learn how to conduct relationships.

Learning theory is based on animal research

Behaviourists believe humans are no different from other animals in terms of how they learn. Others argue that learning theory is an over-simplified explanation of human behaviour. Attachment involves innate predispositions and mental activity that are not considered by learning theory.

Contact comfort is more important than food

Harlow (1959) provides strong evidence that feeding has nothing to do with attachment (see page 38). Infant rhesus monkeys showed a preference for a cloth mother to a wire mother over a wire mother who provided food.

Drive reduction theory is largely ignored today

Drive reduction can only explain a limited number of behaviours and so has lost popularity as an explanation. Furthermore, the theory does not adequately explain how secondary reinforcers work. Secondary reinforcers do not directly reduce discomfort but they are rewarding in themselves.

Bowlby's theory provides a better explanation of attachment

First, it can explain *why* attachments occur, whereas learning theory only explains *how* attachments form. Second, Bowlby's theory offers a better explanation of other research, for example Schaffer and Emerson's finding that infants are not always most strongly attached to the person who feeds them.

KEY TERMS

Classical conditioning
- Learning through association. A neutral stimulus (NS) is consistently paired with an unconditioned stimulus (UCS) eventually becomes the conditioned stimulus (CS), producing a conditioned response (CR).

Learning theory
- A group of explanations (classical and operant conditioning), which explain behaviour in terms of learning rather than inborn tendencies or higher order thinking.

Operant conditioning
- Learning through reinforcement or punishment. If a behaviour is followed by a desirable consequence, then that behaviour is more likely to occur again in the future.

Apply it

Scenario. Ian and his partner Megan are new parents. When their daughter Sara was born Megan gave up work to care for her full-time. Ian has to work long hours as he is the sole source of income for the family. Ian feels his daughter has a much stronger bond with Megan than with him.

How would learning theory explain Sara's attachment behaviour?
(6 marks)

Explanation. Megan is more likely to be the person who feeds Sara. Feeding (UCS) gives Sara feelings of pleasure (UCR). With repeated feeding Sara associates Megan with pleasure and so her mother has become the conditioned stimulus (CS). Ian works long hours so feeds his daughter less often, making it likely Sara will form an association with him. Food is a primary reinforcer for Sara as it reduces the uncomfortable feeling of hunger. Megan has become a secondary reinforcer as Sara has associated feeding with Megan and the removal of hunger. Again, because Ian is not as involved in feeding he is less likely to become the secondary reinforcer and so less likely to form a strong attachment.

KEY TERMS

Continuity hypothesis
- The idea that emotionally secure infants go on to be emotionally secure, trusting and confident adults.

Critical period
- A biologically determined period during which certain characteristics develop. Outside this time window such development will not be possible.

Internal working model
- A mental model of the world which enables individuals to predict and control their environment. In the case of attachment, the model relates to a person's expectations about relationships.

Monotropy (monotropic)
- The relationship the infant has with his/her primary attachment figure is of special significance in emotional development.

Social releaser
- A social behaviour or characteristic, such as smiling, that elicits caregiving and leads to attachment.

Apply it

Scenario. Aisha loves her baby sister and tells everyone about her big eyes and little squashy nose. Aisha enjoys feeding her and helps out with nappy changes. However, she sometimes finds it difficult to soothe her when she cries. Aisha's mother seems to instantly know what the baby needs and is able to calm her much more quickly than other family members.

How could Bowlby's attachment theory explain Aisha's experience? (4 marks)

Explanation. Aisha's baby sister, has social releasers such as big eyes and a little nose that encourage attachment formation. Aisha is motivated to remain in close proximity and interact with her. Although Aisha is involved in caregiving she may lack the level of sensitivity needed to become the primary attachment figure (she often finds it difficult to sooth her). Aisha's mother, however, can quickly identify the baby's needs and so is more likely to form that one special relationship (monotropy) during the critical period of 3 to 6 months. Aisha's sister is likely to form a secondary attachment to her which will play a role in the infant's social development.

Bowlby's monotropic theory of attachment

Bowlby's maternal deprivation theory (see page 43) led him to think about the nature (how attachments form) and function (why attachments form) of the attachment bond.

Why attachments form

In the environment of evolutionary adaptiveness (EEA), parents who are attached to their offspring provide the care needed for survival. Infants with an attachment seek proximity ensuring they are well protected. Those possessing this attachment trait are more likely to survive, reproduce and pass on the trait to the next generation.

How attachments form

- Bowlby argued that who infants attach to is determined by sensitivity. The concept of caregiver sensitivity is an important feature of Ainsworth's work (see page 41) and research into caregiver–infant interactions (see page 35). Infants who do not form an attachment during the **critical period** (around 3–6 months) seem to have difficulty forming attachments later in life.
- **Social releasers** are innate mechanisms that explain how attachments are formed. We are predisposed to find social releasers appealing which elicits a caregiving response.
- **Monotropy** – infants have one special emotional bond, usually to their biological mother. Secondary attachments also form, providing the infant with an emotional safety net which is important for healthy psychological and social development.

The consequences of attachment

The infant forms a mental representation of their monotropic relationship - an **internal working model** which gives an insight into the caregiver's behaviour. The model provides a template for all future relationships. The **continuity hypothesis** predicts strongly attached infants continue to be socially and emotionally competent as adults, whereas adults with insecure childhood attachments have more difficulties.

Evaluation

Support for the continuity hypothesis
The Minnesota parent–child study found infants classified as securely attached were rated highest for social competence, were less isolated, and more popular and empathetic in late adolescence (Sroufe *et al.*, 2005).

Age of attachment is species specific
Young monkeys cling to their mother as she moves around their habitat while human mothers carry their infants. Only when human infants start crawling (around 6 months) is attachment vital to ensure proximity to the caregiver. As attachments in humans develop during this time the concept of attachment as an adaptive function is supported.

Multiple attachments versus monotropy
Rutter (1995) argued that all attachment figures are equally important, integrating to form an internal working model. In contrast Bowlby distinguishes between primary and secondary attachments, but does suggest secondary attachments contribute. Grossmann and Grossmann (1991) found fathers play a key role as secondary attachments in infants' social development.

A sensitive period rather than a 'critical' period
Rutter and Sonuga-Barke (2010) found while it is less likely attachments will form after the critical period it is not impossible (see page 42). Researchers now prefer to use the term **sensitive period** to describe the period of time when the child is most receptive to attachment formation.

Temperament rather than sensitivity determines attachment
Kagan (1984) proposes infants with an 'easy' **temperament** (innate emotional personality) are easier to interact with and so are more likely to form secure attachments. 'Difficult' children aged one to three days old were later judged to be more likely to have insecure attachments (Belsky and Rovine, 1987).

Ainsworth's Strange Situation: Types of attachment

The **Strange Situation** (Ainsworth *et al.*, 1971, 1978) systematically tests the nature of attachment by observing infants' behaviour under conditions of mild stress and novelty.

The Strange Situation

How? 106 middle-class infants aged between 9 and 18 months were placed in a novel environment: a 9 × 9 foot room containing age-appropriate toys. The infant's behaviour is observed across eight episodes.

This enables observation of the infant's response to:

- **Separation anxiety** when the caregiver leaves.
- **Reunion behaviour** when the caregiver returns.
- **Stranger anxiety** when an unknown adult approaches.
- **Willingness to explore** the novel environment (mother as a safe base).

Typically a group of observers view the situation via video or one-way mirror, recording what the infant is doing every 15 seconds.

Showed? Infants observed showed a decline in exploratory behaviour and an increase in crying from situation 2 onwards (parent and child play together). Three main patterns of behaviour were identified, leading to the identification of three main attachment types.

	Secure attachment (Type A)	Insecure-avoidant (Type B)	Insecure-resistant (Type C)
Willingness to explore	High	High	Low
Stranger anxiety	Moderate	Low	High
Separation anxiety	Easy to sooth	Indifferent	Distressed
Reunion behaviour	Enthusiastic	Avoids contact	Seeks and rejects
Percentage of infants	66%	22%	12%

Evaluation

Observations have high reliability

High inter-rater reliability is required for measurements to be seen as meaningful. Ainsworth *et al.* (1978) found .94 agreement between raters (1.0 would be a perfect correlation) when measuring exploratory behaviour.

Real-world application

The Circle of Security Project (Cooper *et al.*, 2005) teaches caregivers to better recognise and understand their infant's experience of distress. The project led to a decrease in the number of caregivers classified as disordered (from 60% to 15%) and an increase in securely attached infants (from 32% to 40%).

Internal validity

The Strange Situation may only measure the quality of one particular relationship. Main and Weston (1981) showed children behaved differently depending on with parent they were with. However, Main (1999) found that, when re-assessed at 9 years of age, attachment type was mainly influenced by the mother. This supports the concept of monotropy and the internal validity of the measurement.

Other types of attachment

Main and Soloman's (1986) analysis of over 200 Strange Situation videotapes identified Type D **insecure-disordered attachment**. Children who do not seem to have a consistent attachment type and who lack a coherent strategy for coping with separation from the caregiver. In a meta-analysis of 80 studies, Van Ijzendoorn et al. (1999) found 15% of infants were classified as Type D.

Maternal reflective functioning

Some studies have found a rather low correlation between measures of secure attachment and maternal sensitivity. Slade *et al.* (2005) found **maternal reflective functioning** (the ability to understand what someone else is thinking and feeling) played a greater role in establishing attachment type.

Apply it

Scenario Tom and his mother participated in a Strange Situation study. Observers noted that Tom showed high willingness to explore and a moderate level of distress when approached by a stranger. Amelia and her mother also took part. Unlike Tom, Amelia did not explore and showed intense distress when with a stranger. Compared to Amelia, Tom showed great enthusiasm when reunited with his mother. Amelia sought comfort but reacted angrily when held.

Based on the behaviours displayed how would observers classify each child's attachment type? (3 marks)

Explanation Tom would be classified as securely attached as he uses his mother as a safe base to explore the room. He is comfortable with social interactions showing enthusiastic reunion behaviour and only moderate distress when with a stranger.

Amelia is showing behaviours associated with insecure-resistant attachment. She shows low willingness to explore and becomes very upset in the presence of a stranger. Her reunion with her mother suggests she is seeking but at the same time rejecting interaction.

Apply it

Scenario. A researcher carried out cross-cultural research to compare the attachment types across two countries: Germany and Japan. Mother-infant pairs were observed in the Strange Situation enabling classifications of secure, insecure-avoidance and insecure-resistant to be made.

Based on Van Ijzendoorn and Kroonenberg's research predict the researcher's findings. (2 marks)

Why should the researcher treat their findings with caution? (4 marks)

Explanation. The researcher may find that for both countries secure attachment is the most common classification. Germany is likely to show more insecure-avoidant than insecure-resistant attachments, while Japanese infants are more likely to be classified as insecure-resistant than insecure-avoidant. However, these findings should be treated with caution as the Strange Situation is based on Western ideas of childcare and attachment behaviours. It is unlikely the Japanese infants will have been left alone before experiencing the Strange Situation and so show extreme distress compared to German children whose parents have encouraged independence. This could result in Japanese children being incorrectly classified as insecure-resistant. Furthermore, the researcher should not mistake culture for country, Van Ijzendoorn and Kroonenberg found more variation within cultures than between them so one study of Germany or Japan cannot be said to represent a whole culture due to the influence of subculture on childrearing practices.

Cultural variations in attachment

Van Ijzendoorn and Kroonenberg (1988) suggest there are **cultural variations** in childrearing practices, although secure attachments are the dominant form.

How? Van Ijzendoorn and Kroonenberg investigated **inter-cultural variations** (differences in attachments between cultures) and **intra-cultural variations** (attachment differences within a culture). They conducted a meta-analysis of 32 studies: over 2,000 Strange Situation classifications in eight different countries.

Showed? Secure attachment was the most common classification in all eight countries. Insecure-avoidant was the next most common – except in Israel and Japan (**collectivist cultures**). **Individualist cultures**, such as Great Britain, West Germany and USA, showed more insecure-avoidant than insecure-resistant classifications. Variation within cultures was 1.5 times greater than the variation between cultures.

Cultural similarities

Tronick *et al.*'s (1992) studied the Efe tribe from Zaire. The tribe live in extended family groups with infants being looked after and breastfed by various women but sleeping with their own mother at night. Despite such different childrearing practices, 6-month-old infants still showed one primary attachment.

Cultural differences

Grossman and Grossman (1991) found German infants tended to be classified as insecurely attached. German culture involves keeping some interpersonal distance and so infants do not engage in proximity-seeking behaviours in the Strange Situation.

Takahashi's (1990) observations of Japanese mother-infant pairs found no insecure-avoidant attachments but 32% were judged insecure-resistant. For 90% of these infants their extreme distress led to the situation being stopped. As Japanese infants are rarely separated from their mother the extreme distress made them appear insecure-resistant.

⚙ Evaluation

Should attachment theory be culturally based?
Rothbaum *et al.* (2000) argued there may be a small set of universal principles, such as attachment ensures protection, but childcare practices will vary naturally. However, Posada and Jacobs (2001) cite cross-cultural evidence supporting the universality of attachment, highlighting that caregiver sensitivity is linked to secure attachment.

Similarities may not be innately determined
An increasingly global culture rather than an innate mechanism may explain similarities in attachment behaviour. Some cultural similarities may be due to the effects of mass media: parents are now able to access childrearing information from all over the world via electronic and print media to inform their parenting.

The impact of subcultures should be considered
Van Ijzendoorn and Sagi's (2001) study of attachment in Tokyo (urban setting) found similar attachment distributions to Western studies whereas studies from rural Japan showed more insecure-resistant classifications. This meta-analysis shows more variation occurs within rather than between cultures.

Cross cultural research involves the use of imposed etics
The Strange Situation assumes willingness to explore, indicates a secure attachment. However, in traditional Japanese culture dependence rather than independence denotes secure attachment.

Attachment research is influenced by American culture
Bowlby and Ainsworth see securely attached infants as maturing into socially and emotionally competent children and adults, with 'competent' implying independence. However, in Japan competence is represented as being group rather than self-oriented.

Bowlby's theory of maternal deprivation

Bowlby (1951, 1953) proposed that prolonged emotional **deprivation** would have long-term consequences in terms of the child's emotional development.

 Key study: 44 juvenile thieves

How? Bowlby (1944) analysed the case histories of 88 maladjusted children attending the Child Guidance Clinic. Half of these children had been caught stealing (the 44 thieves). Bowlby classified 14 of the 44 thieves as affectionless psychopaths – they lacked normal signs of affection, shame or sense of responsibility.

Showed? 86% of the affectionless thieves had experienced early frequent separations from their mothers compared to 17% of the other thieves. 39% of all the thieves had experienced early separations. Bowlby suggested the long-term consequences of deprivation was emotional maladjustment and even mental health problems.

The value of maternal care

Spitz and Wolf (1946) observed how 100 children placed in institutions quickly became severely depressed. Skodak and Skeels (1949) found institutionalised children scored poorly on intelligence tests but showed an improvement of almost 30 points when cared for by inmates in a different institution. Bowlby argued a 'warm, intimate and continuous relationship' with a mother (or permanent mother-substitute) is vital for mental health.

Critical period

Separation from the primary caregiver will only lead to emotional disturbance if it occurs before the age of about two and a half years (for Bowlby, this risk extends to 5 years of age), and if there is no mother-substitute available.

Evaluation

Support for long-term effects

Bifulco et al. (1992) found women who had been separated from their mothers as children were more likely to experience depression or anxiety disorders (25%) compared to women who had no experience of separation (15%). Mental health problems were much greater in women whose loss occurred before the age of 6.

Research had a significant impact on post-war childrearing practices

Before Bowlby's research, children were separated from their parents during hospital stays with visiting being discouraged or forbidden. Robertson and Bowlby (1952) filmed 2-year-old Laura over an 8-day stay in hospital during which she showed frequent distress and begged to go home.

Emotional separation can also have a damaging effect

Radke-Yarrow et al. (1985) studied severely depressed mothers who were physically present but unable to provide suitable emotional care. 55% of the children (mean age 32 months) were insecurely attached compared with 29% of children with non-depressed mothers.

Securely attached children cope better with separation

Bowlby et al. (1956) studied 60 children below the age of 4 who had experienced prolonged hospital stays due to TB. Children had received poor substitute care from nurses and only one family visit a week. As adolescents 63% were judged to be more maladjusted than 'normal' children. Those children with secure attachments were more resilient and so coped better with deprivation.

Deprivation versus privation

Rutter (1981) claimed Bowlby did not make it clear whether the child had formed an attachment that was subsequently broken or if they had never formed an attachment in the first place. Rutter argues **privation** (never forming an attachment) has potentially far more serious consequences than deprivation (loss of an attachment).

KEY TERMS

Deprivation
- The loss of emotional care that is normally provided by a primary caregiver.

	Separations from mother before the age of two		Total
	Frequent	None	
Affectionless thieves	12 (86%)	2 (14%)	14
Other thieves	5 (17%)	25 (83%)	30
All thieves	17 (39%)	27 (61%)	44
Control participants	2 (4%)	42 (96%)	44

▲ Findings from Bowlby's 44 juvenile thieves study.

Apply it

Scenario. Jamie lost his mother to a terminal illness when he was 3 years old. Before her death she had spent a long time in hospital. Jamie rarely visited her as his father felt it would be too upsetting for him to see his mother.

Using Bowlby's theory of maternal deprivation explain how Jamie might be affected by this separation from his mother. (6 marks)

Explanation. Bowlby believed a child who experiences deprivation during the critical period is at risk of later emotional disturbance. As Jamie experienced separation from his mother before the age of 5 Bowlby would argue he could develop difficulties in childhood and adulthood. Bowlby argued, 'mother-love in infancy is as important for mental health as are vitamins and proteins for physical health', implying Jamie will experience poorer mental health than children who have not experienced deprivation. Jamie experienced prolonged separation from his mother prior to her death and so may develop affectionless psychopathy as identified by Bowlby in his study of 44 thieves. This would mean Jamie will lack normal signs of affection, shame or a sense of responsibility.

KEY TERMS

Institutionalisation

- The effect of institutional care, especially how time spent in an institution such as an orphanage can affect the development of children. Possible effects include social, mental and physical underdevelopment. Some of these effects may be irreversible.

Apply it

Scenario. Nadia and Aaron are in the process of adopting a four-month-old infant. The birth mother was unable to look after the child and so she has been cared for by a state orphanage in Russia. Due to a lack of funding the orphanage has few staff and conditions are less than ideal, with limited resources to provide a good standard of physical care and cognitive stimulation.

What insights can institutional research offer Nadia and Aaron regarding their upcoming adoption? (4 marks)

Explanation. Due to the lack of resources in the orphanage the child may be underdeveloped both physically and cognitively. Research suggests lack of emotional care and mental stimulation can lead to developmental delays. They should also be aware that the child may show disinhibited attachment showing overfamiliarity with strangers and attention seeking as they age. However, the child is currently four months old and so still within the sensitive period for attachment formation. Therefore the effects of institutionalisation may not be as extreme if the adoption is completed quickly. Furthermore, research suggests that if Nadia and Aaron can provide high-quality substitute emotional care the effects of institutionalisation can be overcome.

Romanian orphan studies: effects of institutionalisation

In the past, institutions offered little emotional care. Today many institutions strive to avoid this. However, in some countries limited resources mean it is still not possible to offer a good standard of emotional care.

Key study: Rutter and Sonuga-Barke (2010)

How? 165 children who had spent their early lives in Romanian institutions were either adopted before the age of two (111 children) or adopted by the age of four (54 children). Physical, cognitive and social development were tested at 4, 5, 11 and 15 years of age. They were compared to a control group of 52 British children adopted before the age of 6 months.

Showed? At the time of adoption, Romanian children were behind on all developmental measures. By 4 years of age almost all of the early adopted children had caught up with the British children. Significant deficits remained in a substantial minority of the late adoptees: many showed disinhibited attachments and had problems with peers. Forming attachments may make long-term consequences less severe.

Other studies of Romanian orphans

At four and a half years of age Romanian infants adopted by Canadian families were physically smaller and had poorer physical health than a matched control group. However, these difference disappeared by ten and a half years (Le Mare and Audet, 2006).

Zeanah *et al.* (2005) compared 136 Romanian orphans who had spent, on average, 90% of their lives in an institute to a control group of Romanian children who had never been **institutionalised**. The institutionalised children (aged 12–31 months) showed signs of disinhibited attachment.

Effects of institutionalisation

- Physical underdevelopment: lack of emotional care has been found to be the cause of deprivational dwarfism.
- Intellectual underfunctioning: Skodak and Skeels (see page 43) found institutionalised children scored poorly on intelligence tests.
- Disinhibited attachment: a form of insecure attachment characterised by overfriendliness with strangers and attention seeking.
- Poor parenting: Women reared in institutions experienced more difficulties acting as parents (Quinton *et al.*, 1984).

Evaluations

Value of longitudinal studies

By following the development of adopted children it is possible to determine whether the major effects of early institutional care disappear with sufficient time and high quality care.

Research has been used to improve the lives of children in such care

Romanian orphan research highlights the importance of early adoption before the sensitive period for attachment formation. Singer *et al.* (1985) showed early adopted infants are just as securely attached to their adopted mother as non-adopted infants.

Institutionalisation may just be slow development

It may be that the effects of institutionalisation disappear over time if good quality emotional care is provided. Development may continue beyond the time period and so effects may not be irreversible as research suggests.

Deprivation is only one factor

The Romanian orphans also experienced poor physical conditions and the lack of cognitive stimulation impacted on their health and development. Damage may only occur when multiple risk factors are experienced.

Individual differences

Rutter suggests some of the children may have received special attention in the institution, perhaps because they smiled more, meaning they did have some early attachment experiences.

The influence of early attachment

Primary attachment quality is positively correlated with the quality of later relationships.

The role of the internal working model

Interaction with the primary attachment figure teaches the infant what relationships are and how people in relationships treat each other. This forms the **internal working model**, which can predict the behaviour of other people in the future.

Key study: Hazan and Shaver (1987)

How? 205 men and 415 women responded to a love quiz placed in an American news publication asking about current attachment experiences, attachments in childhood and attitudes towards love.

Showed? Attachment classifications were similar to infancy – 56% secure attached, 25% insecure-avoidant, 19% insecure-resistant. Securely attached adults described their love experiences as happy and trusting, having longer lasting relationships (on average 10 years) than insecure-avoidant (6 years) and insecure-resistant (5 years). Securely attached adults tended to have a positive internal working model.

Behaviours influenced by the internal working model

- **Childhood friendships**. The Minnesota child-parent study found securely attached infants were rated highest for social competence, were less isolated, more popular and empathetic as children. Their internal working model provided higher expectations that others would be friendly and trusting, leading to easier relationships.
- **Poor parenting**. Harlow (see page 38) found that infant rhesus monkeys removed from their mother had later difficulties caring for their own offspring. Quinton et al. (see page 44) showed the same is true for humans.
- **Romantic relationships**. Securely attached individuals tended to have a positive internal working model leading to longer, more satisfying relationships (Hazan and Shaver, 1987).
- **Mental health**. The DSM now recognises attachment disorder as a psychiatric condition. Individuals show no preferred attachment figure, an inability to interact and relate to others evident before the age of 5. Experience of extreme neglect or frequent change of caregiver has led to a lack of an internal working model.

Evaluation

Support from longitudinal studies

Simpson et al. (2007) support Hazan and Shaver's findings. Participants assessed as securely attached at 1 year of age were rated as having higher social competence as children, being closer to their friends at age 16 and were more expressive and emotionally attached to their romantic partners in early adulthood.

Research is correlational so cause and effect is not established

Both attachment type and later love-style could be due to innate temperament. An infant's temperament may affect the way a parent responds which determines their attachment type and may also explain issues with relationships later in life.

Low correlations between infant and adult attachment style

Fraley (2002) reviewed 27 samples where infants were assessed in infancy and later reassessed as adults. Correlations ranged from .50 to as low as .10, suggesting attachment type is not stable.

Overly deterministic

Studies have found plenty of instances where insecurely attached children were experiencing happy relationships in adulthood. Simpson et al. (2007) conclude that research does not suggest that 'an individual's past unalterably determines the course of his/her relationships'.

An alternative explanation

Feeney (1999) suggested that adult attachment patterns may result from the current relationship rather than the individual's early attachment type. Rather than the adult attachment type causing the adult's secure relationship, it is the qualities of the adult relationship that is causing the secure attachment.

KEY TERMS

Internal working model
- A mental model of the world which enables individuals to predict and control their environment. In the case of attachment the model relates to a person's expectations about relationships.

Apply it

Scenario. As an infant Marco seemed to avoid social interaction and intimacy with others. He showed little tendency to cling to his caregiver and was happy to explore with or without the caregiver's presence. This behaviour resulted in Marco being classified as insecurely attached.

How might Marco's behaviour as an adult be influenced by his internal working model? (4 marks)

Explanation. Marco's internal working model may mean he has lower expectations that others are friendly and trusting. Therefore, he may have fewer friendships than people who showed secure attachments in infancy. Marco may also have shorter romantic relationships than securely attached people. Hazan and Shaver found relationships lasted, on average, 6 years for insecure-attached individuals compared to 10 years for those classified as securely attached. Should he become a father he may experience parenting difficulties as his internal working model may not provide a reference point from which to form relationships with his own children.

Chapter 4

Psychopathology

- Definitions of abnormality, including deviation from social norms, failure to function adequately, statistical infrequency and deviation from ideal mental health.
- The behavioural, emotional and cognitive characteristics of phobias, depression and obsessive-compulsive disorder (OCD).
- The behavioural approach to explaining and treating phobias: the two-process model, including classical and operant conditioning; systematic desensitisation, including relaxation and use of hierarchy; flooding.
- The cognitive approach to explaining and treating depression: Beck's negative triad and Ellis' ABC model; cognitive behaviour therapy (CBT), including challenging irrational thoughts.
- The biological approach to explaining and treating OCD: genetic and neural explanations; drug therapy.

Key terms (highlight each cell when you can define the term for 3 marks)

Definitions of abnormality	Mental disorders	The behavioural approach to explaining phobias	The behavioural approach to treating phobias	The cognitive approach to explaining depression	The cognitive approach to treating depression	The biological approach to explaining OCD	The biological approach to treating OCD
Deviation from social norms	Phobia	The two-process model	Systematic desensitisation	ABC model (Ellis, 1962)	Cognitive behaviour therapy (CBT)	Genetic: COMT and SERT genes	SSRIs and tricyclics
Failure to function adequately	Depression	Classical conditioning: initiation	Desensitisation hierarchy	Musturbatory thinking	Challenging irrational thoughts	Neurological: Abnormal neurotransmitter levels	Benzodiazepines
Statistical infrequency	Obsessive compulsive disorder (OCD)	Operant conditioning: maintenance	Flooding	Negative schema and triad (Beck, 1967)	Homework	Neurological: Abnormal brain circuits	GABA
Deviation from ideal mental health		Social learning			Behavioural activation		
Cultural relativism		Diathesis stress model			Unconditional positive regard		

Content checklist

1. In each 'describe, apply and evaluate' cell tick when you have produced brief notes.
2. Once you feel you have a good grasp of the topic add a second tick to the cell.
3. When you feel you have complete mastery of the topic and would be able to answer an exam question without the aid of notes highlight the cell.

I am able to…	Describe	Apply	Evaluate
Deviation from social norms and statistical infrequency			
Failure to function adequately			
Deviation from ideal mental health			
Clinical characterisitics of phobia, depression and OCD			
The behavioural two-process model of phobia, including classical and operant conditioning			
Systematic desensitisation of phobia, including relaxation and the use of hierarchy as a behavioural treatment for phobia			
Flooding as a behavioural treatment for phobia			
Cognitive explanation of depression: Beck's (1967) negative triad			
Cognitive explanation of depression: Ellis' (1962) ABC model			
Cognitive treatment for depression: Cognitive Behaviour Therapy (CBT)			
Cognitive treatment for depression: Challenging irrational thoughts			
Biological explanations of OCD: genetic			
Biological explanations of OCD: neurological			
Biological treatment for OCD: drug therapy			

Definitions of abnormality 1

Statistical infrequency

Statistically infrequency refers to conditions that are rare compared to the norm. Many human characteristics fall into a normal frequency distribution. This can tell us what is common or 'normal', and what is uncommon or abnormal. For example, in facing everyday challenges, it is rare to be excessively fearless or fearful and normal to experience some anxiety.

Deviation from social norms

As well as *statistical* norms, there are also *social* norms created by social groups of people about what comprises acceptable standards of behaviour. **Deviation from social norms** is classed as abnormal. Some rules about unacceptable behaviour are implicit whereas others are policed by laws. They also differ over place and time due to **cultural relativism**, e.g. alcohol consumption in public places.

Evaluation of statistical infrequency

Some abnormal behaviour is desirable

The statistical infrequency definition does not distinguish between desirable and undesirable behaviours. Very high IQ is infrequent but is generally considered to be desirable. Equally, depression is relatively common, yet undesirable. We need a means of identifying infrequent *and* undesirable behaviours.

The cut-off point is subjectively determined

We need to determine the dividing line between normality from abnormality and this can be problematic, e.g. what is excessive or too little sleep? The cut-off point is inevitably subjectively determined, but is important for deciding who gets treatment.

Statistical infrequency is sometimes not enough

In some situations a statistical criterion can define abnormality, e.g. uncommonly low intellectual ability may be judged as a mental disorder. However, such a diagnosis is appropriate only if failure to function adequately (see page 48) is also taken into account.

Evaluation of deviation from social norms

Susceptible to abuse

The main difficulty with the deviation from social norms definition is that it varies as social morals and attitudes change over time, e.g. homosexuality was once labelled as a disorder. The mentally ill are thus those individuals who transgress against prevailing social attitudes. Szasz (1974) claimed that this could be used as an excuse to exclude nonconformists from society.

Deviance is related to context and degree

Behaviour considered to be deviant in one setting is considered normal in another, e.g. wearing a swimming costume to college would be deviant but wearing it on a beach would be normal. The distinction between deviance and normality can also be a matter of degree. Wearing a swimming costume to every class would be considered deviant but wearing it once to class during rag week might be considered normal.

Deviance is defined as transgression of the social rules people establish in order to live together. Accordingly, abnormal behaviour is behaviour that damages others. The social deviancy model thus distinguishes between desirable and undesirable behaviour. Other explanations, such as statistical infrequency, do not do take account of the effect that behaviour has on others.

Cultural relativism

Classification systems, such as DSM, draw on social norms of dominant Western, white, middle-class culture hence they are culture-bound. This cultural relativism is acknowledged in DSM-5 (2013), e.g. regarding panic attacks, uncontrollable crying may be symptomatic in some cultures whereas difficulty breathing may be a primary symptom in others. There are no universal standards for labelling a behaviour as abnormal.

KEY TERMS

Cultural relativism
- The view that behaviour cannot be judged properly unless it is viewed in the context of the culture in which it originates.

Deviation from social norms
- Abnormal behaviour is seen as a deviation from implicit rules about how one 'ought' to behave. Anything that violates these rules is considered abnormal.

Statistical infrequency
- Abnormality is defined as those behaviours that are extremely rare, i.e. any behaviour that is statistically infrequent is regarded as abnormal.

Apply it

Scenario. Pete spends up to 60 hours every week video-gaming. His parents complain that this is so extreme that he must be addicted to it.

Using the statistical infrequency definition of abnormality, explain whether Pete's behaviour could be considered abnormal. (4 marks)

Explanation. First, Pete's behaviour would need to be compared to statistical norms of video-gaming time amongst his peers to determine whether 60 hours per week was rare. If it were not he would not be considered abnormal. Nevertheless, 60 hours might mean that he (and his peers) did not function adequately in other ways so statistical infrequency is an insufficient explanation on its own.

KEY TERMS

Deviation from ideal mental health
- Abnormality is defined in terms of mental *health*, behaviours that are associated with competence and happiness. Ideal mental health would include a positive attitude towards the self, resistance to stress and an accurate perception of reality.

Failure to function adequately
- People are judged on their ability to go about daily life. If they can't do this and are also experiencing distress (or others are distressed by their behaviour) then it is considered a sign of abnormality.

Psychopathology: Definitions of abnormality 2

Two more definitions of abnormality are summarised below.

⬡ Failure to function adequately

Failing to cope with everyday living (e.g. eating, washing), i.e. **failure to function adequately**, is a third criterion for judging abnormality. It may cause distress for the individual and/or others around them. If it distresses only others but not oneself, the label of abnormality is inappropriate.

◉ Deviation from ideal mental health

Physical illness is defined in part by looking at the *absence* of signs of physical health (Jahoda, 1958). The **deviation from ideal mental health** definition proposes the *absence* of the following criteria. There is some overlap here with failure to function adequately – for example, in both definitions not being able to cope with stressful situations is a sign of abnormality.

- *Self-attitudes*: having high **self-esteem** and a strong sense of identity.
- *Personal growth and* **self-actualisation**.
- *Integration*, such as being able to cope with stressful situations.
- *Autonomy*: being independent and self-regulating.
- Having an *accurate perception of reality*.
- *Mastery of the environment*: including the ability to love, function at work and in interpersonal relations, adjust to new situations and solve problems.

⬡ Evaluation of failure to function adequately

Limitations: Who judges?

'Failure to function adequately' must be judged by the individual or someone else and they may disagree on the criteria. There is thus a risk that adequately functioning individuals may be classed as abnormal or that dysfunctional people may remain undiagnosed.

Strengths: The behaviour may be functional

Apparently dysfunctional behaviour can be adaptive and functional, e.g. some conditions, such as **depression**, may lead to extra support for the individual. Some cross-dressers make a living from it, yet transvestitism is in the list of mental disorders and is generally regarded as abnormal.

Strengths: Easy to measure objectively

The subjective experience and point of view of the patient is acknowledged. In addition 'failure to function' is also relatively easy to judge objectively because we can list behaviours (can dress self, can prepare meals) and thus decide when treatment is required.

◉ Evaluation of deviation from ideal mental health

Limitations: Unrealistic criteria

According to ideal criteria, most of us are abnormal! Furthermore the criteria are difficult to measure, e.g. capacity for personal growth or environmental mastery. The approach may be an interesting concept but not really useable.

Limitations: Mental health is not the same as physical health

Like physical illnesses, some mental disorders have physical causes (e.g. brain injury) but many result from life experiences. Therefore it is unlikely that we could diagnose mental health and physical health in the same way.

Strengths: It is a positive approach

Deviation from mental health offers an alternative perspective on mental disorder by emphasising the positives rather than the negative. Jahoda's ideas were never espoused by humanistic psychologists or really adopted by mental health professionals but do accord with 'positive psychology'.

Limitations: Cultural relativism

The 'failure to function' criterion is likely to result in different diagnoses when applied in different cultures. For example, self-actualisation is relevant in individualistic cultures but not collectivist ones, Many, if not most, of the criteria are culture-bound because the standard of one culture is being applied in another.

Apply it

Scenario. Mike's flatmate never cleans his room. It is so bad that visitors to the flat remark on the bad smell it causes. Mike's flatmate holds down a good job and is clean and well-presented when he goes to work.

Using the 'failure to function adequately' definition of defining abnormality, explain whether Mike's flatmate could be considered abnormal. (4 marks)

Explanation. Mike's flatmate is failing to function by keeping his room clean but functions well at work. He is unlikely to be causing serious distress to himself or others, in spite of the smell! His behaviour might tip into abnormal if his room became a health hazard to him and his flatmate.

Phobias and OCD

All of us experience depression or phobia or obsessions to some degree, but these are not *clinical* disorders. A clinical disorder will significantly affect a person's day-to-day life over an extended period of time.

Phobias

Phobias are 'anxiety disorders'. Primary symptoms are extreme anxiety and conscious avoidance of a feared object or situation, e.g. agoraphobia, social phobia and specific phobias (about objects or situations).

Behavioural characteristics

A phobic's immediate response to a feared object or situation is avoidance, e.g. in social situations they may freeze or faint. The usual stress response is fight or flight, but for phobics it is fight, flight or freeze. This is distressing and may interfere significantly with the person's daily life.

Emotional characteristics

These are primarily marked, persistent, excessive and unreasonable fear, anxiety and panic. They are cued by the presence or anticipation of a specific object or situation and are out of proportion to the actual danger posed.

Cognitive characteristics

Phobias are characterised by irrational thinking (cognition) and resistance to rational arguments, e.g. a flying phobic is not helped by arguments that flying is relatively safe. Furthermore, the person recognises that their fear is excessive or unreasonable, although this feature may be absent in children.

Depression

Depression is a mood disorder. DSM-5 distinguishes between major depressive disorder and persistent depressive disorder which is longer term and/or recurring. Most people suffer only from depression whereas others experience states of mania that alternate with their depression (bipolar disorder).

Behavioural characteristics

Activity level may be reduced or increased, e.g. some individuals experience reduced energy and increased fatigue, while others become agitated and restless. Some sleep more whereas others experience insomnia.

Emotional characteristics

Formal diagnosis – 'major depressive disorder'. Symptoms include sadness, feeling worthless, low self-esteem, loss of interest and pleasure in usual activities, feelings of despair, lack of control and anger directed towards others or turned inwards on the self, possibly after being hurt and wishing to retaliate.

Cognitive characteristics

Negative emotions are associated with negative *thoughts*, such as a low self-concept, guilt, a sense of worthlessness and a pessimistic view of the world. Such negative thoughts are irrational, they do not accurately reflect reality.

Obsessive compulsive disorder (OCD)

OCD is an anxiety disorder, typically beginning in young adulthood. It has two components: persistent, obsessive thoughts and compulsive behaviours, e.g. intrusive thoughts about contamination and a compulsion to clean.

Behavioural characteristics

Compulsive behaviours reduce anxiety caused by obsessive thoughts. They may be overt, such as hand washing to remove contamination, or covert, such as prayers to avert perceived danger. Failure to carry out the behaviour leads to excessive anxiety. Some compulsions are not preceded by obsessive thoughts.

Emotional characteristics

OCD can cause anxiety and distress, embarrassment and shame.

Cognitive characteristics

Obsessions are recurrent, intrusive and unwelcome thoughts which the individual will, at some point, recognise as excessive and unreasonable.

KEY TERMS

Depression
- A mood disorder where an individual feels sad and/or lacks interest in their usual activities. Further characteristics include irrational negative thoughts, raised or lowered activity levels, difficulties with concentration, sleep and eating.

OCD (obsessive compulsive disorder)
- An anxiety disorder where anxiety arises from both obsessions (persistent thoughts) and compulsions (behaviours that are repeated over and over again). Compulsions are a response to obsessions and are believed to reduce anxiety.

Phobias
- A group of mental disorders characterised by high levels of anxiety in response to a particular stimulus or group of stimuli. The anxiety interferes with normal living.

49

KEY TERMS

Behaviourist
- People who believe that human behaviour can be explained in terms of conditioning, without the need to consider thoughts or feelings.

Classical conditioning
- Learning through association. A neutral stimulus (NS) is consistently paired with an unconditioned stimulus (UCS) eventually becomes the conditioned stimulus (CS), producing a conditioned response (CR).

Operant conditioning
- Learning through reinforcement or punishment. If a behaviour is followed by a desirable consequence, then that behaviour is more likely to occur again in the future.

Two-process theory (model)
- A theory that explains the two processes that lead to the development of phobias – they begin through classical conditioning and are maintained through operant conditioning.

The behavioural approach to explaining phobias

Behaviourists assume behaviour is learned through conditioning, rather than inherited. Behaviourist principles can account for how people develop phobias by applying the **two-process model**. Social learning may also play a part.

 ## The two-process model

Mowrer (1947) proposed the **two-process model** incorporating both **classical** and **operant conditioning** to explain the initiation and persistence of phobias respectively.

Classical conditioning: Initiation

Watson and Rayner (1920) demonstrated initiation of phobia in Little Albert who startled with fear (UCR) to a loud noise (UCS). A UCS was paired several times with a white rat (NS). The rat (CS) eventually elicited fear (CR) in the absence of the loud noise. Little Albert's phobia generalised to other furry objects, e.g. a non-white rabbit.

Operant conditioning: Maintenance

Maintenance involves operant conditioning – the likelihood of a behaviour being repeated is increased if the outcome is rewarding. Escape from the phobic stimulus reduces fear and is negatively reinforcing. Avoidance of the phobic stimulus altogether is positively reinforcing because anxiety is averted.

 ## Social learning

Social learning theory is not part of the two-process model; it is a more recent development of behaviourism. Phobias may also be acquired through observing significant others model behaviour, e.g. a parent responding to a spider with fear may lead a child to imitate similar behaviour because behaviour appears rewarding, i.e. the fearful person gets attention.

 ## Evaluation

Strengths: The importance of classical conditioning

Phobics can often recall a specific incident when their phobia appeared, for example being bitten by a dog (Sue *et al.*, 1994). However not all phobics can do this (Öst, 1987). Sue *et al.* suggest phobias may result from different processes, e.g. agoraphobics were most likely to recall a specific incident, whereas arachnophobics (people who are scared of spiders) were most likely to cite modelling as the cause.

Limitations: Diathesis-stress model

Researchers have found that not everyone who is traumatised by something develops a phobia (Di Nardo *et al.*, 1988). The diathesis-stress model could explain this: we inherit a genetic vulnerability for developing a mental disorder, however it only manifests itself if triggered by a traumatic event. People without this vulnerability would not develop a phobia.

Strengths: Support for social learning

Bandura and Rosenthal (1966) supported the social learning explanation. In the experiment, a model acted as if he was in pain every time a buzzer sounded. Later on, those participants who had observed this showed an emotional reaction to the buzzer, demonstrating an acquired 'fear' response.

Limitations: Biological preparedness

Animals, including humans, are genetically programmed to rapidly learn to fear certain stimuli (e.g. snakes, strangers) because they are potentially life-threatening. This biological preparedness (Seligman, 1970) means that behavioural explanations alone cannot explain the development of phobias.

Limitations: Two-process theory ignores cognitive factors

The cognitive approach proposes that phobias may develop not through conditioning but as the consequence of **irrational thinking**. For example, 'I could become trapped in this lift and suffocate' is an irrational thought that could trigger extreme anxiety and develop into a phobia. Cognitive therapies designed to treat this, such as **CBT**, may be more successful than the behaviourist treatments for certain phobias (Engels *et al.*, 1993).

 ## Apply it

Scenario. A wasp becomes trapped in Becky's hair and stings her painfully several times before she is able to free it. Thereafter she is panicky and has to escape whenever she hears a buzzing insect and avoids going outdoors in case she encounters one.

Apply the two-process model of phobias to explain Becky's buzzing insect phobia. (4 marks)

Explanation. Classical conditioning explains the initiation of Becky's fear. She learned to associate buzzing (NS) with pain (UCS) and the fear it caused (UCR) so that buzzing alone (now the CS) could elicit fear (CR). Operant conditioning maintained her fear. Escaping buzzing insects (and the potential fear) was negatively reinforcing, while avoiding them kept her calm and was positively reinforcing.

The behavioural approach to treating phobias

 Systematic desensitisation (SD)

Phobias may persist because phobics avoid the phobic stimulus so do not unlearn the fear. **Systematic desensitisation** (SD) is based on the following:

Counterconditioning (Wolpe, 1958)

Using classical conditioning, the patient learns a new association that runs *counter* to the original one. They associate the phobic stimulus with relaxation instead of fear, thus becoming desensitised. Wolpe called this 'reciprocal inhibition' because relaxation inhibits the anxiety.

Relaxation

The patient learns relaxation techniques e.g. controlled breathing; visualising a peaceful scene. Progressive muscle relaxation is also used to relax one muscle group at a time.

Desensitisation hierarchy

SD works by gradually introducing the person to the feared situation. At each stage the patient practises relaxation so their anxiety diminishes.

 Flooding

Instead of SD, the patient can be taught relaxation techniques then practise them while being exposed in one long session (2–3 hours) to the phobic object (**flooding**). The exposure can be *in vivo* (actual exposure) or in virtual reality. The fear response has a time limit and, as it is exhausted, a new association between the feared stimulus and relaxation is learned.

 Evaluation of SD

Strengths: Effectiveness of SD

Researchers have found that SD is successful for a range of phobic disorders in up to 75% of patients (McGrath *et al.*, 1990). *In vivo* techniques are the most effective (Choy *et al.*, 2007).

Limitations: Not appropriate for all phobias

Öhman *et al.* (1975) suggest that, due to preparedness, SD may not be as effective in treating phobias with an evolutionary survival component (e.g. fear of the dark) compared to those that do not.

Strengths: General effectiveness of behavioural therapies

Behavioural therapies are relatively fast and less effortful than psychotherapies requiring 'thinking'. They are thus useful for people who lack insight, such as patients with learning difficulties. SD can also be self-administered as effectively and more cheaply than therapist-guided treatment.

 Evaluation of flooding

Limitations: Individual differences

Flooding is not for every patient (or therapist). Even though patients are made aware beforehand that it is traumatic, they may quit during the treatment, which reduces the ultimate effectiveness of the therapy.

Strengths: Effectiveness

Flooding is a quick treatment compared to SD and may be more effective than SD (Choy *et al.*, 2007). However, another review (Craske *et al.*, 2008) concluded that SD and flooding were equally effective so, either way, flooding has some therapeutic benefit.

Limitations: Relaxation may not be necessary

Exposure and anticipation of success might be more important than relaxation. Klein *et al.* (1983) found no difference in effectiveness of SD with supportive psychotherapy for patients with either social or specific phobias, suggesting that generating hopeful expectancies that the phobia can be overcome is key.

Limitations: Symptom substitution

Behavioural therapies remove symptoms but may not address their underlying cause, so 'symptom substitution' may occur, e.g. a smoker may quit but then comfort-eat because the anxiety underlying smoking was not dealt with.

KEY TERMS

Flooding
- A form of behavioural therapy used to treat phobias and other anxiety disorders. A client is exposed to (or imagines) an extreme form of the threatening situation under relaxed conditions until the anxiety reaction is extinguished.

Systematic desensitisation
- A form of behavioural therapy used to treat phobias and other anxiety disorders. A client is gradually exposed to (or imagines) the threatening situation under relaxed conditions until the anxiety reaction is extinguished.

Apply it

Scenario. A student with social phobia is terrified of giving oral presentations in class.

Using the principles of SD, explain how a therapist could help this student to overcome their fear. (4 marks)

Explanation. The therapist would apply counterconditioning to substitute fear with relaxation. The student would identify a hierarchy of feared situations relating to giving oral presentations. They would also be taught to master relaxation techniques. Each step of the hierarchy would then be faced while maintaining relaxation until the most feared step was manageable.

KEY TERMS

ABC model
- A cognitive approach to understanding mental disorder, focusing on the effect of irrational beliefs on emotions.

Negative triad
- A cognitive approach to understanding depression, focusing on how negative expectations (schema) about the self, world and future lead to depression.

Schema
- A cognitive framework that helps organise and interpret information in the brain. A schema helps an individual to make sense of new information.

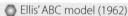

Activating event (A)	Activating event (A)
⬇	⬇
Rational belief (B)	Irrational belief (B)
⬇	⬇
Healthy emotion (C)	Unhealthy emotion (C)

▲ *Ellis' (1962) ABC model*

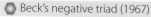

Negative view of the self

Negative view of the future ⬌ Negative view of the world

▲ *Beck's (1967) Negative triad*

Apply it

Scenario. Anita is the youngest child in a family of high achievers and has never matched their accomplishments. She often feels very low in spirits. During her first driving lesson, she experiences road-rage from other drivers and immediately decides to give up.

Apply Beck's (1967) concepts of negative schema and negative triad to explain the cognitive processes that led to Anita's decision. (4 marks)

Explanation. Anita's history of feeling like a failure has led her to develop a pessimistic framework (negative schema) for interpreting events. When she encounters a new failure, the schema is activated and she thinks in a depressive way: 'I am a bad driver. Everyone thinks so. I will never be able to drive.'

The cognitive approach to explaining depression

Cognitive approaches focus on how *irrational* thinking leads to mental disorder. Cognitive explanations are particularly appropriate for depression.

⬡ Beck's negative triad (1967)

Beck believed that depression follows thinking that is negatively biased, coupled with a sense of lack of control.

Negative schema

Negative **schemas** are acquired in childhood and activated in conditions resembling those in which they were learned e.g. expecting to fail when tested. They lead to *cognitive biases* in thinking, e.g. over-generalisation – reduced feelings of self-worth based on one piece of negative feedback.

The negative triad (Beck, 1967)

Negative schemas and cognitive biases maintain the **negative triad**: a pessimistic and irrational view of three key elements in a person's belief system:
- The self, e.g. 'I'm unattractive and boring'.
- The world, e.g. 'No-one wants my company'.
- The future, e.g. 'I am always going to be on my own'.

⬡ Ellis' ABC model (1962)

In his **ABC model**, Ellis proposed that the key to depression lies in irrational beliefs:

A: Activating event, e.g. you get a low grade.

B: rational or irrational belief, e.g. 'I didn't work hard' vs 'My tutor is a sadist'.

C: consequence – rational beliefs lead to healthy emotions (e.g. acceptance); irrational beliefs lead to unhealthy emotions (e.g. depression).

Musturbatory thinking

This is the source of irrational beliefs that certain things *must* be true for an individual to be happy. Ellis identified the three most important irrational beliefs:
- *I must* be approved of or accepted by people I find important.
- *I must* do well or very well, or I am worthless.
- The world *must* give me happiness, or I will die.

Such 'musts' need to be challenged in order for mental healthiness to prevail.

⬡ Evaluation of the cognitive approach to explaining depression

Strength: Research support for the role of irrational thinking

When asked to interpret written material, depressed participants made more errors in logic than non-depressed participants (Hammen and Krantz, 1976). Depressed participants who were given negative automatic-thought statements became increasingly depressed (Bates *et al.*, 1999). Both studies support hypotheses derived from the cognitive approach.

Limitations: Blames the patient rather than situational factors

Responsibility for depression and recovery rests with the individual. Situational factors, e.g. being in a stressful job, may be side-lined. In this case, altering thinking patterns does not deal with the problem's root cause.

Strengths: Practical applications in therapy

Cognitive explanations presented here have both been usefully applied in CBT which is consistently found to be the best treatment for depression, especially when used in conjunction with drug treatments (e.g. Cuijpers *et al.*, 2013). This lends support to the underlying explanation.

Limitations: More complex explanations

The diathesis-stress approach suggests that a genetic propensity for depression renders individuals more vulnerable to the effects of a negative environment, which then leads to negative irrational thinking. The success of drug therapies for depression suggests that neurotransmitters play an important role. Cognitive explanations alone do not account for these possibilities.

The cognitive approach to treating depression

Cognitive explanations of depression form the basis of **cognitive-behaviour therapy** (CBT). The aim of therapy is to turn irrational thoughts into rational ones and develop coping strategies leading to *behavioural* change.

 Cognitive-behaviour therapy (CBT), Ellis (1962)

Challenging irrational thoughts

Ellis called his CBT-based therapy 'rational emotional behavioural therapy' (REBT) because the therapy resolves emotional and behavioural problems. He extended his ABC model to ABCDEF:

  D: Disputing irrational thoughts and beliefs.

  E: Effects of disputing and effective attitude to life.

  F: Feelings (emotions) that are produced.

REBT focuses on challenging irrational thoughts and replacing them with rational ones, e.g.:

* *Logical disputing* – self-defeating beliefs do not follow from the event.
* *Empirical disputing* – self-defeating beliefs are inconsistent with reality.
* *Pragmatic disputing* – the pointlessness of self-defeating beliefs.

Effective disputing changes self-defeating beliefs into more rational beliefs, replacing *catastrophising* with more rational interpretations of events.

Homework

Patients are often asked to complete homework outside therapy sessions to test irrational beliefs against reality and put new rational beliefs into practice.

Behavioural activation

Based on the assumption that being active leads to rewards that act as an antidote to depression, CBT often involves encouraging patients to become more active and engaged in pleasurable activities.

Unconditional positive regard

If a client feels worthless, they will be less willing to consider change. If the therapist provides respect for the client without judgement (i.e. *unconditional positive regard*), a change in beliefs and attitudes should be facilitated.

 Evaluation

Strengths: Research support

Ellis (1957) claimed an average of 27 sessions to complete treatment and a 90% success rate. REBT and CBT do well in outcome studies of depression, e.g. Cuijpers *et al.* (2013) found that CBT was superior to no treatment in 75 studies.

Limitations: Individual differences

CBT works less well with people who have high levels of irrational beliefs that are both rigid and resistant to change (Elkin *et al.*, 1985), or when realistic stressors cannot be resolved by therapy (Simons *et al.*, 1995). The directness of REBT does not suit everyone; some people want to share their worries without expending the cognitive effort necessary for recovery (Ellis, 2001).

Strengths: Support for behavioural activation

Babyak *et al.* (2000) randomly assigned 156 depressed adults to four months of aerobic exercise, drug treatment or both. All patients improved, but six months later, the exercise group had lower relapse rates than the medication group, especially if they had continued with an exercise regime.

Strengths: Combination with alternative treatments

Cuijpers *et al.* (above) found that CBT was especially effective when used with drug therapy, e.g. SSRIs which may alleviate symptoms enough to allow the patient to focus on the demands of CBT.

Limitations: The Dodo Bird effect

The *Dodo Bird effect* was named after the Dodo in Lewis Carroll's *Alice in Wonderland* who decided that everyone should win. Rosenzweig (1936) argued that therapeutic effectiveness was due mainly to common factors in different psychotherapies, such as talking to a sympathetic person.

KEY TERMS

Cognitive-behaviour therapy (CBT)

* A combination of cognitive therapy (a way of changing maladaptive thoughts and beliefs) and behavioural therapy (a way of changing behaviour in response to these thoughts and beliefs).

Apply it

Scenario. A person in poor physical condition believes that they will never be any better.

How might a cognitive therapist encourage a depressed client to dispute this conclusion on logical, empirical and pragmatic grounds and with what aim in mind? (4 marks)

Explanation. Logically it does not follow that this person cannot change their situation. Empirically, there is abundant evidence that many people in a similar position have made big improvements. Pragmatically, maintaining the irrational belief is self-destructive. The therapist's aim would be to replace the person's irrational belief with a rational one that leads to more positive thoughts and actions.

The biological approach to explaining OCD

 Genetic explanations

The COMT gene

The COMT **gene** produces the enzyme, which regulates the production of dopamine, a **neurotransmitter** implicated in OCD. One COMT gene variation more common in OCD patients results in lower activity of the COMT gene and higher levels of dopamine (Tükel *et al.*, 2013).

The SERT gene

The SERT gene affects the transport of serotonin (see page 53), also implicated in OCD, lowering levels of this neurotransmitter. Ozaki *et al.* (2003) found a mutation of this gene in two unrelated families where six of the seven family members had OCD.

Diathesis-stress

Individual genes may create a vulnerability (a diathesis) for OCD, which is only expressed if particular stressors are present. Some people could possess gene variations but suffer no stressors and, therefore, no ill effects.

 Neural explanations

Abnormal levels of neurotransmitters

Dopamine levels may be abnormally high in people with OCD since dopamine-enhancing drugs induce stereotyped movements resembling compulsive behaviours of OCD in animals (Szechtman *et al.*, 1998). Lower serotonin levels are associated with OCD: antidepressant drugs that increase serotonin can reduce OCD symptoms (Pigott *et al.*, 1990).

Abnormal brain circuits

Several areas in the frontal lobes of the brain are thought to be abnormal in people with OCD, e.g. the orbitofrontal cortex (OFC) sends 'worry' signals to the thalamus. These are normally suppressed by the caudate nucleus but, if this is damaged, the thalamus is alerted and confirms the 'worry' to the OFC creating a worry circuit.

 Evaluation

Strengths: Family and twin studies

Compared to the general population, people with a first-degree relative with OCD have a five times greater risk of having the illness at some time (Nestadt *et al.*, 2000). Compared to non-identical twins, identical twins are more than twice as likely to develop OCD if their co-twin has it (Billett *et al.*, 1998). **Concordance rates** are never 100% however, so environmental factors must contribute (the **diathesis-stress model**).

Limitations: Tourette's syndrome and other disorders

Genes may merely predispose individuals towards obsessive-type behaviour. Pauls and Leckman (1986) argued that OCD is one expression of the same gene that determines Tourette's syndrome. OCD symptoms are also present in autism and anorexia nervosa, and two out of every three OCD patients also experience at least one episode of depression (Rasmussen and Eisen, 1992). There is, therefore, no one gene directly and exclusively responsible for OCD.

Strengths: Research support for genes and OFC

Many studies demonstrate the genetic link to abnormal levels of neurotransmitters. Compared to unrelated healthy people, OCD patients and their close relatives had reduced grey matter in key regions of the brain, including the OFC (Menzies *et al.*, 2007). Anatomical differences are inherited and these may lead to OCD in certain individuals.

Limitations: Alternative explanations

The two-process model is a credible, alternative, behaviourist explanation for OCD, e.g. a link between dirt and anxiety persists because compulsions such as hand-washing reduce the anxiety. This explanation is supported by an improvement rate in up to 90% of cases following treatment for OCD called exposure and response prevention (ERP) (Albucher *et al.*, 1998).

Apply it

Scenario. Identical twin Della shows symptoms of OCD, while her co-twin, Delia, is symptom-free.

Explain how genetic explanations of OCD could account for this. (4 marks)

Explanation. Della and Delia are genetically identical so they may have inherited the COMT or SERT gene. These affect dopamine and serotonin production respectively and are implicated in OCD. The difference between the twins might be explained by diathesis stress. Both of them may have the same inherited vulnerability (a diathesis) but only Della experienced a stressor which triggered its expression while Delia escaped it and suffered no ill effects.

The biological approach to treating OCD

 Drug therapy

Antidepressants: SSRIs

Low levels of the neurotransmitter serotonin are associated with depression as well as OCD so antidepressants are used to increase levels of serotonin in both disorders. They may normalize the 'worry circuit' described previously. Antidepressants also reduce anxiety associated with OCD. Selective serotonin re-uptake inhibitors (SSRIs, e.g. *Prozac*) are currently the preferred drug for treating anxiety disorders (Choy and Schneier, 2008). They increase levels of the serotonin thus regulating mood and anxiety.

Antidepressants: Tricyclics

The antidepressant tricyclic *clomipramine* (brand name *Anafranil*) is today primarily used in the treatment of OCD rather than depression. Tricyclics block the mechanism that re-absorbs both serotonin and noradrenaline, prolonging their activity. Tricyclics have the advantage of targeting more than one neurotransmitter, however they have greater side effects so are used as a second-line treatment for patients where SSRIs were not effective.

Anti-anxiety drugs

Benzodiazepines (BZs, e.g. *Valium*) are commonly used to reduce anxiety. BZs slow down the activity of the central nervous system by enhancing the activity of the neurotransmitter **GABA** (gamma-amino butyric-acid). This is the neurotransmitter that has a general quietening effect on many of the neurons in the brain by reacting with special sites (called GABA receptors) on the outside of neurons.

Other drugs

Recent research has found that D-Cycloserine has an effect on reducing anxiety and thus may be an effective treatment for OCD, particularly when used in conjunction with psychotherapy. D-Cycloserine is an antibiotic used in the treatment of tuberculosis. It also appears to enhance the transmission of GABA and thus reduce anxiety (Kushner *et al.*, 2007).

 Evaluation

Strength: Effectiveness

Soomro *et al.* (2008) reviewed 17 studies of the use of SSRIs with OCD patients and found them to be more effective than placebos in reducing the symptoms of OCD up to three months after treatment, i.e. in the short term. However, most studies are only of three to four months' duration, and therefore little long-term data exists (Koran *et al.*, 2007).

Limitations: Drug therapies are preferred to other treatments

Drug therapy generally requires less time and effort than therapies such as CBT, which requires patients to invest time and effort into tackling their problems. It is also relatively cheaper and requires less monitoring. Furthermore, some benefit may derive from simply talking with a doctor during consultations (the 'Dodo Bird effect').

Limitations: Side effects

All drugs have side effects, e.g. nausea, headache and insomnia during SSRI use (Soomro *et al.*, 2008) and hallucinations following tricyclic antidepressant use. Possible side effects of BZs include increased aggressiveness, long-term impairment of memory and possible addiction. Side effects may amount to costs that outweigh benefits and thus stop a patient taking a drug.

Limitations: Not a lasting cure

In a review of treatments for OCD, Koran *et al.* (2007) suggested that, although drug therapy may be more commonly used, psychotherapies such as CBT should be tried first. Drug therapy may be efficient in the short term but it does not provide a lasting cure, as indicated by the fact that patients relapse within a few weeks if medication is stopped (Maina *et al.*, 2001).

KEY TERM

GABA (gamma-aminobutyric acid)
- A neurotransmitter that regulates excitement in the nervous system, thus acting as a natural form of anxiety reducer.

 Apply it

Scenario. Imagine that you are a health professional tasked with helping a patient who is troubled by OCD.

What key points would you make to help the patient decide between drug treatments and CBT? (4 marks)

Explanation. Drug treatments are a relatively quick and cost-effective way of treating symptoms associated with OCD. However, they have side effects of differing severity. They may also be a 'quick fix' lasting only a few months. CBT requires much greater investment of time and effort but may be more effective in the long term. A compromise position might be to try drug therapy in the short term to enable the patient to take a more considered view of their situation and decide what to do in the longer term.

Chapter 5

Approaches in psychology

3.2.1. Approaches in psychology

AS and A Level

- Origins of Psychology: Wundt, introspection and the emergence of psychology as a science.
- Learning approaches: the behaviourist approach, including classical conditioning and Pavlov's research, operant conditioning, types of reinforcement and Skinner's research; social learning theory including imitation, identification, modelling, vicarious reinforcement, the role of meditational processes and Bandura's research.
- The cognitive approach: the study of internal mental processes, the role of schema, the use of theoretical and computer models to explain and make inferences about mental processes. The emergence of cognitive neuroscience.
- The biological approach: the influence of genes, biological structures and neurochemistry on behaviour. Genotype and phenotype, genetic basis of behaviour, evolution and behaviour.

A Level only

- The psychodynamic approach: the role of the unconscious, the structure of personality, id, ego and superego, defence mechanisms including repression, denial and displacement, psychosexual stages.
- Humanistic psychology: free will, self-actualisation and Maslow's hierarchy of needs, focus on the self, congruence, the role of conditions of worth. The influence on counselling psychology.
- Comparison of approaches.

Key terms (highlight each cell when you can define the term for 3 marks)

Origins of psychology (Wundt)	Learning approaches: the behaviourist approach (Pavlov, Skinner)	Learning approaches: social learning theory (Bandura)	The cognitive approach	The biological approach	(A Level only) The psychodynamic approach (Freud)	(A Level only) Humanistic psychology (Maslow)	(A Level only) Comparison of approaches
Empiricism	Behaviourist	Identification	Cognitive	Biological approach	Defence mechanisms	Conditions of worth	Determinism
Introspection	Classical conditioning	Imitation	Cognitive neuroscience	Evolution	Psychoanalysis	Congruence	Nature
Scientific method	Operant conditioning	Modelling	Computer model	Gene	Psychodynamic	Free will	Nurture
	Punishment	Social learning theory	Inference/ inferring	Genotype and phenotype	Unconscious	Hierarchy of needs	Science
	Reinforcement	Vicarious reinforcement	Schema	Natural selection		Humanistic	
			Theoretical model	Neurochemistry		Self and self-actualisation	

Content checklist

1. In each 'describe, apply and evaluate' cell tick when you have produced brief notes.
2. Once you feel you have a good grasp of the topic add a second tick to the cell.
3. When you feel you have complete mastery of the topic and would be able to answer an exam question without the aid of notes highlight the cell.

I am able to...	Describe	Apply	Evaluate
AS and A Level			
Origins of psychology: Wundt, introspection and the emergence of psychology as a science			
Learning approaches: the behaviourist approach, including classical conditioning and Pavlov's research, operant conditioning, types of reinforcement and Skinner's research			
Learning approaches: social learning theory including imitation, identification, modelling, vicarious reinforcement, the role of meditational processes and Bandura's research			
The biological approach: the influence of genes, biological structures and neurochemistry on behaviour. Genotype and phenotype, genetic basis of behaviour, evolution and behaviour			
The cognitive approach: the study of internal mental processes, the role of schema, the use of theoretical and computer models to explain and make inferences about mental processes. The emergence of cognitive neuroscience.			
A Level only			
The psychodynamic approach: the role of the unconscious, the structure of personality, id, ego and superego, defence mechanisms including repression, denial and displacement, psychosexual stages			
Humanistic psychology: free will, self-actualisation and Maslow's hierarchy of needs, focus on the self, congruence, the role of conditions of worth. The influence on counselling psychology.			
Comparison of approaches			

The origins of psychology

Wilhem Wundt (1982–1920) and introspection

Wundt believed that the human mind could be studied scientifically. He established psychology as a science and experimentation as the method of choice. He thought the human mind was constructed of basic elements of sensation and perception; an approach known as 'structuralism'. He used **introspection** to access mental processes.

The emergence of psychology as a science

Wundt's approach was based on **empiricism**. This is a hallmark of the **scientific method**, and thus helped to establish scientific psychology as a discipline. Wundt also adopted two further scientific assumptions: that behaviour is caused (the assumption of determinism) and thus predictable.

The scientific method in psychology

Scientific method refers to the use of investigative techniques that are:

- objective: preconceptions or biases do not influence data collection
- systematic: measurement and recording of empirical data are carried out with precision and control
- replicable: they can be repeated by other researchers to determine whether the same results are obtained. Non-replicable (unreliable) results cannot be accepted as trustworthy.

The research process also necessitates the use of reason to explain observations. The development of scientific theories and the constant testing and refining of them through further research completes the scientific cycle.

Evaluation

Limitations: Wundt's methods are unreliable

Introspection involves 'non-observable' processes (e.g. memory, perception) which are not easily reproducible. In contrast, behaviourists such as Pavlov, could achieve reproducible results, based on publicly observable behaviour, leading to explanatory principles that could be generalised to all human beings.

Limitations: Introspection is not particularly accurate

Introspection is not always possible; we may have little knowledge of the processes underlying our behaviour. Studies of implicit attitudes (prejudice) corroborate this. A person may be implicitly sexist, and react to the opposite sex accordingly, but introspection would not reveal this because they are not consciously aware of it.

Strengths of a scientific approach to psychology

Scientific method:

- relies on empirical, objective, systematic methods so is less biased.
- is based on determinism, and is thus able to establish causes of behaviour.
- is self-correcting: explanations that are unreliable, or no longer fit the evidence, can be refined or abandoned.

Limitations of a scientific approach to psychology

- High levels of objectivity and control may tell us little about how people act in more natural environments.
- Much psychological subject matter is not directly unobservable. Of all the sciences, psychology is, therefore, probably the most open to interpretation.
- Critics such as humanistic psychologists say that applying the assumptions of scientific method is largely inappropriate because it is reductionist whereas human behaviour is more than the sum of its parts.

Strengths: Introspection is still useful in psychology

Csikszentmihalyi and Hunter (2003) recently used introspection to measure 'happiness'. Teenage participants were given beepers signalling them at random times during the day to write down their thoughts and feelings preceding the beep. Teens were generally more unhappy than happy, but tended to be happier when they were focusing on a challenging task.

KEY TERMS

Empiricism

- The belief that all knowledge is derived from sensory experience. Generally characterised by the use of the experimental method in psychology.

Introspection

- The process by which a person gains knowledge about their own mental and emotional states as a result of the examination or observation of their conscious thoughts and feelings.

Scientific method

- The use of investigative methods that are objective, systematic and replicable, and the formulation, testing and modification of hypotheses based on these methods.

Apply it

Scenario. In a study of perception, several participants are asked to describe their inner sensations and experiences while viewing a visual illusion and what they say is recorded.

How would a structuralist, such as Wundt, use the records to construct an understanding of this experience? What difficulties might this present them with? (4 marks)

Explanation. The researcher would combine accounts and look for patterns amongst them which would give clues about the nature of this type of perception. Understanding of this is likely to be poor because participants are using introspection: everyone's reports are likely to be different and not everyone is equally aware of their inner thought processes.

KEY TERMS

Classical conditioning

- Learning through association. A neutral stimulus (NS) is consistently paired with an unconditioned stimulus (UCS) eventually becomes the conditioned stimulus (CS), producing a conditioned response (CR).

Operant conditioning

- Learning through reinforcement or punishment. If a behaviour is followed by a desirable consequence, then that behaviour is more likely to occur again in the future.

Reinforcement

- A term used in psychology to refer to anything that strengthens a response and increases the likelihood that it will occur again in the future.

The behaviourist approach

Behaviourists argue that much behaviour results from conditioning which involves the organism forming learned associations between stimuli in the environment and the responses they make to them.

◐ Classical conditioning and Pavlov's research

Animals (including humans) have innate reflexes consisting of an *unconditioned stimulus* (UCS, e.g. food) and an *unconditioned response* (UCR, e.g. salivation). In **classical conditioning**, a *neutral stimulus* (NS, e.g. a buzzer) is presented just before the UCS several times. The NS becomes capable of eliciting the UCR without the UCS. The NS becomes a *conditioned stimulus* (CS) and the UCR a *conditioned response* (CR). Pavlov (1927) trained dogs to salivate to the sound of a buzzer in this way.

◐ Operant conditioning

Organisms spontaneously produce different behaviours, and these have *consequences*. **Operant conditioning** (Skinner, 1938) is the process by which behaviour is changed by its consequences.

◐ Types of reinforcement: Positive and negative reinforcement

Reinforcement strengthens a response making it more likely to re-occur. Positive reinforcers are pleasant, e.g. praise for effort. Negative reinforcers remove something unpleasant, e.g. a pain-killer removes pain. Both types increase the frequency of the preceding response.

◐ Evaluation

Strengths: Systematic desensitisation is effective

Systematic desensitisation is an effective, classical conditioning-based therapy for phobias such as fear of spiders. The learned anxious response (CR) associated with the feared situation (CS) is gradually replaced with another CR of relaxation so that the patient is no longer anxious.

Limitations: Classically conditioned associations cannot be achieved with equal ease

CS–CR associations cannot be established with equal ease. Animals are biologically *prepared* (Seligman, 1970) to learn associations that aid survival very rapidly (e.g. rotten food with sickness) but *unprepared*, therefore slower, to learn other associations (e.g. a buzzer with food). This challenges the idea that any NS can become associated with any UCR.

Strengths: Cause and effect can be established

Skinner used the highly controlled experimental method to discover causal relationships between variables. By manipulating the consequences of behaviour (the independent variable), he could measure the effects on an organism's behaviour (the dependent variable) thus establishing confidence in a cause and effect relationship between them.

Limitations: Limited applicability of animal research to human behaviour

Critics claim that Skinner's research using rats and pigeons tells us little about *human* behaviour which results from free will rather than positive and negative reinforcement. Skinner, however, argued that free will is an illusion and what we believe are behaviours chosen through free will are actually the product of external influences that determine our behaviour.

Limitations: A limited perspective on behaviour?

Critics complain that treating human behaviour as a product of conditioning underplays the importance of other factors, such as cognition or emotional states, in shaping behaviour. Skinner rejected this, arguing that internal states are scientifically untestable. He asserted that complex behaviours such as our interactions with each other or pathological behaviour could be explained by our reinforcement history.

Apply it

Scenario. Shortly after eating breakfast with coffee, while listening to music, a traveller is seasick during a ferry crossing. Following this the smell and taste of coffee induce nausea but the music does not.

Apply what you know about classical conditioning to explain this outcome. (4 marks)

Explanation. Sickness is a natural UCR to the UCS of disorienting motion. The previously NS of coffee has become a CS for nausea due to its accidental pairing with seasickness (UCR), which is now a CR. We are biologically prepared to associate smells and tastes with potentially toxic, nausea-inducing substances but not with music which is harmless.

Social learning theory: Bandura (1986)

Bandura (1986) believed that new patterns of behaviour could be acquired not only through conditioning, but also by observing one's own and others' behaviour and its consequences. He named this **social learning theory**.

◯ Modelling

In order for social learning to take place, someone must perform the behaviour to be learned (**modelling**). A *live* model might be a parent, teacher or peer. A *symbolic* model is someone portrayed in the media, for example a TV character.

◯ Imitation

Modelled behaviour can be observed and later reproduced by the individual through **imitation**. Key determinants of imitation are (i) the characteristics of the model, (ii) the observer's perceived ability to perform the behaviour and (iii) the observed consequences of the behaviour.

◯ Identification

Identification is the degree to which an individual feels similar to the model and likely to experience the same consequences of its behaviour. Shutts *et al.* (2010) suggest that children are more likely to identify with, and preferentially learn from, models who are similar to them, e.g. same-sex models.

◯ Vicarious reinforcement

Bandura and Walters (1963) showed that children who observed a model rewarded for aggressive behaviour were more likely to imitate it than children who had observed a model punished for the same thing. They called this **vicarious reinforcement**; individuals do not need to experience rewards or punishments directly in order to learn.

◯ The role of mediational processes

Bandura (1986) emphasised internal, mediational processes that take place between a stimulus and response. For social learning to take place, the observer must form mental representations of the modelled behaviour and its probable consequences. They might imitate the learned behaviour *provided* the expectation of positive consequences is greater than the expectation of negative ones.

◯ Evaluation

Strengths: Social learning theory has useful applications

The probability of engaging in criminal behaviour should increase when we are exposed to criminal models, identify with them and develop expectations of positive consequences for our own criminal behaviour. Ulrich (2003) found evidence for this in delinquent peer groups.

Strengths: Research support for the importance of identification

Fox and Bailenson (2009) manipulated identification using computer generated 'virtual' humans. These models looked either similar or dissimilar to the individual participants. Participants who viewed their virtual model exercising engaged in more exercise in the 24 hours following the experiment than participants who viewed their virtual model merely loitering or a dissimilar model exercising. Greater identification with a model led to more learning.

Limitations: A problem of causality

Having deviant attitudes *prior* to exposure to deviant role models could explain delinquency. Siegel and McCormick (2006) suggest that young people who possess deviant attitudes seek out peers with similar attitudes before experiencing their deviant behaviours, so the former may be more influential than the latter.

Limitations: A problem of complexity

The power of social learning may be over-emphasised as we are exposed to many different influences, for example genetic predispositions and the mass media, making it difficult to show that *one* particular thing (social learning) is the main causal influence.

KEY TERMS

Identification
- The extent to which an individual relates to a model or a group of people and feels that they are similar to them. Identification means that the individual is more likely to imitate the model's or the group's behaviour.

Imitation
- The action of using someone or something as a model and copying their behaviour.

Modelling
- A form of learning where individuals learn a particular behaviour by observing another individual performing that behaviour.

Social learning theory
- Learning through observing others and imitating behaviours that are rewarded.

Vicarious reinforcement
- Learning that is not a result of direct reinforcement of behaviour, but through observing someone else being reinforced for that behaviour.

Apply it

Scenario. Jack and Jess are 10 year-old siblings. Jack tends to be badly behaved after watching violent television programmes and has been fighting at school. Jack's mum is puzzled because Jess watches the same programmes but doesn't appear to be as affected by them.

Using social learning theory, explain Jack's behaviour and suggest why Jess does not behave in the same way after watching violent programmes on TV. (4 marks)

Explanation. It is likely that Jack identifies more strongly than Jess does with the violent role models on TV. He is therefore more likely to internalise their behaviour and imitate it, especially if he expects the consequences of that to be rewarding. Jess probably does not identify with the violent models and does not imitate them because she sees no pay-off in it.

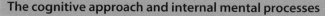

KEY TERMS

Cognitive
- Relating to mental processes such as perception, memory and reasoning.

Cognitive neuroscience
- An area of psychology dedicated to the underlying neural bases of cognitive functions.

Computer model
- Refers to the process of using computer analogies as a representation of human cognition.

Schema
- A cognitive framework that helps organise and interpret information in the brain. A schema helps an individual to make sense of new information.

Apply it

Scenario. After observing real counsellors at work, cognitive scientists develop a computerised counsellor which they claim can ask questions in a way that is indistinguishable from real counsellors. In pilot tests, participants rate the capability of the computerised counsellor as very low.

Apply what you know about cognitive models of human behaviour to explain the clients' dissatisfaction. (3 marks)

Explanation. Cognitive models of complex human behaviour tend to concentrate on information flow through predictable systems. Real human interaction is much more complex than this. Computer models fail to incorporate unpredictable, emotional and motivational influences on behaviour, therefore they do not closely resemble real-life, everyday behaviour.

The cognitive approach and internal mental processes

Much **cognitive** psychology comprises the 'information processing' approach which explains human cognition using computing metaphors. It concerns internal mental processes like attention, perception, memory and problem solving. These cannot be studied directly and must be inferred, so cognitive psychologists develop theories about how they underpin observed behaviour.

The role of schemas

A **schema** is a cognitive framework that helps organise and interpret information. Schemas allow us to take shortcuts in processing information, however, they may lead us to ignore information that does not fit our schema or fill in gaps if information is missing. An example of this is a stereotype which is difficult to modify, even when challenged by conflicting information.

 The role of theoretical and computer models

Theoretical models, such as the working memory model (Baddeley and Hitch, 1974), are simplified, often diagrammatic representations, of a cognitive process. They guide researchers who refine them as understanding improves, e.g. the working memory model first consisted of three main sections with a fourth (the episodic buffer) added by Baddeley (2000).

Computer models – Developments in computing led to a focus on **computer models** representing cognitive processes, e.g. information stored on the hard disk is like long-term memory and RAM (Random Access Memory) corresponds to working memory. Computer models can be used to simulate human processing and test our understanding of a particular cognitive process.

The emergence of cognitive neuroscience

Invention of non-invasive neuroimaging techniques, such as positron emission tomography (PET) and functional magnetic resonance imaging (fMRI) have enabled **cognitive neuroscience** to improve understanding of the living brain and its activity during cognition e.g. when people feel guilty, certain brain regions associated with social emotions are active (Burnett *et al.*, 2009).

Evaluation

Strengths: The cognitive approach has many useful applications

In social psychology, *social* cognition research has improved understanding of errors and biases in interpretation of the causes of others' behaviour. The cognitive approach to psychopathology can explain dysfunctional behaviour and give rise to treatments for illnesses such as depression.

Strengths: The cognitive approach is scientific

Cognitive psychologists favour rigorous scientific method and experimentation for creating theories and models of cognition. Conclusions are thus based on more than introspection which can give a misleading picture of mental processes, especially if they are not consciously accessible.

Limitations: Rigidity of computer models

There are important differences between the computerised information processing compared to the human mind. Computers do not make mistakes, ignore available information or forget anything that has been stored. Humans, on the other hand, do all of these things, making direct comparisons difficult.

Limitations: Ignores emotion and motivation

The cognitive approach can tell us *how* different cognitive processes take place, but not *why* they do. There is over-dependence on information-processing analogies which ignore human emotions and motivation.

Limitations: Laboratory studies lack ecological validity

Much cognitive psychology research might be criticised as lacking ecological validity, i.e. it fails to generalise to other settings, e.g., some memory experiments involve tasks such as remembering random word lists or digits. It is unlikely that we would be able to generalise findings from such studies to everyday memory.

The biological approach

The **biological approach** to psychology focuses on genetics, **neurochemistry**, the nervous and endocrine systems and **evolution** of behaviour.

Biological influences on behaviour

The influence of genes on behaviour

Genes carry the instructions for a particular characteristic (such as intelligence). Heredity is the passing of characteristics from one generation to the next through the genes. The argument about the relative contribution of genes and environmental influences to characteristics is called the nature–nurture debate.

Genotype is the unique genetic code that comprises an individual's DNA. **Phenotype** is the physical expression of the genotype.

'Heritability' is the amount of variability in a trait in a population that can be attributed to individual genotypic differences. Studies of identical twins suggest that 60–80% of the variability in intelligence could be genetic.

The influence of biological structures on behaviour

Neurons and the nervous system

Nervous systems transmit impulses via nerve cells (neurons). They comprise:

* The central nervous system (CNS) – the brain and spinal cord.
* The peripheral nervous system (PNS) – the somatic and autonomic nervous systems.

The brain

The cerebrum makes up about 85% of the brain and is divided into two hemispheres each with four lobes. Its outer surface, the cerebral cortex, is responsible for 'higher-order' functions such as thought and language.

The influence of neurochemistry on behaviour

Nerve impulses travel between neurons via the synapse by means of neurotransmitters. Some are excitatory (e.g. dopamine) and others inhibitory (e.g. serotonin).

Hormones are chemicals produced by glands (e.g. the pituitary gland), comprising the endocrine system. The brain signals glands to release hormones directly into the bloodstream and stimulate receptors on 'target cells' to alter their activity

Evolution and behaviour

Darwin argued that individuals who have physical and behavioural characteristics that enable them to survive and reproduce pass them to the next generation. Through this process of evolution by natural selection, successive generations become better adapted to their environment.

Evaluation

Strengths: The importance of the scientific method

Scientific method allows biological psychologists to replicate research studies to check their soundness.

Strengths: Applications of the biological approach

Research into neurochemical imbalance in depression has led to effective drug treatments. Research into circadian rhythms has led to a better understanding of the psychological impact of shift work.

Limitations: The biological approach is reductionist

Neurochemical and hormonal explanations of mental disorders are reductionist and arguably ignore cognitive, emotional and cultural influences.

Limitations: The dangers of genetic explanations

Genetic explanations of behaviour may be poorly understood and potentially abused, e.g. screening could identify those with a genetic predisposition for criminality but underplay the complexity of causes leading to discrimination.

KEY TERMS

Biological approach
* Views humans as biological organisms and so provides biological explanations for all aspects of psychological functioning.

Evolution
* Refers to the change over successive generations of the genetic make-up of a particular population. The central proposition of an evolutionary perspective is that the genotype of a population is changeable rather than fixed, and that this change is likely to be caused by the process of natural selection.

Gene
* A part of the chromosome of an organism that carries information in the form of DNA.

Genotype
* The genetic make-up of an individual. The genotype is a collection of inherited genetic material that is passed from generation to generation.

Neurochemistry
* The study of chemical and neural processes associated with the nervous system.

Phenotype
* The observable characteristics of an individual. This is a consequence of the interaction of the genotype with the environment.

Apply it

Scenario. Laura's friends describe her as a fitness fanatic. She spends most of her spare time preparing for and running in increasingly demanding marathons, which she finds personally very rewarding.

How might this behaviour be explained on genetic and neurochemical levels? (4 marks)

Explanation. Laura may have a genotype that predisposes her to athleticism such that she needs to be active much of the time. She may also run in order to achieve a neurochemical 'high'. As she becomes fitter, this becomes harder to achieve so she has to push herself harder and harder.

The psychodynamic approach

Freud's psychoanalytic theory and the unconcscious

Psychodynamic theorists believe that most behaviour is driven by unconscious motivation. Sigmund Freud believed the unconscious reveals itself in e.g. dreams and neurotic symptoms. Psychoanalysis is the psychotherapy derived from this approach.

The structure of personality

Freud divided the mind into three interacting structures.

The id – contains the libido and operates according to the pleasure principle, demanding immediate gratification regardless of circumstances.

The ego – mediates between the id and the superego.

The superego – consists of the conscience and the ego-ideal, which are internalised standards of what is good and bad behaviour respectively.

Defence mechanisms

If the id threatens to overwhelm the ego or superego, defence mechanisms may be triggered. These 'fixes' protect the individual from anxiety.

Repression – unconscious blocking of unacceptable thoughts and impulses.
Denial – refusal to accept reality.
Displacement – re-directing feelings onto an innocent person or object.

Psychosexual stages

Personality develops through psychosexual stages, each driven by the need to express sexual energy (libido) through different parts of the body and the pleasure that comes from its discharge. The stages are: oral (0–2 years), anal (2–3 years), phallic (3–6 years), latency (6–12 years) and genital (12+ years).

Evaluation

Strengths: Psychoanalysis – a pioneering approach

Freud championed case studies and observations rather than introspection. He demonstrated the potential of *psychological* rather than biological treatments for disorders such as depression and anxiety. In a review of psychotherapy studies, deMaat *et al.* (2009) concluded that psychoanalysis produced significant improvements in symptoms that lasted years after treatment.

Strengths: Scientific support for the psychoanalytic approach

Critics of psychoanalysis often claim there is no scientific evidence for psychoanalysis and that its claims are not testable or falsifiable. However, in a review of 2,500 studies, Fisher and Greenberg (1996) claimed that experimental tests of psychoanalysis lent support for the existence of unconscious motivation and defence mechanisms.

Limitations: Psychoanalysis is a gender-biased approach

Freud's views of women and of female sexuality were less developed than his views on male sexuality. This lack of detailed attention to women is problematic, nevertheless, Freud treated many female patients.

Limitations: Psychoanalysis is a culture-biased approach

Sue and Sue (2008) argue that psychoanalysis, with its emphasis on gaining personal insight through therapy, has little relevance for people from non-Western cultures. In China, for example, a person who is depressed or anxious avoids thoughts that cause distress rather than discuss them openly. This contrasts with the Western belief that open discussion and insight are helpful.

Strengths: Psychoanalysis – a comprehensive theory

One of the main strengths of psychoanalysis is the comprehensive nature of the theory. As well as its therapeutic applications, it can explain aspects of normal and abnormal behaviour that other theories cannot, e.g. humour, religious behaviour, dreams and appreciation of the Arts and literature. No other theory in psychology has been able to achieve such breadth.

Apply it

Scenario. Gerry is trying to quit smoking because he knows it is bad for him. For several weeks he succeeds but then meets an old smoking companion who presses him to smoke. Gerry successfully resists and feels pleased.

Apply Freud's concepts of id, ego and superego to explain Gerry's resistance to the temptation to smoke. (4 marks)

Explanation. Gerry enjoys smoking and this satisfies the immediate, pleasure-seeking of the id. However, because his ego is in touch with reality he knows it is bad for him. Temptation causes a tension between the id and ego, but also with the superego, which stands in judgement of the ego's actions. Resistance to temptation activates the ego-ideal which makes Gerry feel good about himself.

Humanistic psychology

Humanistic psychologists emphasise conscious experience and **free will**.

 Maslow's theory

Hierarchy of needs

Maslow focused on the importance of personal growth and fulfilment of needs. His **hierarchy of needs** can be represented as a pyramid. The most basic, 'deficit needs' (physiological and safety) are at the base, followed by love and belongingness and esteem needs. Each level must be fulfilled before a person can move up to the highest 'growth need' of **self-actualisation**.

Self-actualisation

Maslow described self-actualisers as creative, accepting of others and accurate perceivers of the world around them. They have *peak experiences*. Rogers used 'self-actualisation' to describe when a person's 'ideal self' is congruent with their *real* self and they become a 'fully functioning person'.

The self and self-congruence

The **self** – how we perceive ourselves; 'ideal self' – what we aspire to be. **Congruence** occurs when these match well, leading to feelings of self-worth. A poor match leads to incongruence, and lower self-worth. Complete congruence is rare and people may thus use defence mechanisms to protect themselves from the discomfort of incongruence.

Conditions of worth

These are requirements that we perceive significant others expect us to meet if we are to be seen positively by them. Rogers claimed that failure to meet **conditions of worth** results in incongruence and lower self-worth.

The influence on counselling psychology

Rogers (1959) developed the client-centred approach to counselling. He argued that, with support, we could solve our own problems, become a fully functioning person and potentially achieve self-actualisation. Counsellors provide a supportive environment aimed at dissolving conditions of worth, moving the client toward authenticity and self-congruence.

Evaluation

Strengths: Maslow's hierarchy is linked to economic development

Hagerty (1999) found support for a relationship between Maslow's need levels and countries' economic growth. In the early stages of growth there were lower level needs. In more advanced countries *esteem* and *self-actualisation* were greater (e.g. shown by levels of educational enrolment).

Strengths: Research support for conditions of worth

Harter *et al.* (1996) discovered that teenagers who feel that they have to fulfil certain conditions in order to gain their parents' approval were more likely to develop depression and lose touch with their self. This supports Rogers' concept of 'conditions of worth' in relation to psychological health.

Limitations: Humanistic research methods

Scientific evaluation of the humanistic approach is difficult because evidence for it tends to be correlational. Some studies have shown personal growth following humanistic counselling, but not that the therapy *caused* the changes, thus failing to meet a fundamental requirement of scientific psychology.

Limitations: The humanistic approach is unrealistic

Critics argue that this approach is idealised and does not adequately acknowledge negative behaviour. Encouraging people to focus on self-development rather than their situation may be unrealistic or inappropriate in modern society.

Limitations: Cultural differences in the hierarchy of needs

Cross cultural studies have confirmed that Europeans and Americans focus more on personal identity in defining their self-concept, whereas Chinese, Japanese and Koreans define self-concept more in terms of social relationships (Nevis, 1983). The hierarchy of needs therefore appears not to be universal.

KEY TERMS

Conditions of worth
- Conditions imposed on an individual's behaviour and development that are considered necessary to earn positive regard from significant others.

Congruence
- If there is similarity between a person's ideal self and self-image, a state of congruence exists. A difference represents a state of incongruence.

Free will
- The ability to act at one's own discretion, i.e. to choose how to behave without being influenced by external forces.

Hierarchy of needs
- The motivational theory proposed by Abraham Maslow, often displayed as a pyramid. The most basic needs are at the bottom of the pyramid and higher needs at the top.

Humanistic
- Refers to the belief that human beings are born with the desire to grow, create and love, and have the power to direct their own lives.

Self
- Our sense of personal identity, used synonymously with the terms 'self-image' and 'self-concept'

Self-actualisation
- A term used in different ways. Rogers used it as the drive to realise one's true potential. Maslow used it to describe the final stage of his hierarchy of needs.

Apply it

Scenario. Al knows her parents are proud of the career she has chosen but she is unhappy in it. One day she has a serious accident. As soon as she recovers, she leaves her job to pursue her dream of travelling the world.

Apply Rogers' concepts of conditions of worth, self, ideal self and congruence to explain Al's decision. (4 marks)

Explanation. Al attempted to fulfil her parents' conditions of worth by pursuing the career that they valued. However, this ideal self was a poor fit to her self and the incongruence of the two left her unfulfilled. The accident made her re-assess her conditions of worth, achieve greater congruence between her self and ideal self and become a fully functioning, authentic person.

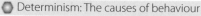

Determinism
- Behaviour is determined by external or internal factors acting upon the individual.

Nature
- Behaviour is seen to be a product of innate (biological or genetic) factors.

Nurture
- Behaviour is a product of environmental influences.

Science
- A systematic approach to creating knowledge. The method used to gain scientific knowledge is called scientific method.

Apply it

Using every combination of the six approaches covered in this spread, outline **one** similarity and **one** difference between each combination (2 marks each), for example:

- Psychodynamic vs social learning
- Cognitive vs biological
- Humanistic versus behavioural
- Biological versus psychodynamic

Comparison of approaches

The six major approaches to psychology have some common philosophical ground as well as important differences. Three of the most important ways to compare them are defined below.

💮 Determinism: The causes of behaviour

Determinism refers to the belief that behaviour is determined by forces other than the individual's will to do something. Many of the approaches covered in this chapter represent a determinist view, because they suggest that our behaviour is determined by, for example, biology, early experience or rewards. 'Free will' is used to refer to the alternative end of the spectrum, where the individual is seen as being capable of self-determination. As with most debates in psychology, the answer usually lies somewhere in between – our behaviour is probably a mixture of the two extremes.

💮 Nature and nurture: the role of innate and experiential factors

Human behaviour is either the product of a person's genes and biology (**nature**) or what they experience as a result of interacting with the environment (**nurture**). It is rare that behaviour is entirely one or the other alone. More usually, the question of 'nature or nurture' lies in looking at the way in which nature and nurture interact.

💮 Psychology as science

Psychology is often defined as the '**science** of behaviour', and most psychologists have adopted the scientific method as the most appropriate way of studying human behaviour. However, because psychology lies at the intersection of many other different disciplines, such as biology, philosophy and sociology, the application of scientific methods is not universal across the subject. For example, psychologists who are allied with biology may adopt the methods associated with the natural sciences, whereas psychologists who are more allied with philosophy or sociology may not always see scientific methodology as appropriate to their areas of interest.

An overview

APPROACH	Basic assumptions
Behaviourist	• External forces in the environment shape our behaviour (i.e. it is *determined*). • Explanations of behaviour emphasise the role of nurture more than nature. • Behaviourism aligns itself strongly with the scientific method.
Social learning	• Behaviour is learned as a result of the observations of others (i.e. it is *determined*). • Explanations of behaviour emphasise the role of nurture more than nature. • Social learning aligns itself with the scientific method but research can lack validity.
Cognitive	• Thought processes determine behaviour (i.e. some degree of control over behaviour). • Explanations of behaviour emphasise the role of nature *and* nurture. • Cognitive psychology aligns itself with the scientific method despite some inference.
Biological	• Physiological and/or inherited factors determine behaviour. • Explanations of behaviour emphasise the role of nature more than nurture. • Biological psychology aligns itself strongly with the scientific method.
Psychodynamic	• Unconscious factors beyond our conscious control determine behaviour. • Explanations of behaviour emphasise the role of nature *and* nurture. • Psychodynamic psychology does not really align itself with the scientific method.
Humanistic	• Behaviour is under our conscious control (i.e. we have free will). • Explanations of behaviour emphasise the role of nature *and* nurture. • Humanistic psychology mostly rejects the use of the scientific method.

A Level only (applies to Psychodynamic and Humanistic rows)

Biopsychology

3.1.2.1 Biopsychology (Year 1/AS) 4.2.2 Biopsychology (Year 2/A Level)

AS and A Level
- The divisions of the nervous system: central and peripheral (somatic and autonomic).
- The structure and function of sensory, relay and motor neurons. The process of synaptic transmission, including reference to neurotransmitters, excitation and inhibition.
- The function of the endocrine system: glands and hormones.
- The fight-or-flight response including the role of adrenaline.

A Level only
- Localisation of function in the brain and hemispheric lateralisation: motor, somatosensory, visual, auditory and language centres; Broca's and Wernicke's areas, split-brain research, plasticity and functional recovery after trauma.
- Ways of studying the brain: scanning techniques, including functional magnetic resonance (fMRI), electroencephalogram (FEGs) and event related potentials (ERPs); post-mortem examinations.
- Biological rhythms: circadian, infradian and ultradian and the difference between these rhythms. The effect of endogenous pacemakers and exogenous zeitgebers.

Key terms (highlight each cell when you can define the term for 3 marks)

Divisions of the nervous system	Structure and function of neurons	Function of the endocrine system	Fight-or-flight response	Localisation of function and hemispheric lateralisation	Ways of studying the brain	Biological rhythms
Central	Sensory	Glands	Adrenaline	Motor and somatosensory areas	fMRI	Circadian
Peripheral	Relay	Hormones		Visual and auditory centres	EEG	Infradian
Somatic	Motor			Language centres: Broca's areas, Wernicke's area	ERP	Ultradian
Autonomic	Neuro-transmitters				Post-mortem	Endogenous pacemakers
	Excitation			Plasticity		Exogenous zeitgebers
	Inhibition			Functional recovery		

Content checklist

1. In each 'describe, apply and evaluate' cell tick when you have produced brief notes.
2. Once you feel you have a good grasp of the topic add a second tick to the cell.
3. When you feel you have complete mastery of the topic and would be able to answer an exam question without the aid of notes highlight the cell.

I am able to...	Describe	Apply	Evaluate
AS and A Level			
The divisions of the nervous system: central and peripheral (somatic and autonomic)			
The structure and function of sensory, relay and motor neurons			
The process of synaptic transmission including reference to neurotransmitters, excitation and inhibition			
The function of the endocrine system; glands and hormones			
The fight-or-flight response including the role of adrenaline			
A Level only			
Localisation of function in the brain: motor, somatosensory, visual, auditory, language centres; Broca's area and Wernicke's area			
Hemispheric lateralisation and split-brain research			
Plasticity and functional recovery after trauma			
Ways of studying the brain: scanning techniques including fMRI, EEGs, ERPs, post-mortem examinations			
Biological rhythms: circadian, infradian and ultradian and the difference between these rhythms			
The effect of endogenous pacemakers and exogenous zeitgebers			

KEY TERMS

Autonomic nervous system (ANS)
- Governs the brain's involuntary activities (e.g. stress response, heartbeat) and is self-regulated (autonomous). It is divided into the sympathetic branch (fight or flight) and the parasympathetic branch (rest and digest).

Brain
- The part of the central nervous system that is responsible for coordinating sensation, intellectual and nervous activity.

Central nervous system (CNS)
- Comprises the brain and spinal cord. It receive information from the senses and controls the body's responses.

Peripheral nervous system
- The part of the nervous system that is outside the brain and spinal cord.

Somatic nervous system
- The part of the peripheral nervous system responsible for carrying sensory and motor information to and from the central nervous system.

Spinal cord
- A bundle of nerve fibres enclosed within the spinal column and which connects nearly all parts of the body with the brain.

Apply it

Scenario. Tasmin loves rollercoasters, she explains she enjoys the adrenaline rush they give her, the feeling of her heart racing and breathlessness. Once she has ridden the rollercoaster she finds she quickly returns to a 'normal' state and so queues up to ride again and again.

Use your knowledge of the peripheral nervous system to explain Tasmin's experience of riding the rollercoaster. (3 marks)

Explanation. When Tasmin is on the ride the sympathetic branch of her autonomic nervous system (ANS) is responding causing fight or flight. This explains Tasmin's experience of an 'adrenaline rush' leading to her heart rate increasing and shallow breathing which causes her to feel breathless. After the ride is over the parasympathetic branch of her ANS relaxes Tasmin as the emergency has ended. Her heart rate slows and breathing will return to normal.

The nervous system

The human nervous system is divided into the central nervous system (CNS) and the **peripheral nervous system**. These two divisions are further subdivided into different components each with a different function.

The central nervous system (CNS)

The **CNS** is made up of the **brain** and **spinal cord**. It has two main functions: the control of behaviour and the regulation of the body's physiological processes.

The spinal cord

Relays information between brain and body enabling the brain to monitor and regulate bodily processes and coordinate voluntary movements. Spinal nerves connect the spinal cord to the body. Circuits of nerve cells perform simple involuntary reflexes, e.g. pulling your hand away when something is hot. If the spinal cord is damaged, body parts supplied by the spinal nerves below the damage will be cut off from the brain and unable to function.

The brain

The brain consists of four main areas:

- The **cerebrum** is divided into four lobes: the frontal lobe (speech, thought and learning), temporal lobe (hearing and memory), parietal lobe (processing sensory information) and occipital lobe (visual information). It is split into two cerebral hemispheres which communicate through the corpus callosum.

- The **cerebellum** is involved in control of motor skills and balance. Abnormalities of this area can cause speech difficulties, motor problems and epilepsy.

- The **diencephalon** contains the thalamus which relays nerve impulses from the senses to the brain. The hypothalamus, also in the diencephalon, has many functions including regulation of body temperature, hunger and thirst. It also links the endocrine system to the nervous system controlling the release of hormones from the pituitary gland.

- The **brain stem** regulates automatic functions such as breathing and heartbeat. Motor and sensory neurons travel through the brain stem, allowing impulses to pass between the brain and spinal cord.

The peripheral nervous system

Consist of all nerves outside the CNS. Their function is to relay nerve impulses to and from the CNS and the rest of the body. There are two main divisions: the **somatic nervous system** and the **autonomic nervous system** (ANS).

The somatic nervous system

Consists of 12 pairs of cranial nerves and 31 pairs of spinal nerves which are both sensory (relay messages to the CNS) and motor (relay information from the CNS to the body). The system is also involved in involuntary reflex actions that do not require the CNS.

The autonomic nervous system (ANS)

Regulates involuntary actions such as heartbeat and digestion. Divided into two parts: the sympathetic (uses noradrenaline which has stimulating effects) and the parasympathetic nervous system (uses acetylcholine which has an inhibiting effect).

- **The sympathetic nervous system (SNS).** Neurons from the SNS travel to virtually every organ and gland preparing the body for fight-or-flight response: stored energy is released, pupils dilate and sweating increases. Less important processes, like digestion, are slowed.

- **The parasympathetic nervous system (PNS).** Works in opposition to the SNS relaxing the body once the emergency has passed: heart rate slows and blood pressure reduces. The PNS is called rest and digest as it is involved in energy conservation and digestion (following its inhabitation by the SNS).

Neurons and synaptic transmission

The average human brain contains around 100 billion neurons and, on average, each neurone is connected to 1000 other neurons.

 The structure and function of neurons

Neurons can be one of three types: **sensory**, **relay** or **motor neurons**. Neurons can vary from a few millimetres up to one metre in length:

- Dendrites at one end of the neuron receive signals from other neurons or sensory receptors.
- The **cell body** is the control centre of the neuron. From the cell body the nerve impulse travels along the **axon**.
- In many nerves, including those in the CNS, the axon is insulated by a **myelin sheath** which increases the speed of nerve transmission.

Sensory neurons

These neurons carry nerve impulses from sensory receptors to the spinal cord and brain where impulse are translated into sensations. Not all sensory information travels to the brain; some neurons end in the spinal cord allowing reflex actions to occur.

Relay neurons

Allow sensory and motor neurons to communicate with each other. They lie entirely within the brain and spinal cord.

Motor neurons

Responsible for direct and indirect muscle contraction. Axons project outside the CNS forming **synapses** with muscles. When stimulated, **neurotransmitters** are released that bind to receptors on the muscle triggering muscle contraction. Contraction strength depends on the rate of firing of the axons that control it. Muscle relaxation is caused by inhibition of the motor neuron.

 Synaptic transmission

Synaptic vesicles, at the end of the presynaptic axon, contain neurotransmitters. When an **action potential** reaches the synaptic vesicles, neurotransmitters are released into the **synaptic gap** through a process called **exocytosis**.

Neurotransmitters diffuse across the synaptic gap and bind onto specialised **receptors** on the surface of the postsynaptic neuron. Once activated the receptor molecules produce either **excitatory** or **inhibitory** effects on the postsynaptic neuron.

The quicker the **re-uptake** of the neurotransmitter into the presynaptic neuron the shorter the excitatory or inhibitory effect. Enzymes can deactivate neurotransmitters after they have stimulated receptors.

 Excitatory and inhibitory neurotransmitters

A nerve cell can receive excitatory and inhibitory messages simultaneously. Adding up the excitatory and inhibitory input (**summation**) determines whether or not the cell fires.

Excitatory neurotransmitters

Acetylcholine and noradrenaline act as 'on switches' making the postsynaptic cell more likely to fire. An excitatory neurotransmitter binding with a postsynaptic receptor causes an electrical charge resulting in an **excitatory postsynaptic potential** (EPSP).

The strength of an EPSP can be increased by:

- *Spatial summation.* A large number of EPSPs are generated at many different synapses on the postsynaptic neuron at the same time.
- *Temporal summation.* A large number of EPSPs are generated at the same synapse.

Inhibitory neurotransmitters

Serotonin and GABA are 'off switches'. **Inhibitory postsynaptic potentials** (IPSP) occur when these neurotransmitters bind to postsynaptic receptors, making it less likely the cell will fire.

KEY TERMS

Motor neurons
- Form synapses with muscles and control their contractions.

Neurotransmitter
- Chemical substances that play an important part in the workings of the nervous system by transmitting nerve impulses across the synapse.

Relay neurons
- The most common type of neuron in the CNS. They allow sensory and motor neurons to communicate with each other.

Sensory neurons
- Carry nerve impulses from sensory receptors to the spinal cord and the brain.

Synapse
- The conjunction of the end of the axon of one neuron and the dendrite or cell body of another.

Synaptic transmission
- The process by which a nerve impulse passes across the synaptic cleft from one neuron (the presynaptic neuron) to another (the postsynaptic neuron).

Apply It

Scenario. Jarred is cooking a meal for his family. He uses a tea towel to take a dish out of the oven. Unfortunately the towel slips and his hand touches the edge of the dish. It is so hot he instantly relaxes his grip and the dish, along with the food it contains, crashes to the floor.

Using your understanding of the structure and function of neurons to explain why Jarred reacted in this way. (3 marks)

Explanation. Sensory neurons receive information (heat, pain) from the sensory receptors in the skin on Jarred's hand. The sensory neurons carry these nerve impulses to the CNS. Relay neurons in the CNS allow sensory neurons to communicate with motor neurons. Motor neurons form synapses with muscles enabling Jarred to react appropriately to events in the environment, in this case letting go of the dish as it is painful to hold. This seems to be a reflex action and so the sensory neurons involved may terminate in the spinal cord rather than the brain, allowing for a faster reaction without the delay of sending impulses to the brain.

KEY TERMS

Endocrine system
- A network of glands throughout the body that manufacture and secrete hormones.

Hormones
- The body's chemical messengers. They travel through the bloodstream, influencing many different processes including mood, the stress response and bonding between mother and newborn baby.

Pituitary gland
- The 'master gland', whose primary function is to influence the release of hormones from other glands.

Apply it

Scenario. Mr Ray is planning a health and well-being lesson for his Year 7 class. He decides to teach about the effects of hormones, especially as they will soon be approaching puberty.

Suggest suitable information Mr Ray may wish to focus on in the lesson. (3 marks)

Explanation. Mr Ray should explain that glands within the body are responsible for the release of hormones and that these hormones regulate activity of the organs and tissues in the body. He could introduce the class to the pituitary gland as this gland, under control of the hypothalamus, influences the release of hormones from other glands. As his students are nearing the age of puberty he may wish to focus on the glands of the reproductive system explaining that in females the ovaries produce oestrogen and progesterone while in men, the testes produce testosterone.

The endocrine system

The **endocrine system** works closely with the nervous system to regulate the physiological processes of the human body.

 Endocrine glands

A feedback mechanism ensures stable concentrations of **hormones** in the bloodstream:
- A 'releasing hormone' from the hypothalamus signals the **pituitary gland** to secrete a stimulating hormone', which signals the target gland to secrete *its* hormone.
- As levels of this hormone rise, the secretion-releasing hormones shut down. The target gland then slows secretion of its hormone.

 Hormones

Target cells have receptors specific to a certain hormone, meaning they can only be influenced by that hormone. Too much or little hormones, and release of hormones at the wrong time can result in dysfunction of bodily systems.

 The pituitary gland

The pituitary gland is a 'master gland' regulating many bodily functions by releasing hormones that influence the release of hormones from other glands or by directly causing changes in the physiological processes in the body.

Hormones produced by the pituitary gland

The pituitary gland has two main parts, each releasing different hormones which act on different target glands or cells. For example:
- **Anterior pituitary**. Releases ACTH which stimulates the adrenal glands to produce cortisol. It also produces luteinising hormone (LH) and follicle-stimulating hormone (FSH) involved in reproduction.
- **Posterior pituitary**. Releases oxytocin which stimulates contraction of the uterus during childbirth, and plays a role in mother–infant bonding.

 The adrenal glands

Located above the kidneys, each gland is made up of the adrenal cortex (outer part) and the adrenal medulla (inner part).

Hormones produced by the adrenal glands

Each region has different functions, for example hormones released from the adrenal cortex are vital for life, while those released by the adrenal medulla are not.
- **Adrenal cortex**. Produces cortisol which regulates or supports important bodily functions such as cardiovascular and anti-inflammatory functions. Cortisol production increases in response to stress.
- **Adrenal medulla**. Releases adrenaline and noradrenaline, preparing the body for fight or flight by increasing heart rate and blood flow (adrenaline) and constricting blood vessels to increase blood pressure (noradrenaline).

 The reproductive organs

Ovaries (part of the female reproductive system) and testes (the male reproductive glands) are major components of the reproductive system.

Ovaries

Ovaries are responsible for the production of eggs and for the hormones oestrogen and progesterone. Progesterone has been associated with heightened social awareness of opportunities (forming allies) or threats (from enemies), both beneficial during pregnancy.

Testes

Testes produce the hormone testosterone which is responsible for growth of facial hair, deepening of voice and growth spurt during puberty. The hypothalamus instructs the pituitary gland on how much testosterone needs to be produced by the testes. Testosterone also plays a role in sex drive, sperm production, muscle strength maintenance and overall health and well-being in men.

The fight-or-flight response

The **fight-or-flight response** is a survival response enabling the organisms to react quickly in dangerous situations.

The amygdala and hypothalamus

The amygdala associates sensory signals with emotions such as fear or anger. This sends a distress signal to the hypothalamus, which triggers the body's response to stress through the sympathetic nervous system.

Response to acute (sudden) stressors

- **The sympathetic nervous system (SNS)**. When triggered the SNS sends a signal to the adrenal medulla to release adrenaline into the bloodstream.
- **Adrenaline**. This hormone prepares the body for fight or flight. Heart rate increases and blood pressure rises. Breathing becomes more rapid, increasing oxygen intake. Blood sugar (glucose) and fats flood into the bloodstream supplying energy to parts of the body.
- **The parasympathetic nervous system**. Reduces the stress response. Heart rate and breathing slow down, blood pressure reduces and digestion begins again.

Response to chronic (ongoing) stressors

If a stressor continues the initial surge of adrenaline subsides and the hypothalamus activates the HPA axis.

- **'H' – Hypothalamus**. Chronic stress leads to the hypothalamus releasing *corticotrophin-releasing hormone (CRH)* into the bloodstream.
- **'P' – Pituitary gland**. CRH causes the pituitary gland to produce and release adrenocorticotrophic hormone (ACTH).
- **'A' – Adrenal glands**. ACTH stimulates the adrenal cortex to release cortisol, leading to quick bursts of energy and lower sensitivity to pain as well as impaired cognitive function and lowered immune response.
- **Feedback**. The hypothalamus and pituitary gland have special receptors that monitor cortisol levels; if levels are too high CRH and ACTH levels are reduced to return cortisol to a normal level.

Evaluation

Negative consequences of the fight-or-flight response

Stressors in modern life rarely require a heightened physical response. Repeated activation of the SNS can lead to physical damage to blood vessels and eventually heart disease. Too much cortisol leads to suppression of the immune response, making the body more vulnerable to infection.

Most animals initially display a freeze response

Gray (1988) proposes that before confronting or fleeing a stressor most animals (including humans) display the freeze response. By freezing the animal is hyper-vigilant, which has an adaptive advantage as new information is sought, allowing the best possible response to be made for that particular threat.

A genetic basis to sex differences in the fight-or-flight response

The SRY gene, which promotes aggression, is only present on the male Y chromosome. This may prime the fight-or-flight response in males. Females do not have the Y chromosome and this, along with the action of oestrogen and oxytocin, may prevent the fight-or-flight response to stress.

The 'tend and befriend' response

Female response to stress is characterised by tend (nurturing) and befriend (forming protective alliances) behaviours. Research with rats suggests the release of oxytocin increases relaxation and reduces fearfulness and so decreasing the fight-or-flight response.

Gender differences in stress response may be exaggerated

Von Dawans et al.'s (2012) study found that in both genders acute stress increased cooperative and friendly behaviour. This could be because humans are social animals and it is the protective nature of human social relationships that has allowed our species to survive.

Apply it

Scenario. Mikala, Daniella and Lucy are about to give a presentation to the class. They are all feeling very nervous as they want to perform well in front of their classmates. As they stand in front of the class Lucy whispers to Mikala, 'My mind has gone blank, I can't remember anything!' Mikala responds by reassuring her she is going to be fine and reminds her she can use her flash cards as a prompt. Daniella said she would sit behind the laptop to manage the slideshow as, 'there was no way she would be able to talk to the class'.

Using your knowledge of the fight-or-flight response explain the students' different responses to the stress of giving a presentation in class. (3 marks)

Explanation. Daniella seems to be fleeing the situation as she has almost removed herself from the threat of giving a presentation as she is sitting behind the laptop changing slides. Rather than fight or flight Lucy is showing the freeze response – a kind of stop, look and listen behaviour which is preventing her acting in the situation as she is unable to begin the presentation. Mikala is showing 'tend and befriend' as her response to Lucy is nurturing and will help build alliances.

KEY TERMS

Broca's area
- An area in the frontal lobe of the brain, usually in the left hemisphere, related to speech production.

Localisation of function
- Refers to the belief that specific areas of the brain are associated with specific cognitive processes.

Motor cortex
- A region of the brain responsible for the generation of voluntary motor movements.

Somatosensory cortex
- A region of the brain that processes input from sensory receptors in the body that are sensitive to touch.

Wernicke's area
- An area in the temporal lobe of the brain important in the comprehension of language.

Localisation of function

Localisation of function refers to the belief that specific functions such as language, memory and hearing have specific locations in the brain.

⬡ Visual centres in the brain

The primary visual centre is located in the **visual cortex** in the **occipital lobe** of the brain. Photoreceptors in the retina detect changes in light, sending nerve impulses along the optic nerve. Most nerve impulses terminate in the thalamus which relays information to the visual cortex. The visual cortex in the right hemisphere receives input from the left visual field while the visual cortex in the left hemisphere receives input from the right visual field. Different areas of the cortex process different types of visual information such as colour, shape or movement.

⬡ Auditory centres in the brain

Most of the auditory centre is located in the **auditory cortex** which lies within the **temporal lobes** in both hemispheres. In the cochlea (found in the inner ear) sound waves convert to nerve impulses which travel along the auditory nerve. Impulses first arrive at the brain stem for basic decoding, e.g. the duration and intensity of a sound. They pass to the thalamus for further processing and are relayed to the auditory cortex for recognition.

⬡ The motor cortex

Located in the **frontal lobe**, along the precentral gyrus, the **motor cortex** generates voluntary motor movements. The motor cortex in the right hemisphere controls movement on the left side of the body, the motor cortex in the left hemisphere controls movement on the right side. Different regions of the motor cortex control different parts of the body. The regions are ordered by body part, e.g. the region that controls foot movement is located next to the region that controls the leg.

⬡ The somatosensory cortex

Found in the **parietal lobe**, along the postcentral gyrus, the **somatosensory cortex** detects sensory events around the body. The postcentral gyrus processes touch information. Using sensory information from the skin the somatosensory cortex produces sensations of touch, pressure, pain and temperature localised to specific body regions. As with the motor cortex, sensory information from one side of the body is processed by the cortex in the opposite side of the brain.

⬡ Language centres in the brain

A neural loop known as the **arcuate fasciculus** runs between Broca and Wernicke's language centres: Broca's area is responsible for speech production and Wernicke's area is responsible for the processing of spoken language.

Broca's area

Broca studied patients with similar brain injuries to the left frontal hemisphere who could understand speech but not produce it verbally or in written form. **Broca's area** is located in the posterior portion of the frontal lobe in the left hemisphere and is responsible for speech production. The motor region, located in Broca's area, is close to the area that controls the mouth, tongue and vocal cords. Later research has found two regions in Broca's area, one involved in language, the other in responding to demanding cognitive tasks.

Wernicke's area

Wernicke discovered an area in the posterior portion of the left temporal lobe responsible for understanding language. Patients with a lesion in this area could speak but were unable to understand language. The sensory region, located in **Wernicke's area**, is close to regions responsible for auditory and visual input. This input is thought to be transferred to Wernicke's area where it is recognised as language and associated with meaning.

⬡ Evaluation

Support for language centres in the brain

Research into aphasia (inability/impaired ability to understand or produce speech) supports the different functions of language centres in the brain. In most cases, patients with expressive aphasia (an inability to produce language) have brain damage in Broca's area. Receptive aphasia (an impaired ability to understand spoken and written language) is usually the result of damage to Wernicke's area. Such studies demonstrate the role different language centres play in our use of language.

There are individual differences in language areas

Different patterns of brain activity have been observed in individuals carrying out various language activities. For example, Bavelier *et al.* (1997) found large variability in activation across individuals, with activity being recorded in the right temporal lobe as well as the left frontal, temporal and occipital lobes. Furthermore, Harasty *et al.* (1997) found women have proportionally larger Broca's and Wernicke's areas than men.

Language production may not be confined to Broca's area alone

Re-examination of the preserved brains of two of Broca's patients found that other areas besides Broca's area could have contributed to their speech difficulties. MRI imagining (not available at the time of Broca's research) revealed the true extent of lesions in the brains, suggesting that language and cognition involve networks of brain regions rather than being localised to specific areas.

Communication may be more important that localisation

How brain areas communicate with each other may be more important than associating specific brain regions with particular functions. Wernicke himself suggested that although different brain regions had different functions they must interact with each other to produce complex behaviours. For example, Dejerine (1892) reported a case where damage to the connection between the visual cortex and Wernicke's area led to a loss in the ability to read. Complex behaviours result from the movement of stimuli through various structures in the brain before a response is produced.

Challenges to localisation: equipotentiality

The equipotentiality theory proposes that while basic motor and sensory functions are localised, higher mental functions are not. Lashley (1930) claimed that following injury, intact areas of the cortex could take over functions usually carried out by damaged areas: it is the extent of the damage rather than the location of the damage that determines the effects of the injury. This theory has received some support from research into brain plasticity and functional recovery (see page 73).

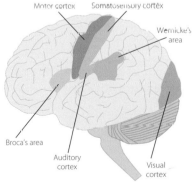

▲ *Areas of the brain*

Apply it

Scenario. Dr Suresh is researching the effects of head injury in patients displaying speech difficulties. She has arranged for each patient to undergo an fMRI to identify which regions of the brain are active when completing different cognitive tasks. She plans to compare the activity recorded to a control group of adults with no known head injury.

What activities could Dr Suresh ask the sample to attempt during the fMRI? What differences might she find between the patients and the control group? (4 marks)

Explanation. While in the fMRI participants' ability to understand speech could be tested. This could be done by asking patients to hold up a certain number of digits, for example, 'hold up three fingers': if they understand speech they should hold up three fingers for the researcher to see. A control group following this instruction should show brain activity in the area known as Wernicke's area which is located in the posterior portion of the left temporal lobe. In comparison, if the patients with head injuries are unable to understand the instructions then this area of the brain may be damaged and so activation in this area may be greatly reduced or non-existent. She plans to compare the activity recorded to a control group of adults with no known head injury.

KEY TERMS

Hemispheric lateralisation
- Refers to the fact that some mental processes are mainly specialised to either the right or left hemisphere of the brain. For example, the left hemisphere is dominant for language and speech.

Split-brain research
- Research that studies individuals who have been subjected to the surgical separation of the two hemispheres of the brain as a result of severing the corpus callosum.

Apply it

Scenario. In an attempt to treat his severe epileptic seizures, patient X underwent a surgical procedure to cut the nerve fibres forming the corpus callosum. A psychologist decided to test the effect of splitting the two hemispheres. Patient X was asked to focus on a central dot while the psychologist presented an image in either the left or right visual field. Each time the psychologist asked patient X whether they could see anything.

Use your knowledge of split-brain research to predict what Patient X would answer when an image was presented in this left visual field and on a second trial, when an image was presented in his right visual field. (4 marks)

Explanation. When the image is presented in patient X's right visual field the patient would be able to say they had seen the image. This is because information from the right visual field is processed in the left hemisphere which also contains the language centres so patient X is able to give a verbal response. However, when the image is presented in the left visual field the patient would say they cannot see the image. Information from the left visual field is processed by the right hemisphere which can see the image but has no language centre to respond.

Lateralisation and split-brain research

Lateralisation suggests different hemispheres have different specialisations. **Split-brain research** aims to identify functions unique to each hemisphere.

 ## Hemispheric lateralisation

Neural mechanisms for some functions are localised primarily in one hemisphere. For example, the left hemisphere is dominant for language and speech (Broca's area and Wernicke's area, see page 70). We are able to talk about things we have experienced in the right hemisphere (e.g. face recognition) as the hemispheres are connected by the **corpus callosum**.

 ## Split-brain research

Sperry and Gazzaniga's research (1967)

How? The split-brain patient focused on a dot in the centre of the screen while information was displayed in the left or right visual field. Without seeing their hands, patients responded with either their left hand (right hemisphere control) or right hand (left hemisphere control), or verbally (left hemisphere control).

Showed? If a picture of a dog was flashed in the right visual field, the patient would verbally answer dog: the left hemisphere had received visual information and language centres located there responded. However, if a picture of a cat was flashed in the left visual field the patient was unable to respond verbally as the right hemisphere has no language centre and due to severing of the corpus callosum the left hemisphere could not receive information from the right hemisphere.

What have we learnt from split-brain research?

The left hemisphere is responsible for speech and language, and the right hemisphere specialises in visuo-spatial processing and face recognition. Research has also suggested that rather than the brain being localised (discrete regions with specific functions) connectivity between different regions is as important.

 ## Evaluation

Advantages of hemispheric lateralisation

Rogers *et al.* (2004) found domestic chickens showed enhanced ability to perform two tasks at the same time: finding food and being vigilant for predators. This suggests lateralisation enhances brain efficiency in cognitive tasks that demand simultaneous but different use of both hemispheres. However, very little empirical evidence has been found.

Lateralisation and immune system functioning

Tonnessen *et al.* (1993) reported a small but significant relationship between handedness and immune disorders. In support, Morfit and Weekes (2001) found that left handers had a higher incident of immune disorders in their immediate families than did right handers.

Lateralisation changes with age

Szaflarski *et al.* (2006) found language became more lateralised to the left hemisphere as children aged but after the age of 25 lateralisation decreased with each decade of life. Using extra processing resources of the other hemisphere may compensate for age-related declines in function.

Language may not be restricted to the left hemisphere

Turk *et al.* (2002) reported the case of JW, a split-brain patient who developed the capacity to speak out of the right hemisphere. This contradicts previous research that suggested the right hemisphere was unable to handle even basic language functions.

Limitations of split-brain research

Many studies contain as few as three participants, with some being based on one single case study (Andrewes, 2001). Research conclusions have been drawn from patients with a confounding physical disorder or have been found to have a less complete sectioning of the two hemispheres than originally thought.

Brain plasticity and functional recovery

Functional recovery refers to the moving of functions from one damaged brain area to other undamaged areas following head trauma.

Brain plasticity

- **Life experience**. Frequently used nerve pathways develop stronger connections, while neurons that are rarely used die. Boyke *et al.* (2008) found increases in grey matter in the visual cortex of 60-year-olds learning to juggle, but if they stopped practising these changes were reversed.
- **Video games**. Kühn *et al.* (2014) studied changes to the hippocampus and cerebellum of participants playing Super Mario for at least 30 minutes each day for two months. A significant increase in grey matter was seen suggesting game play led to new synaptic connections in areas involved in spatial navigation, strategic planning, working memory and motor performance.
- **Meditation**. Davidson *et al.* (2004) compared eight Tibetan monks with 10 student volunteers. When meditating for short periods the monks (experienced in meditation) showed much greater activation of gamma waves even before they began meditating, suggesting prior meditation had led to permanent changes in their brain.

Functional recovery after trauma

Research with stoke victims has suggested that over time the brain is able to re-wire itself. Neurons next to a damaged brain area can form new circuits in an attempt to take over some of the functions that were lost.

Mechanisms for recovery

Regenerative developments in brain function may occur following trauma. There are two mechanisms that make this is possible:

- **Neuronal masking**. Wall (1977) suggests when surrounding brain cells are damaged, the rate of input to **dormant synapses** increases. 'Unmasking' the dormant synapses can open connections to previously inactive regions of the brain which over time leads to the development of new structures.
- **Stem cells**. Implanting stem cells may directly replace dead or dying cells. Alternatively the stem cells secrete growth factors that somehow 'rescue' the injured cells. A third suggestion is that the transplanted stem cells form a neural network linking an uninjured brain area with the damaged region.

Evaluation

Animal studies supporting brain plasticity
Kempermann *et al.* (1998) found rats living in complex environments showed an increased number of neurones, especially in the **hippocampus**, compared to rats kept in laboratory cages.

Human studies supporting brain plasticity
MRI scans of London taxi drivers revealed a greater amount of grey matter in the brain compared to a control group. The **posterior hippocampus** of taxi drivers was significantly larger, with its volume being positively correlated with the amount of time they had been a taxi driver (Maguire *et al.* 2000).

Animal studies supporting functional recovery
Rats who had stem cells transplanted into an injury site showed clear development of neuron-like cells in that brain area. A solid stream of stem cells was also identified migrating to the brain's site of injury (Tajiri *et al.*, 2013).

Age differences in functional recovery
However, Elbert *et al.* (2001) conclude that children have a much greater capacity for neural reorganisation than adults, as evidenced by the extended practice adults need in order to produce functional changes following brain injury.

Educational attainment and functional recovery
Schneider *et al.* (2014) found that out of 214 patients who had achieved disability-free recovery (DFR) after 1 year, 39.2% had 16 or more years of education. Only 9.7% of patients with less than 12 years of education achieved DFR after 1 year.

KEY TERMS

Brain plasticity
- The brain's ability to modify its own structure and function as a result of experience: developing new connections and discarding weaker ones.

Functional recovery
- The recovery of abilities and mental processes that have been compromised as a result of brain injury or disease. There are two mechanisms for recovery: neuronal masking and stem cells.

Apply it

Scenario. At the age of 48 Simon, a university lecturer, suffered a major stroke in the left side of his brain. Damage to the language centres found in the left hemisphere meant he was unable to form words and found it very difficult to communicate with others. When Simon was physically well he began a therapeutic programme involving bi-weekly speech therapy which was supported by family and friends helping Simon practise the activities set by his therapist on a daily basis. After a year Simon was able to utter a short sentence. Four years later, Simon is able to use a wide range of simple sentences and is overjoyed to have regained his ability to talk.

How might psychologists explain the progress Simon has made following his brain injury? (4 marks)

Explanation. Brain plasticity can be used to explain the recovery of function shown by Simon following his stroke. Life experiences, such as repeatedly practising speech techniques, have changed Simon's neuronal structure and function, meaning he is able to regain functions that were previously lost, in his case speech. Increased rates of input to dormant synapses in Simon's brain 'unmasks' these synapses, opening connections to the previously inactive areas of the brain. Before his stroke Simon was a university lecturer, which may have increased his likelihood of experiencing functional recovery. For example, Schneider *et al.* (2014) found patients with the equivalent of a college education were more likely to show rapid recovery than those whose level of education did not reach the end of high school.

KEY TERMS

Electroencephalogram (EEG)

- A method of recording changes in the electrical activity of the brain using electrodes attached to the scalp. There are four basic EEG patterns: alpha waves, beta waves, delta waves and theta waves.

Event-related potential (ERP)

- A technique that takes raw EEG data and uses it to investigate cognitive processing of a specific event. It achieves this by taking multiple readings and averaging them in order to filter out all brain activity that is not related to the appearance of the stimulus.

Functional magnetic resonance imaging (fMRI)

- A technique for measuring brain activity while a person performs a task. It detects changes in blood oxygenation and flow that indicate increased neural activity.

Post-mortem examinations

- Ways of examining the brains of people who have shown particular psychological abnormalities prior to their death in an attempt to establish the possible neurobiological cause for this behaviour.

Apply it

Scenario. Roberta and Jamal are discussing their research projects. Roberta has been gathering recordings of brain activity in head trauma patients to identify differences in brain waves between patients and normal patterns of activity. Jamal shows Roberta recordings of blood flow in particular area of the brain gathered as participants performed visual tasks.

Identify the different scanning techniques used and suggest one limitation that may be faced when using each techniques. (3 + 3 marks)

Explanation. One problem Roberta may face when using an EEG is that she is only able to detect activity on the brain' surface and so she is unable to determine any effects of the trauma experienced in deeper regions of the brain. Jamal is using fMRI. However, this only shows localised activity and ignores the neural networks involved in responding to stimuli. Any conclusions drawn may not be a complete explanation of neural activity in response to a stimulus.

Ways of studying the brain

Neuroscientists uses a variety of methods to study the functions of brain areas.

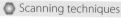 Post-mortem examinations

Post-mortem examination of 'Tan' revealed lesions in the area of the brain now known as Broca's area (see page 70). HM was unable to store new memories, examination after death found lesions in the hippocampus (Annese *et al.* (2014) see page 26). Cotter *et al.* (2001) reported reduced number of glial cells in the frontal cortex of people who had suffered from depression.

⬡ Scanning techniques

Functional magnetic resonance imaging (fMRI)

fMRIs measure changes in blood flow as specific tasks are performed to produce a map of areas of the brain involved in particular mental activities.

Electroencephalogram (EEG)

Electrodes on the scale detect small electrical charges resulting from brain activity. Alpha waves indicate a relaxed state. Beta waves (also seen in REM sleep) denote physiological arousal. Delta and theta waves occur in deeper stages of sleep.

Event-related potentials (ERPs)

The brain's electrical activity in response to repeated presentations of a target stimulus are averaged enabling neural activity in response to that stimulus being detected against any background neural 'noise'. ERPs can be divided into two categories: **Sensory ERPs** occur within the first 100 milliseconds after presentation of the stimulus, reflecting an initial response to the stimuli. **Cognitive ERPs** are generated after the initial response and reflect information processing as the stimulus is evaluated.

⬡ Evaluation

Post-mortems allow examination of deeper brain regions

For example, Harrison (2000) claims post-mortem examinations have discovered structural abnormalities in schizophrenic brains and provided evidence of changes in neurotransmitter systems implicated in the disorder.

However, post-mortem examinations are at risk of confounding influences

The brain being studied can be influenced by factors such as circumstances of death, drug treatments, age at death and time lapsed before the post-mortem.

fMRIs are non-invasive

Therefore making them safer as it does not expose the brain to potentially harmful radiation. In addition, they are useful when investigating phenomena people could not report verbally.

However, blood flow is not a direct measure of mental activity

fMRI's focus on localised activity also overlooks the brain's neural networks. Communication between different brain areas is most critical to mental function.

EEGs are useful in clinical diagnosis

For example, epileptic seizures are associated with sudden changes in brain activity in otherwise normal EEG readings.

However, EEGs cannot measure deeper brain regions

The EEG signal is unable to pinpoint the exact area in which electrical activity is occurring as neighbouring electrodes simultaneously detect the activity. Non-human animal studies have placed electrodes in structures such as the hippocampus but this is too invasive to be carried out on humans.

ERPs provide a continuous measure of processing

The participant can be presented with different types of stimuli to determine how processing is affected. ERPs are also able to measure stimuli processing in the absences of behavioural responses.

However, ERPs are difficult to detect

A number of trials are needed to gain meaningful data. Furthermore, readings are restricted to neocortex activity and so important electrical activity occurring deep in the brain is undetected.

Circadian rhythms

Every bodily cell contains clocks that are synchronised by the master circadian pacemaker, the suprachiasmatic nuclei (SCN) located in the hypothalamus. Environmental cues continually reset this clock through photoentrainment. Light sensitive cells in the retina send messages about light levels to the SCN which uses this information to co-ordinate the activity of the entire circadian system.

 ### The sleep–wake cycle

The strongest sleep drives occur around 2–4am and 1–3pm. Sleep deprivation increases the strength of circadian dips experienced. This homeostatic drive increases gradually throughout the day, reaching a peak in late evening. The internal body clock is **free-running**. Major alterations in sleep and wake schedules such as jet lag and shift work can cause the biological clock to become out of balance.

Free-running circadian rhythm

Michael Siffre spent long periods of time underground isolated from external cues such as light, clocks and radio. His free-running rhythm lengthened to just over 24 hours. During his final underground stay, aged 60, his body clock ticked more slowly sometimes stretching to 48 hours.

 ### Other circadian rhythms

Core body temperature

Over 24 hours core body temperature gradually drops (low point 36°C around 4:30am) and rises (high point 38°C around 6pm). Between 2pm and 4pm most people experience a slight drop in core temperature which may explain feelings of post-lunch sleepiness.

Hormone production

The production and release of melatonin from the pineal gland follows a **circadian rhythm**. Melatonin production increases during darkness, leading to sleepiness. When light melatonin decreases, the person wakes.

 ### Evaluation

Research support for the importance of light

Hughes (1977) studied four participants stationed at the British Antarctic Station. At the end of the summer, cortisol levels followed normal patterns (high point on waking, low point at bedtime). After three months of continuous darkness levels now peaked at noon. However, participants in the Arctic, who also experience prolonged winter darkness, showed no such disruption.

Real-world application: Chronotherapeutic medications

These drugs ensure the right concentration is released at the time it is most needed. For example, the risk of heart attack is greatest during the early hours after waking. Medication can be administered before a person goes to sleep but the drug is not released until the vulnerable period of 6am to noon (Evans and Marain, 1996).

Issues with research methodology

Early free-running cycle studies assumed participants were isolated from variables that might affect their circadian rhythms. However, Czeisler et al. (1999) showed it is possible to alter participants' circadian rhythms down to 22 hours and up to 28 hours using artificial light.

Genetic differences in length and onset of circadian cycles

Czeisler et al. (1999) found circadian cycles can vary from 13 to 65 hours. Duffy et al. (2001) identified 'morning people' who prefer to rise early (6am) and go to bed early (10pm) and 'evening people' who would rather wake later (10am) and go to bed later (1am).

Temperature may be more important than light in setting circadian rhythms

Buhr et al. (2010) explain that the SCN transforms information about light levels into neural messages that set the body's temperature. Fluctuations in body temperature over a 24-hour period set the timing of cells and therefore cause tissues and organs to be active or inactive.

KEY TERMS

Circadian rhythms
- A pattern of behaviour that occurs or recurs approximately every 24 hours, and which is set and reset by environmental light levels.

Sleep–wake cycle
- Alternating states of sleep and waking that are dependent on the 24-hour circadian cycle.

 ### Apply it

Scenario. Tina has begun a new career as a nurse working in the Accident and Emergency centre of a local hospital. By her own admission she has found working night shifts a challenge. She feels extremely sleepy at work and finds it difficult to sleep during the daytime. She is concerned this is affecting her performance at work as well as her ability to drive safely to and from the hospital.

Using your knowledge of circadian rhythms explain the problems Tina is facing. What advice could you offer her to reduce these difficulties? (6 marks)

Explanation. Tina's internal body clock has become out of balance with external cues. Melatonin production is increased during periods of darkness, leading to feelings of sleepiness. This means Tina will find it difficult to feel alert while working the night shift. Furthermore, attempts to sleep during the daytime are hindered by a decrease in melatonin and so Tina will feel too alert to sleep. If these problems continue then over time Tina will become sleep deprived and she will feel an increasing need to sleep, which could lead to accidents either at work or when driving. Tina could consider using artificial lights to alter her circadian cycle. Turning lights on as soon as she wakes could help her feel more alert. She should also reduce the amount of light when she is trying to sleep during the day. An eye mask or black-out blinds on her windows may help to increase melatonin production, leading to feelings of sleepiness.

KEY TERMS

Infradian rhythms

- Rhythms that have a duration of over 24 hours, and may be weekly, monthly or even annually.

Ultradian rhythms

- Cycles that last less than 24 hours, such as the cycle of sleep stages that occur throughout the night.

Ultradian and Infradian rhythms

As well as circadian rhythms we also experience **ultradian rhythms** (less than 24 hours) and **infradian rhythms** (longer than 24 hours).

Ultradian rhythms

Sleep stages

Our sleep follows a pattern of alternating REM and NREM sleep. REM (rapid eye movement) involves an increase in brain activity with EEG readings resembling that of a person awake. Dreaming is most likely to occur in this stage. NREM is made up of sleep stages 1 to 4 with stages 3 and 4 being deep sleep, characterised by slow delta waves on EEG recordings. This cycle repeats itself every 90–100 minutes with different sleep stages having different durations. Each cycle ends in a final stage of REM.

The Basic Rest Activity Cycle (BRAC)

Kleitman (1969) suggested the 90-minute cycle seen during sleep continues during wakefulness: moving from a state of alertness to a state of fatigue every 90 minutes. Research suggests we can focus for a period of 90 minutes but towards the end of this period we experience a loss of concentration, fatigue and hunger as the body begins to run out of resources. Kleitman points to everyday examples to support the existence of the BRAC cycle such as workers' 10.30am coffee break dividing the morning (9am to 12pm) into two 90-mininute phases.

Infradian rhythms

Weekly rhythms

Seven-day cycles have been seen in male testosterone levels which are elevated at the weekend and in young couples' sexual activity, again showing an increase at the weekend. The frequency of births is higher on week days than weekends. Although Halberg *et al.* (2002) reported a seven-day rhythm of blood pressure and heart rate in humans there is a lack of substantial evidence for the presence of weekly infradian rhythms that influence human behaviours.

Monthly rhythms

The human menstrual cycle is about one month in length, on average 28 days. However, Refinetti (2006) reports individual differences in length, with some women experiencing shorter cycles (23 days) than other women (36 days). Ovulation occurs roughly half way through the cycle when oestrogen levels peak and usually lasts for 16 to 32 hours. Following the ovulation phase, progesterone levels increase to prepare the uterus for the possible implantation of an embryo.

Annual rhythms

In most animals the seasons regulate annual rhythms, for example the migration of certain species during the winter months. Magnusson (2000) found seasons variations in mood in humans, especially women, with some becoming severely depressed during winter months (seasonal affective disorder). Trudeau (1997) reported an annual rhythm in human deaths, with most deaths occurring in January. Incidents of heart attacks vary seasonally, peaking in winter months.

Apply it

Scenario. Ali has volunteered to take part in a sleep study. She will be spending one night in a sleep laboratory during which an EEG will measure electrical activity in her brain. Ali is interested to learn what is happening in her brain while she is sleeping.

Explain what Ali is likely to learn from the EEG readings. (3 marks)

Explanation. Ali's EEG will show that she experiences an ultradian rhythm while asleep with cycles repeating every 90 to 100 minutes. During each cycle her brain activity will show periods of NREM and REM sleep. In her first cycle Ali would move from light stage 1 sleep, through to stage 2 sleep and into the deeper sleep stages (3 and 4) before returning to stage 2 and then entering a period of REM. During REM sleep Ali's EEG recordings would be similar to the EEG recordings of a person awake.

Evaluation

Support for the BRAC: elite performers

Ericsson *et al.* (2006) found elite violinists limited their practice sessions to no more than 90 minutes at a time and napped frequently to recover from practice sessions spaced across the day. This pattern was also found among other musicians, athletes, chess players and writers.

Individual differences in sleep stages

Sleep differences may be biologically determined, possibly under genetic influence. Tucker *et al.* (2007) recorded large differences in sleep duration, time to fall asleep and time spent in each sleep stage (especially deep sleep) of participants spending 11 nights in a controlled laboratory environment. As all participants experienced the same the sleep environment findings imply differences were at least partially biologically determined.

Evidence for exogenous cues controlling the menstrual cycle

Research has suggested a woman's pheromones can affect the menstrual cycle of women close by. Russell *et al.* (1980) rubbed daily sweat samples from one group of women on the upper lips of a second group of women, who were kept separate from the sweat donors. The menstrual cycles of the women became synchronised suggesting exogenous cues can also control the menstrual cycle.

Evidence that the menstrual cycle influences human mate choice

Penton-Voak *et al.* (1999) found that when picking a long-term partner, women generally preferred 'slightly feminised' faces, believed to represent a preference for kindness and cooperation. However, in the ovulatory phase of their cycle women preferred more masculine faces, implying a preference for 'good genes' that may be passed to any offspring resulting from a short-term liaison.

Unfounded belief in lunar rhythms

Arliss *et al.* (2005) found that many midwives believe more babies are born during a full moon while surveys of mental health workers found a persistent belief that the full mood can alter behaviour (Vance, 1995). However, Foster and Roenneberg (2008) report that while occasional studies have found correlations there is no evidence of a causal relationship between phases of the moon and human behaviour.

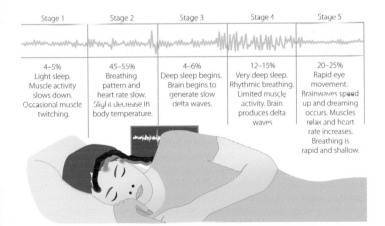

Stage 1	Stage 2	Stage 3	Stage 4	Stage 5
4–5%	45–55%	4–6%	12–15%	20–25%
Light sleep. Muscle activity slows down. Occasional muscle twitching.	Breathing pattern and heart rate slow. Slight decrease in body temperature.	Deep sleep begins. Brain begins to generate slow delta waves.	Very deep sleep. Rhythmic breathing. Limited muscle activity. Brain produces delta waves	Rapid eye movement. Brainwaves speed up and dreaming occurs. Muscles relax and heart rate increases. Breathing is rapid and shallow.

KEY TERMS

Endogenous pacemakers
- Mechanisms within the body that govern the internal, biological bodily rhythms.

Exogenous zeitgebers
- Environmental cue, such as light, that helps to regulate the biological clock in an organism.

Apply it

Scenario. On returning to England, following a holiday in the USA, Eric found his sleep-wake pattern was disrupted. He feels sleepy during the day but wakes up in the middle of the night.

Using your knowledge of endogenous pacemakers and exogenous zeitgebers explain Eric's experiences. (3 marks)

Explanation. Eric has jet lag because his internal sleep-wake cycle, originating from the SCN, has become out of sync with environmental cues (exogenous zeitgeber). Light usually entrains the sleep-wake cycle to a 24-hour pattern of sleeping during darkness and wakefulness during the day which offers and adaptive advantage. But, we are not able to adapt to rapid changes in zeitgebers resulting from flying across time zones. Eric is experiencing the effects of increased melatonin during daylight so feels sleepy when he should feel awake.

Endogenous pacemakers and exogenous zeitgebers

To maintain co-ordination with the external world, **exogenous zeitgebers** reset **endogenous pacemakers** on a daily basis.

 ## Endogenous pacemakers

The suprachiasmatic nucleus (SCN)

Located in the hypothalamus, the SCN is a 'master clock' generating circadian rhythms. Spontaneous synchronicity of SCN neurons ensure all biological clocks receive correctly time-co-ordinated signals. Without SCN control, peripheral clocks cannot maintain a circadian rhythm for long.

The SCN links to brain regions that control sleep and arousal. Information about changes in external light levels are sent via the optic nerve to the SCN. In response, the SCN regulates the manufacture and secretion of melatonin in the pineal gland. If our biological clock is running too slow then morning light automatically adjusts the clock, leading to wakefulness.

The pineal gland

The pineal gland receives signals from the SCN to increase production and secretion of melatonin at night. Melatonin is a hormone that inhibits brain mechanisms that promote wakefulness. In the morning, as light levels increase, melatonin decreases and wakefulness occurs. Our cycle of sleep and wakefulness originates internally but the activity of the SCN is synchronised with the light-dark rhythm of the external world.

 ## Exogenous zeitgebers

Light

Certain cells in the retina of the eye detect light intensity. A small number of retinal cells contain the protein melanopsin which carry signals to the SCN to set the daily body clock. The sleep–wake cycle of most blind people is still influenced by light because connections exist between the eye and the SCN that do not involve those parts of the visual system on which perception of light depends.

Social cues

We are able to compensate for the absence of natural zeitgebers (e.g. light) by responding to social cues, such as mealtimes and social activities. Klein and Wegmann (1974) found the circadian rhythms of air travellers adjusted more quickly if they went outside more at their destination, possibly because they were exposed to social cues that acted as zeitgebers.

 ## Evaluation

Animal studies have demonstrated the importance of the SCN

Morgan (1995) bred hamsters with circadian rhythms of 20 hours. SCN neurons from these 'abnormal' hamsters were transplanted into the brains of normal hamsters. These normal hamsters now showed a 20-hour rhythm. In a reverse experiment, abnormal hamsters who received SCN neurons from normal hamsters changed to a 24-hour rhythm.

Separate rhythms

In some circumstances rhythms controlled by the SCN can become desynchronised. Aldcroft spent 25 days with no access to daylight or other zeitgebers. Her core body temperature maintained a 24-hour cycle but her sleep-wake cycle lengthened to 30 hours, with periods of sleep as long as 16 hours (Folkard, 1996).

Support for the role of melanopsin

Some blind people are able to reliably entrain their circadian rhythm in response to light despite being unable to see images. This suggests the pathway from retinal cells containing melanopsin to the SCN is still intact. People without light perception show abnormal circadian entrainment, providing further evidence for the importance of this pathway.

Using light exposure to avoid jet lag

Burgess *et al.* (2003) found that participants exposed to continuous bright light shifted their circadian rhythm back by 2.1 hours, those exposed to intermittent bright light shifted by 1.5 hours while a third group exposed to dim light shifted by 0.6 hours. The continuous bright light group felt sleepier 2 hours earlier in the evening and awoke 2 hours earlier in the morning, which was closer to the local time conditions after an east-west flight. This suggests exposure to bright light prior to travel can decrease readjustment time on arrival in the new time zone.

The role of artificial light as a zeitgeber

Participants kept a sleep log and wore devices to measure movement in order to monitor their sleep–wake and activity rest patterns. Participants working under normal 'warm' artificial light showed synchronisation to natural sunrise on free days. In contrast, those working under blue-enriched light synchronised to office hours during their free days, indicating that light is the dominant zeitgeber for the SCN and entrainment depends on its spectral composition (Vetter *et al.*, 2011).

Chapter 7

Research methods

3.1.3 Research Methods

Methods

- Experimental method. Types of experiment, laboratory and field experiments; natural and quasi experiments.
- Observational techniques. Types of observation: naturalistic and controlled observation; covert and overt observation; participant and non-participant observation.
- Self-report techniques. Questionnaires; interviews, structured and unstructured.
- Correlations. Analysis of the relationship between co-variables.
- The difference between correlations and experiments

Scientific processes

- Aims: stating aims, the difference between aims and hypotheses.
- Hypotheses: directional and non-directional.
- Sampling: the difference between population and sample; sampling techniques including: random, systematic, stratified, opportunity and volunteer; implications of sampling techniques, including bias and generalisation.
- Pilot studies and the aims of piloting.
- Experimental designs: repeated measures, independent groups, matched pairs.
- Observational design: behavioural categories; event sampling; time sampling.
- Questionnaire construction, including use of open and closed questions; design of interviews.
- Variables: manipulation and control of variables, including independent, dependent, extraneous, confounding; operationalisation of variables.
- Control: random allocation and counterbalancing, randomisation and standardisation.
- Demand characteristics and investigator effects.
- Ethics, including the role of the British Psychological Society's code of ethics; ethical issues in the design and conduct of psychological studies; dealing with ethical issues in research.
- The role of peer review in the scientific process.
- The implications of psychological research for the economy.

Data handling and analysis

- Quantitative and qualitative data; the distinction between qualitative and quantitative data collection techniques.
- Primary and secondary data, including meta-analysis.
- Descriptive statistics: measures of central tendency – mean, median, mode; calculation of mean, median and mode; measures of dispersion; range and standard deviation; calculation of range; calculation of percentages; positive, negative and zero correlations.
- Presentation and display of quantitative data: graphs, tables, scattergrams, bar charts.
- Distributions: normal and skewed distributions; characteristics of normal and skewed distributions.
- Introduction to statistical testing: the sign test.

Content checklist

Column 1: tick when you have produced brief notes.
Column 2: tick when you have a good grasp of this topic.
Column 3: tick during the final revision when you feel you have complete mastery of the topic.

	1	2	3
Methods			
Experimental method: laboratory and field experiments; natural and quasi experiments			
Observational techniques: naturalistic and controlled observation; covert and overt observation; participant and non-participant observation			
Self-report technique: questionnaires; interviews, structured and unstructured			
Correlations. analysis of the relationship between co-variables			
The difference between correlations and experiments			
Scientific processes			
Aims: stating aims, the difference between aims and hypotheses			
Hypotheses: directional and non-directional			
Sampling: the difference between population and sample; random, systematic, stratified, opportunity and volunteer sampling; bias and generalisation			
Pilot studies and the aims of piloting			
Experimental designs: repeated measures, independent groups, matched pairs			
Observational design: behavioural categories; event sampling; time sampling			
Questionnaire construction, open and closed questions; design of interviews			
Variables: manipulation and control of variables, including Independent, dependent, extraneous, confounding; operationalisation of variables			
Control: random allocation and counterbalancing, randomisation and standardisation			
Demand characteristics and investigator effects			
Ethics, including the role of the British Psychological Society's code of ethics; ethical issues in the design and conduct of psychological studies; dealing with ethical issues in research			
The role of peer review in the scientific process			
The implications of psychological research for the economy			
Data handling and analysis			
Quantitative and qualitative data; the distinction between qualitative and quantitative data collection techniques			
Primary and secondary data, including meta-analysis			
Descriptive statistics: measures of central tendency – mean, median, mode; calculation of mean, median and mode; measures of dispersion; range and standard deviation; calculation of range; calculation of percentages; positive, negative and zero correlations			
Presentation and display of quantitative data: graphs, tables, scattergrams, bar charts			
Distributions: normal and skewed distributions; characteristics of normal and skewed distributions			
Statistical testing: the sign test			

Research methods

Method/technique		Nature and use	Advantages (+) and limitations (−)
Experiments	Lab experiment	IV manipulated to observe effect on DV, highly controlled.	+ Can draw causal conclusion. + Extraneous variables minimised. + Can be easily replicated. − Contrived, tends to lack mundane realism. − Investigator and participant effects.
	Field experiment	More natural (or ordinary) surroundings, IV directly manipulated by experimenter to observe effect on DV, some control.	+ Can draw causal conclusion. + Usually higher ecological validity. + Avoids some participant effects. − Less control. − May have demand characteristics.
	Natural and quasi experiments	IV not directly manipulated, it is one that would vary anyway. Participants not randomly allocated.	+ Allows research where the IV can't be manipulated for ethical/practical reasons. + Enables psychologists to study 'real' problems. − Cannot demonstrate causal relationships. − Inevitably many extraneous variables. − Investigator and participant effects.
Observational techniques	Naturalistic observation	Everything left as normal, all variables free to vary.	+ Study behaviour where can't manipulate variables. + High ecological validity. − Poor control of extraneous variables. − Observer bias. − Low inter-observer reliability can be a problem.
	Controlled observation	Some variables controlled by researcher, e.g. the environment.	+ Can manipulate variables to observe effects. − Less natural, reduced ecological validity can be a problem. − Investigator and demand characteristics. − Observer bias. − Low inter-observer reliability can be a problem.
	Covert observation	Observer operates under cover.	+ Demand characteristics controlled. − Ethical issues, e.g. consent.
	Overt observation	Participants are aware they are being observed.	+ Demand characteristics. − Fewer ethical concerns re consent.
	Participant observation	The observer becomes a member of the observed participants.	+ Can give detailed insights. − Researcher may lose impartiality.
	Non participant observation	The observer stays apart from the observed participants.	+ Greater objectivity. − Possible greater observer bias.
Self-report techniques	Questionnaires	Set of written questions.	+ Can be easily repeated, so lots of people can be questioned. + Respondents may be more willing to reveal personal information. + Does not require specialist administrators. − Leading questions, social desirability bias. − Biased samples.
	Interviews	Unstructured interviews where the interviewer develops questions in response to respondent's answers, conducted in real time.	+ More detailed information collected through in-depth questioning. + Can access unexpected information. − Social desirability bias, interviewer bias, inter-interviewer reliability, leading questions. − Requires well-trained personnel.
Studies using a correlational analysis		Co-variables examined for positive, negative or zero association.	+ Can be used when not possible to manipulate variables. + Can rule out a causal relationship. − People often misinterpret correlations. − There may be other, unknown variables.

The experimental method

The experiment is the 'gold standard' of scientific method and is the only research method that allows researchers to show cause and effect.

About experiments

All psychological research begins with a research **aim**. This is usually to answer a question about an aspect of human behaviour. Psychologists use specialised terms in which to state aims and questions, and these are **operationalised** I.e. defined in measurable terms. A research aim might be to find out whether studying with the TV on or off affects students' learning.

In an **experiment** to investigate this, the **independent variable (IV)** is the presence or absence of TV and the **dependent variable (DV)** is a measure of learning.

A research **hypothesis** should always include the two (or more) levels of the IV. A hypothesis is different to the aim of the experiment and is a precise statement of what the research outcome is likely to be, in this case a statement of how the independent affects the dependent variable. The hypothesis should be:

Students who do a memory task with the TV on produce work which is of lower quality than those who do the same task without the TV on.

Psychologists typically devise **standardised procedures** such that each participant experiences the same thing in each condition, otherwise the results might vary because of changes in procedure rather than because of the IV. They will also control other potential sources of interference called **extraneous variables**, such as time of day (people might do better on a test in the morning than in the afternoon, so all participants should do the test at about the same time of day).

Apply it

Two experiments are described below. For each experiment, answer the following questions:

1. Identify the IV and DV (including both levels of the IV). (2 marks)
2. Explain how you could operationalise the IV and DV. (2 marks)
3. Identify **one** possible extraneous variable (EV). (1 mark)

Study A In order to study the effects of sleep deprivation, students are asked to limit their sleep to five hours a night for one night and then sleep normally for the next night. Each day the students' cognitive abilities are assessed using a memory test.

Study B Participants are told they are taking part in a study about public speaking, but the real aim is to see how people respond to encouragement by others. Some participants speak in front of a group of people who smile at them, while others talk to people who appear disinterested. Afterwards, the speakers' satisfaction with their performance is measured.

Suggested answers

A. 1. IV – amount of sleep: 5 hours or normal amount.
   2. DV – memory test scores.
   3. EV – number of hours each student habitually sleeps.
B. 1. IV – audience behaviour: smiling or disinterested.
   2. DV – self-assessed satisfaction with performance.
   3. EV – previous experience of public speaking.

KEY TERMS

Aims
• A statement of what the researcher(s) intend to find out in a research study.

Dependent variable (DV)
• A measurable outcome of the action of the independent variable in an experiment.

Experiment
• A research method where causal conclusions can be drawn because an independent variable has been deliberately manipulated to observe the causal effect on the dependent variable.

Extraneous variable (EV)
• In an experiment, any variable other than the independent variable that might potentially affect the dependent variable and thereby obscure the results.

Hypothesis
• A precise and testable statement about the assumed relationship between variables. Operationalisation is a key part of making the statement testable.

Independent variable (IV)
• Some event that is directly manipulated by an experimenter in order to test its effect on another variable – the dependent variable (DV).

Operationalisation
• Ensuring that variables are in a form that can be easily tested. A concept such as 'educational attainment' needs to be specified more clearly if we are going to investigate it. For example it might be operationalised as 'GCSE grade in Maths'.

Standardised procedures
• A set of procedures that are the same for all participants in order to be able to repeat the study. This includes standardised instructions – the instructions given to participants to tell them how to perform the task.

Confounding variable

- A variable which systematically affects the DV but is not the IV. Changes in the DV due to a confounding variable render the research outcome meaningless. To 'confound' means to cause confusion.

Control

- Refers to the extent to which any variable is held constant or regulated by a researcher.

External validity

- The degree to which a research finding can be generalised to: other settings (ecological validity); other groups of people (population validity); other times (historical validity).

Internal validity

- The degree to which an observed effect was due to the experimental manipulation rather than other factors such as confounding/ extraneous variables.

Validity

- Refers to whether an observed effect is a genuine one.

Control of variables

Studies in psychology often involve a trade-off between **control** and realism. Some psychologists argue that we can only discover things about behaviour if we uncover cause-and-effect relationships in highly controlled **laboratory** experiments. Others argue that studies in the natural environment are better for understanding how life is actually lived.

Control

Confounding variables

A **confounding variable** is an uncontrolled extraneous variable (EV) that exerts an unwanted and systematic effect on a DV. Consider an experiment to test memory (DV) for material learned while being subjected to some or no background noise (IV). If the test with background noise took place in the morning and the one without in the afternoon, any differences between groups could be due to time of testing rather than noise level.

Extraneous variables

Extraneous variables, sometimes called nuisance variables, fluctuate unpredictably and can be a source of unwanted 'noise' that obscures the effect being tested. Individual differences, such as motivational or emotional states, may constitute EVs and must be controlled if possible.

Realism

The term **mundane realism** refers to how well an experiment mirrors 'real-life', everyday settings. Learning word lists in a memory experiment may not tell us much about everyday, real-world memory. Such lack of realism may be the price researchers pay for high levels of control.

Generalisation

The point of realism is generalisation of results beyond the particular unique research setting to everyday life (the 'real world'). Generalisation may be limited if the materials, procedures or setting used in the study are contrived or if the participants have unique characteristics.

Apply it

Scenario: An area of study that has interested psychologists is *massed versus distributed practice*, i.e. whether learning is better if you practise something repeatedly all in one go (massed) or space your periods of practice (distributed). For example:

School students were required to recall nonsense syllables on 12 occasions spread over either 3 days or 12 days (Jost, 1897). Recall was higher when spread over 12 days.

Present arguments for why this study could be viewed as having both high and low external validity. (4 marks)

Suggested answers: Any two of:

Place (ecological validity). Low: memory in the research setting may not reflect contexts in which memorising is needed in everyday life. High: People sometimes have to learn what might seem like nonsense syllables, e.g. chemical element abbreviations in the Periodic Table.

People (population validity). Low: Students may not be representative of other groups of people. High: Students may fairly represent many types of learner.

Time (historical validity). Low: Findings may not apply across different time periods e.g. now that there is high dependence on electronic devices to store materials. High: Memory for abstract material may always be necessary to people.

Validity

Validity means meaningfulness or relevance. It involves the issues of control, realism and generalisability.

Internal validity refers to the extent to which the design of a study is a relevant and appropriate way of testing what it should be testing. Poor control, confounding variables, participant reactivity and investigator effects are all threats to internal validity.

External validity refers to the extent to which research findings can be generalised across contexts, people and time:

- Place (**ecological validity**). Findings can be generalised from the research setting to other settings, most importantly to everyday life.
- People (**population validity**). Findings can be generalised to people different from the original sample.
- Time (**historical validity**). Findings apply across different time periods.

External validity is affected by internal validity – you cannot generalise the results of a study that was low in internal validity because the results have no real meaning for the behaviour in question.

Hypothesis testing and other things

A hypothesis is a testable statement of what the researcher believes to be true. It is not a research prediction or aim and is not stated in the future tense. At the end of a study the researcher decides whether the evidence collected supports the hypothesis or not.

◉ Directional and non-directional hypotheses

A **directional hypothesis** states the expected *direction* of the results, e.g. people who average 8 or more hours of sleep per night have better marks in class tests than people who sleep for less than this. (Note this hypothesis has been **operationalised**.) A **non-directional hypothesis** states that there is a difference between two conditions but does not state the direction of the difference, e.g. people who average 8 hours or more hours of sleep per night have *different* marks in class tests than people who sleep for less than this.

Psychologists use a directional hypothesis when past research (a theory or a study) suggests the direction of an effect. They use a non-directional hypothesis when there is no past research or past research is contradictory.

◉ Pilot studies and the aims of piloting

A **pilot study** is a small-scale, dry-run of a research design before doing the real thing. Its purpose is to identify flaws so that they can be dealt with before going to the time and expense of conducting a full-scale study.

◉ Confederates

A researcher may use another person (a **confederate**), who knows the purpose of the study and is trained to play a role in it, e.g. Milgram used a confederate to play the role of the experimenter in his studies of obedience. The real participants are not told the confederate's true identity unless they are debriefed.

KEY TERMS

Confederate
- An individual in a study who is not a real participant and has been instructed how to behave by the investigator.

Directional hypothesis
- States the direction of the difference between two conditions.

Non-directional hypothesis
- States that there is a difference between two conditions without stating the direction of the difference.

Pilot study
- A small-scale trial run of a study to test any aspects of the design, with a view to making improvements.

Apply it

1. Read the statements below and identify which are aims and which is a hypothesis. (1 mark each)
   a. Younger people have better memories than older people.
   b. To see if blondes have more fun than brunettes
   c. Do people who sleep with a teddy bear sleep longer than people who don't?
   d. Positive expectations lead to differences in performance.
2. For each of the following, decide whether it is a directional or non-directional hypothesis. (1 mark each)
   a. Boys score differently on aggressiveness tests than girls.
   b. Students who have a computer at home do better in exams than those who don't.
   c. People remember the words that are early in a list better than the words that appear later.
   d. Words presented in a written form are recalled differently from those presented in a pictorial form.
3. Now write your own. Below are research aims for possible experiments. For each one write an operationalised hypotheses and state whether it is directional or non-directional. (2 marks each)
   a. Do girls watch more television than boys?
   b. Do teachers give more attractive students higher marks on essays than students who are less attractive?

Answers:
1. a. and d. are hypotheses, b is an aim and c. is a question.
2. a. and d. are non-directional, b. and c. are directional.
3. a. Eight year-old boys and girls differ in the daily average hours of television they watch each day (non-directional).
   b. Teachers award higher grades to 14-year-old students rated above average on attractiveness compared to those who are rated average or below average (directional).

KEY TERMS

Counterbalancing
- An experimental technique used to overcome order effects when using a repeated measures design. Counterbalancing ensures that each condition is tested first or second in equal amounts.

Experimental design
- A set of procedures used to control the influence of factors such as participant variables in an experiment.

Independent groups design
- Participants are allocated to two (or more) groups representing different levels of the IV. Allocation is usually done using random techniques.

Matched pairs design
- Pairs of participants are matched in terms of key variables such as age and IQ. One member of each pair is allocated to one of the conditions under test and the second person is allocated to the other condition.

Order effect
- In a repeated measures design, an extraneous variable arising from the order in which conditions are presented, e.g. a practice effect or fatigue effect.

Random allocation
- Allocating participants to experimental groups or conditions using random techniques.

Repeated measures design
- Each participant takes part in every condition under test, i.e. each level of the IV.

Experimental design

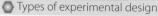 Types of experimental design

Type of experimental design	Limitations	Method of dealing with the limitations
Repeated measures Participants take part in all conditions, for example: • Each participant learns with the TV on and with the TV off. • We compare the performance (DV) under the two conditions.	1. **Order effects:** Participants may do better on the second condition because of the practice effect. They may do worse on the second condition because of the boredom effect. 2. When participants do the second test they may guess the hypothesis and may alter their behaviour.	Researchers may use two equivalent tests to reduce a practice effect. **Counterbalancing**, using the ABBA design, is always used as a precaution against order effects. A cover story about the purpose of the test can prevent participants from guessing the hypothesis.
Independent groups Participants are placed in different (independent) groups. Each group does one of two conditions: • Group A does the task with TV on. • Group B does the task with the TV off. • We compare the performance (DV) of the two groups.	1. Participant variables (e.g. individual differences) are less controlled. This introduces more variation due to EVs and may even introduce a confounding variable. 2. More participants are needed than in a repeated measures design because there are two separate groups.	**Randomly allocate** participants to conditions which should distribute participant variables (that might otherwise influence the outcome) randomly. Random allocation to conditions can be decided by tossing a coin.
Matched pairs design A compromise is to use two groups of participants matched participants on relevant variables. One member of the pair is allocated to Group A and the other to Group B. The procedure is then the same as for independent groups.	1. It is very time-consuming to find sufficient participants matched on key variables. 2. Matching is always imperfect and there is a risk that key variables may be missed.	Restrict the number of variables to match participants on to make it easier. Conduct a pilot study to assess relevant variables on which to match participants.

Strengths of each experimental design tend to be complementary to the limitations of the other designs, e.g. a limitation of repeated measures is the risk of order effects, therefore a strength of independent groups and matched pairs designs is that there are no order effects.

Apply it

For each of the following experiments a–c, identify the experimental design that has been used. Explain **one** limitation of using this experimental design in each case. (1+1 mark each)

a. Hamsters are tested to see if one genetic strain is better at finding food in a maze than another.

b. Reaction time is tested before and after a reaction time training activity to see if test scores improve after training.

c. Students are put in pairs based on their GCSE grades and then one member of the pair is given a memory test.

Suggested answers:

a. Independent groups. Poorer control over individual differences may obscure the effect of the IV on the DV.

b. Repeated measures. Practice may improve reaction times over and above improvements due to training leading to an over-estimation of the training effect.

c. Matched pairs design. Matching on grades may not be as appropriate as matching on a pre-test of memory ability.

Laboratory and field experiments

All experiments have an independent variable (IV) and a dependent variable (DV). An experiment permits us to study cause and effect. It involves the manipulation of an IV and observing consequent changes in the DV, while keeping EVs constant. If the IV is the only thing that is changed then it must have caused any change in the DV.

 Laboratory experiment

A **laboratory experiment** is conducted in a controlled environment. Participants are *aware* that they are taking part in an experiment, but may not know the aims of the study (risk of participant reactivity). Laboratory experiments also often involve contrived materials such as nonsense syllables and may thus lack mundane realism.

Field experiment

A **field experiment** is conducted in an environment not controlled by the experimenter, e.g. 'home ground' for participants. The IV is still deliberately manipulated by the researcher who also measures the DV. Participants may not be aware that they are participating in an experiment so their behaviour may be more natural.

Evaluation of laboratory and field experiments

Strengths: High in control. Good control of the IV makes experiments high in **internal validity** and potentially more easily replicated to check the reliability of findings.

Strengths: Cause and effect. Well-designed experiments lead to greater confidence that any observed changes in the DV *are* caused by the IV. Laboratory and field experiments are the only methods that allow us to claim cause and effect with any certainty.

Limitations: Low in ecological validity. High control may make the experimental situation very unlike everyday experience, so the measures used and participants' behaviour may not be generalisable to other contexts. Such studies may lack mundane realism.

Limitations: Demand characteristics. If participants know they are being studied, or find themselves facing something unfamiliar, they may change their behaviour in line with the perceived demands of the situation. This poses a threat to the validity of the experiment.

Limitations: Ethical issues. If participants don't understand what an experiment is for, they may not be able to give fully informed consent to taking part, therefore their ethical rights may not be properly protected.

KEY TERMS

Field experiment
- An experiment conducted on the participant's 'home ground' and in which the IV is controlled by the experimenter.

Laboratory experiment
- An experiment carried out in a controlled setting and in which the experimenter controls the IV.

Apply it

Answer these questions about the experiment described below.

1. Identify the IV and DV. (2 marks)
2. Was the task required of participants contrived? (1 mark)
3. Was the study conducted in a natural setting? (1 mark)
4. Was the setting high or low in mundane realism? (1 mark)
5. Did the participants know they were being studied? (1 mark)
6. Were the participants brought into a special situation, or did the experimenter go to them? (1 mark)
7. What relevant variable might not have been controlled? (1 mark)
8. Do you think this was a lab or field experiment? (1 mark)

Study. Participants were children aged between 3 and 5 years. Each child was taken on its own to an experimental room containing toys including a 5-foot inflatable Bobo doll and a mallet. The experimenter invited the 'model' (another adult) to join them and then left the room for about 10 minutes. Half of the children watched the model playing aggressively with the Bobo doll while the others watched the model play non-aggressively with the doll. Later they were given an opportunity to play with toys including the Bobo doll and were observed through a one-way mirror. The children who saw the aggressive behaviour were more likely to behave aggressively (Bandura *et al.*, 1961).

Suggested answers

1. IV – Behaviour of the adult model. DV – behaviour of the children following exposure to the model.
2. Yes, the aggression modelled by adult models was carefully 'choreographed' and the opportunity for children to copy it was carefully arranged.
3. No, the setting was controlled by the researcher.
4. Arguably in between – children are often exposed to aggressive models on TV but, hopefully, rarely to real-life adult models behaving in such contrived ways.
5. No, children were unaware of the researcher's hypothesis.
6. This was a special laboratory situation arranged by the researcher.
7. Children's previous experience of watching aggressive models might have varied.
8. This was a laboratory experiment.

KEY TERMS

Natural experiment

- A research method in which change in the IV and its effects on a DV occur fortuitously. In a true experiment, the IV can be manipulated and random allocation of participants to conditions by the experimenter occurs but, as this is not possible here, causal conclusions must be tentative.

Quasi-experiments

- Studies that are 'almost' experiments. They are similar to natural experiments but can be pre-planned. Lack of manipulation of the IV and of random allocation means that causal conclusions can only tentatively be drawn.

Natural and quasi-experiments

Natural experiment

A **natural experiment** is conducted when it is not possible, for ethical or practical reasons, to deliberately change an IV. The IV varies 'naturally'. The DV is gathered after the event, e.g.:

- **Effects of TV** Before 1995, people living on the island of St Helena had no TV. Its arrival enabled researchers to see how exposure to Western programmes might influence behaviour – Charlton *et al.* (2000) found little difference in either pro- or anti-social behaviour after the introduction of TV.

Quasi-experiment

In a **quasi-experiment** the IV occurs naturally and the DV may be measured in a laboratory. The IV pre-exists and cannot be manipulated, e.g.:

- **Gender differences** Sheridan and King (1972) tested obedience by asking student participants to give electric shocks of increasing strength to a puppy. All the females and 54% of male participants delivered the maximum shock. The naturally occurring IV was gender and the DV was shock level.

Evaluation

Strengths: Opens up research possibilities

Quasi- and natural experiments allow research where IV can't be manipulated for ethical or practical reasons. They enable psychologists to study 'real' problems such as the effects of a disaster on health with higher mundane realism and ecological validity.

Limitations: Doubts over cause and effect

Lack of control over the IV means that we cannot be certain that changes in the DV were caused by the IV, e.g. if there were uncontrolled **confounding variables** then observed changes in the DV might not be due to the IV.

Limitations: Pre-existing sample bias

In an experiment with an **independent groups design** participants are **randomly allocated** to conditions. This is not possible in natural or quasi-experiments. This means that there may be pre-existing, uncontrolled differences between groups of participants that could act as confounding variables.

Limitations: Unique characteristics of participants

The sample studied may have unique characteristics, e.g. the people of the St Helena lived in a pro-social community so may have been resistant to TV violence. Unique characteristics of the sample mean that the findings can't be generalised to others (low **population validity**).

Suggested answers for Apply it:

1. a. IV – the reading schemes; DV reading ability. b. natural experiment. c. IV is pre-existing but can vary. d. high validity due to the field setting.
2. a. IV – type of personality; DV – obedience rate. b. quasi experiment. c. IV is a pre-existing difference between people. d. medium validity, the IV occurs naturally but the measure of obedience is contrived.
3. a. IV – the type of maths programme; DV – end of term achievement in maths. b. field experiment. c. IV is manipulated, children are randomly allocated to groups, setting is 'home ground'. d. high validity due to the field setting.
4. a. IV – nature of advertisement; DV – level of gender stereotyping. b. laboratory experiment. c. IV is directly manipulated, laboratory setting. d. medium validity, advertisements are commonplace but the IV is self-report (risk of social desirability bias).

Apply it

Four studies are described below. In each study (a) Identify the IV and DV (2 marks), (b) identify whether it is a laboratory, field, natural or quasi-experiment (1 mark), (c) explain your decision (2 marks), and (d) explain why you think the study would have high, medium or low validity (2 marks).

1. Two primary schools use different reading schemes. A psychological study compares the reading scores at the end of the year to see which scheme was more effective.
2. People who score high on the authoritarian personality scale are compared with people low on the authoritarian personality scale in terms of how willing they are to obey orders in a Milgram-type study.
3. Children take part in a trial to compare the success of a new maths programme. The children are placed in one of two groups – a group receiving the new maths programme or a group receiving the traditional one – and taught in these groups for a term.
4. The effect of advertisements on gender stereotypes is studied by showing children ads with women doing feminine tasks or neutral tasks and then asking them about gender stereotypes.

More problems with experiments

 Demand characteristics

Orne invented the term **demand characteristics** to describe *'The totality of cues that convey the experimental hypothesis to the [participant] become determinant's of the [participant's] behaviour'* (Orne, 1962).

In an experiment participants may actively look for clues as to how they should behave. These clues are demand characteristics. They convey the experimental hypothesis to participants. Demand characteristics may act as an extraneous (confounding) variable, e.g.:

- A participant is given two memory tests, one in the morning and one in the afternoon. Participants might correctly work out that the IV is the effect of time of day on performance. This might lead the participant to try to perform the same on each test.

 Investigator effects

Investigator effects are variables, hopefully unconsciously, introduced by the researcher, sometimes leading to a fulfilment of their expectations. Such variables act as extraneous or confounding variables, e.g.:

Rosenthal and Fode (1963): asked students to train rats to learn the route through a maze. Students were told that rats were either 'fast learners' or 'slow learners'. In fact there were no differences between the rats. Maze-learning results fitted students' expectations about the rats' performance.

Investigators may also design a study so that a particular result is more likely, e.g. they may not use **standardised procedures**, leaving room for the results to vary as desired.

 Dealing with these problems

Single blind design

The participant is not aware of the research aims and/or of which condition of the experiment they are receiving. This prevents the participant from seeking cues about the aims and reacting to them.

Double blind design

Both the participant and the person conducting the experiment are 'blind' to the aims. Therefore neither of them can influence the results.

Experimental realism

If an experimental task is sufficiently engaging, the participant may pay attention to the task and not the fact that they are being observed.

 Participant variables

A **participant variable** is a characteristic of participants. Examples include age, intelligence, motivation, experience, gender. They act as EVs in an independent groups design and may become confounding variables if not controlled. When a repeated measures design is used, participant variables are controlled.

 Situational variables

Situational variables are features of a research *situation* that may influence participants' behaviour and thus act as EVs or confounding variables. **Order effects** are one example. Improved participant performance may be due to practice (a confounding variable) rather than the IV.

KEY TERMS

Demand characteristics
- Cues that make participants unconsciously aware of the aims of a study or help participants work out what the researcher expects to find. They may become EVs or confounding variables.

Investigator effects
- Anything a researcher unintentionally does that has an effect on data collected in a study. They may be direct, as in influencing participants' behaviour, or indirect, e.g. in data interpretation. They may become EVs or confounding variables.

Apply it

Using the study described below, give an example of a possible
(a) demand characteristic,
(b) investigator effect, (c) participant variable and (d) situational variable.
(1 mark each)

For each one, if you can, suggest how the problem might be dealt with.

Study 2 Participants were given a list of adjectives describing Mr Smith. One group had positive adjectives first, followed by negative adjectives. The other group had the adjectives in reverse order. They were all then asked to describe Mr Smith.

Suggested answers:

a. Participants may detect the order of adjectives and decide to ignore one kind when describing Mr Smith.
b. The investigator may have designed the materials in a way that makes the purpose of the study too obvious. c. Participants in one group might be more eager to please than the ones in the other group. d. All of these problems could be overcome by improving the realism of the task and by using a double blind procedure.

KEY TERMS

Bias
- A systematic distortion.

Generalisation
- Applying the findings of a particular study to the population.

Opportunity sample
- A sample of participants produced by selecting people who are most easily available at the time of the study.

Population
- The group of people that has the characteristics the researcher is interested in and from which a sample is drawn. The group of people about whom generalisations can be made.

Random sample
- A sample of participants produced by using a random technique such that every member of the target population being tested has an equal chance of being selected.

Sampling
- The selection of participants from the target population intended to produce a representative group from that population.

Stratified sample
- A sample of participants produced by identifying subgroups according to their frequency in the population. Participants are then selected randomly from the subgroups.

Systematic sample
- A sample obtained by selecting every *n*th person (where *n* is any number). This can be a random sample if the first person is selected using a random method; you then select every *n*th person after that.

Volunteer sample
- A sample of participants that relies solely on volunteers to make up the sample. Also called a self-selected sample.

Sampling

 Populations and samples

In any study the **population** is the group of individuals a researcher is interested in, for example 'babies in the Western world', 'teenagers living in Bristol'. The researcher usually cannot study everyone in the population so selects a smaller group, or **sample**. This sample should represent the population so that **generalisations** about the population can be made.

Opportunity sample. A sample of participants produced by selecting people who are most easily available at the time of the study. It is quick and convenient but inevitably **biased** because the sample is essentially self-selected.

Random sample A sample of participants produced using a random technique such that every member of the target population has an equal chance of being selected. Potential participants may be assigned a number then a random number generator is used to decide which to select. This method is likely to produce the most representative sample and generalisable findings, but is still open to bias if selected individuals refuse to take part.

Stratified sample Groups (strata) participants are selected according to their frequency in the population (e.g. boys and girls, or age groups: 10–12 years, 13–15, etc.). Participants are randomly selected from each stratum in proportion to their occurrence in the target population. Unlike opportunity sampling, this method is more likely to represent the underlying population but is limited by our understanding of which sub-groups are important.

Systematic sample A method of obtaining a representative sample by selecting every 5th or 10th person, for example, from a list beginning with a randomly selected number. It is less biased than an opportunity sample but, like a random sample, may become biased if selected participants refuse to take part.

Volunteer sample A sample of participants recruited by word of mouth or advertisement. This is a quick and easy sampling method but the sample may be biased because of the special characteristics of volunteers.

Apply it

Identify the sampling method in each of the studies below and in each case identify **one** advantage in using that sampling method. Each question is worth 3 marks.

1. A researcher wishes to study memory in children aged between 5 and 11. He selects some suitable children from a local school.
2. A study on sleep habits identifies various subgroups in the population and then randomly selects members from each subgroup.
3. A class of psychology students conducts a study on memory. They put up a notice in the sixth-form common room advertising for participants.
4. A researcher studied IQ in primary school children by selecting the first five names in each class register for every school he visited.

Suggested answers:

1. Opportunity sample. Quick and convenient.
2. Stratified random sampling. Captures representatives from all subgroups.
3. Volunteer sample. Targets a wide participant base.
4. Systematic sample. Likely to minimise sampling bias.

Ethical issues

⬡ British Psychological Society (BPS) code of conduct

UK psychologists are guided by the British Psychological Society (BPS) *Code of Ethics and Conduct* (BPS, 2009) and the *Code of Human Research Ethics* (BPS, 2014). This enables them to balance the need to do research with the rights of participantsbased on four principles:

1. Respect for the dignity and worth of all persons.
2. Competence – Ability to work to a high professional standard.
3. Responsibility – To clients, the public and to the science of Psychology.
4. Integrity – Report research findings honestly and accurately. Alert the BPS to instances of misconduct.

⬡ Ethical issues

Informed consent. Participants must be given comprehensive information about the nature and purpose of a study and their role in it so that they can make an informed decision about whether to participate. However, some information might be withheld if revealing it would influence participants' behaviour in unwanted ways.

Deception occurs when aspects of the research aim and procedures are concealed from participants so they cannot give informed consent. Some deception is arguably harmless and can be compensated for by debriefing.

Right to withdraw. Participants have the right to withdraw from a study at any time and for any reason and to refuse the researcher permission to use any data they produce. Loss of participants this way may bias the study's findings.

Protection from harm. Participants should not experience negative effects, such as physical injury, or psychological effects, such as embarrassment The researcher may not be able to anticipate harm beforehand so a study should be stopped immediately as soon as it becomes apparent.

Confidentiality (and anonymity). Participants have a right to protection of personal information and the Data Protection Act makes confidentiality a legal right. The researcher must ensure that individuals' identity is protected at any point in the research process.

Privacy. Participants have the right to control information about themselves. This may be difficult for researchers to ensure, for example in covert observation. If privacy is invaded, confidentiality should be protected.

Apply it

Piliavin *et al.* (1969) investigated the behaviour of bystanders in an emergency situation to see how quickly they would offer help to someone (a confederate) who collapsed on a New York subway train. The confederate either acted as if he was drunk or as if he was disabled. Observers recorded how long it took for anyone to offer help. There was no opportunity to debrief participants.

1. Identify two ethical issues raised in the study described above. (2 marks)
2. Consider to what extent they are acceptable from the researcher's point of view. (2 marks)
3. Consider to what extent they are acceptable from the participants' point of view. (2 marks)
4. Decide whether the study was ethically acceptable, or not, giving your reasons. (2 marks)

Suggested answers:

1. Informed consent was not obtained and participants had no opportunity to withdraw at the time of the study or afterwards (by withdrawing data).
2. Informing participants of the purpose of the study would prevent the researchers from observing genuine responses to an emergency. Deception was therefore necessary to make the situation realistic for participants. Researchers might also argue that the cost to participants was outweighed by the importance of the research.
3. Participants may have been distressed by witnessing an emergency but may also gain from reflecting on the situation and thus be better prepared to react appropriately in the future.
4. Understanding factors that increase or decrease bystander apathy is important for individuals who may need help and for the greater good. The costs of this research for a few participants therefore have positive consequences for many others like them.

KEY TERMS

Cost–benefit analysis
- A systematic approach to estimating the negatives and positives of any research.

Debriefing
- A post-research interview designed to inform participants of the true nature of the study and to restore them to the state they were in at the start of the study. It may also be used to gain useful feedback about the procedures in the study. Debriefing is not an ethical issue; it is a means of dealing with ethical issues.

Ethical issues
- Questions of right and wrong. They arise in research where there are conflicting sets of values between researchers and participants concerning the goals, procedures or outcomes of a research study.

Ethics committee
- A group of people within a research institution that must approve a study before it begins.

Ethical guidelines (code of conduct)
- A set of principles designed to help professionals behave honestly and with integrity.

Presumptive consent
- A method of dealing with lack of informed consent or deception, by asking a group of people who are similar to the participants whether they would agree to take part in a study. If this group of people consents to the procedures in the proposed study, it is presumed that the real participants would also have agreed.

Apply it

Using the bystander apathy example in the previous spread, suggest ways in which the researchers might have made the study more ethically acceptable. (3 marks)

Suggested answer:

The researchers could have used role play or videos of emergencies in a controlled setting, then asked participants to explain their reactions to the situation. Alternatively, they could stage an emergency in a situation where it was possible to debrief participants afterwards, gain consent retrospectively, or allow participants to withdraw data. These procedures should help to ensure that no lasting harm is caused to participants.

Dealing with ethical issues

 Strategies for dealing with ethical issues

BPS Ethical guidelines (code of conduct)
The BPS regularly updates its **ethical guidelines (code of conduct)** and requires BPS members to abide by them.

Cost–benefit analysis
In a **cost–benefit analysis** we judge the costs of doing the research against the benefits. The costs and benefits may be judged from an individual, group or societal point of view. Benefits for the individual, group or society must ultimately outweigh costs.

Ethics committees
All institutions where research takes place have an **ethics committee** which must approve any study before it begins. The committee weighs up the benefits of the research against the possible costs to the participants. Members of the committee often include lay people as well as experts in the field.

 Evaluation

Ethical guidelines are open to interpretation
This 'rules and sanctions' approach is inevitably rather general because of the impossibility of covering every situation that a researcher may encounter. Guidelines also absolve the researcher from individual responsibility because they can simply say, 'I followed the guidelines so my research is acceptable'.

Difficulties with cost–benefit analysis
It is difficult, if not impossible, to predict both costs and benefits prior to conducting a study or even afterwards. How are costs and benefits quantified? How much does personal distress cost? Resolving such issues will always involve some subjective judgement.

 Dealing with specific ethical issues

Ethical issue	How to deal with it	Limitations
Informed consent	Participants are asked to formally indicate their agreement to participate by, for example, signing a document which contains comprehensive information concerning the nature and purpose of the research and their role in it. An alternative is to gain **presumptive consent**. Researchers can also offer the right to withdraw.	If a participant is given information about a study this may invalidate the purpose of the study. Even if researchers have obtained informed consent, that does not guarantee that participants really do understand what they have let themselves in for. The problem with presumptive consent is that what people expect that they will or will not mind can be different from actually experiencing it.
Deception	The need for deception should be approved by an ethics committee, weighing up benefits (of the study) against costs (to participants). Participants should be fully **debriefed** after the study. This involves informing them of the true nature of the study. Participants should be offered the opportunity to discuss any concerns they may have and to withhold their data from the study – a form of retrospective informed consent.	Cost–benefit decisions are flawed because they involve subjective judgements, and the costs are not always apparent until after the study. Debriefing can't turn the clock back – a participant may still feel embarrassed or have lowered self-esteem.
The right to withdraw	Participants should be informed at the beginning of a study that they have the right to withdraw at any point in the study, including withdrawing any data they have contributed.	Participants may feel their withdrawal would spoil the study. In many studies participants are paid or rewarded in some way, and may not feel able to withdraw.

Observational techniques

⬡ Types of observation

Naturalistic and controlled observation

In a **naturalistic observation** behaviour is studied on familiar, 'home ground' for participants, e.g. an infant in a nursery or an animal's natural habitat.

In **controlled observation** some variables in the environment are manipulated by the researcher. Participants are likely to know they are being studied and the study may be conducted in a laboratory.

⬡ Overt and covert observation

In **overt observation** the individual is aware of being observed.

In a **covert observation** participants do not know they are being observed before or during the study. They may be informed afterwards.

⬡ Participant and non-participant observation

In **non-participant observation**, the observer watches and/or listens from a distance and does not interact with the people being observed.

In **participant observation** the observer is part of the group being observed.

⬡ Evaluation

Limitation: Observer bias

Observer bias occurs if observers' values and preconceptions threaten the objectivity of their observations.

Strength: Inter-observer reliability

Inter-observer reliability. In all observations collecting and interpreting findings collaboratively can greatly improve trustworthiness of findings.

Naturalistic observation

+ Naturalistic observation gives a realistic picture of natural, spontaneous behaviour rather than what participants claim they would do or say. It is likely to be high in ecological validity (though this may be less so if participants know they are being observed).

− Lack of control over a myriad of variables leaves the reasons for people's behaviour open to interpretation.

Controlled observation

+ This allows observers to concentrate on specific aspects of behaviour, leading to greater confidence in the validity of interpretations of observations.

− Control may make the environment feeling unfamiliar to participants and thus affect their behaviour, making observations invalid.

Covert observation

+ Participants are unaware of being observed so their behaviour is natural.

− People should be observed only where they expect to be seen by others, but that is open to interpretation and privacy may be invaded.

Overt observation

+ Overt observation overcomes ethical issues such as invasion of privacy.

− Participant reactivity is a risk if people know they are being observed and that can reduce the validity of the observations.

Participant observation

+ Participant observation may provide 'insider' insights into behaviour that may not otherwise be gained. This can improve the richness of the data.

− The presence of the observer will inevitably change the group dynamic so that behaviour will not be the same as if the observer was unseen.

Non-participant observation

+ Non-participant observers are likely to be more objective because they are not part of the group being observed.

− Special insights into behaviour from the 'inside' may not be gained, thus reducing the informativeness of the data.

KEY TERMS

Controlled observation
- A form of investigation in which behaviour is observed but under conditions where certain variables have been organised by the researcher.

Covert observations
- Observing people without their knowledge. Knowing that behaviour is being observed is likely to alter a participant's behaviour.

Inter-observer reliability
- The extent to which there is agreement between two or more observers involved in observations of a behaviour.

Naturalistic observation
- An observation carried out in an everyday setting, in which the investigator does not interfere in any way but merely observes the behaviour(s) in question.

Non-participant observation
- The observer is separate from the people being observed.

Observer bias
- Observers' expectations affect what they see or hear. This reduces the validity of the observations.

Overt observation
- Observational studies where participants are aware that their behaviour is being studied.

Participant observation
- Observations made by someone who is also participating in the activity being observed, which may affect their objectivity

Apply it

In the study described below decide whether it involved observations that were (a) naturalistic or controlled (1 mark), (b) overt or covert (1 mark), (c) participant or non-participant (1 mark).

Mary Ainsworth (1967) studied 26 mothers and their infants who lived in six villages in Uganda. She observed the mothers in their own homes interacting as they normally would with their infants.

Suggested answer:

a. Naturalistic

b. Overt

c. Non-participant.

KEY TERMS

Behavioural categories
- Dividing a target behaviour (such as stress or aggression) into a subset of behaviours.

Event sampling
- An observational technique in which a count is kept of the number of times a certain behaviour (event) occurs.

Structured observation
- A researcher uses various systems to organise observations, such as behavioural categories and sampling procedures.

Time sampling
- An observational technique in which the observer records behaviours in a given time frame, e.g. noting what a target individual is doing every 15 seconds or 20 seconds or 1 minute. The observer may select one or more behavioural categories to tick at this time interval.

EXPO	exploration when with owner
EXPS	exploration when with stranger
PLYO	playing when with owner
PLYS	playing when with stranger
PASO	passive behaviours when with owner
PASS	passive behaviours when with stranger
CONTO	physical contact with the owner
CONTS	physical contact with the stranger
SBYO	standing by the door when with owner
SBYS	standing by the door when with stranger

▲ *The list of behavioural categories used to assess dogs and their owners. Such a list is called a behaviour checklist or a coding system (because each behaviour is given a code to make it easier to record).*

Observational design

Observational studies can be naturalistic or controlled, overt or covert, participant or non-participant, and structured or unstructured.

⬡ Unstructured observations

The researcher records all relevant behaviour but has no system.

+ There may be too much to record, or only the most eye-catching behaviour may be recorded, so the most important or relevant behaviours may be missed.

− This approach is useful in new research areas to determine what behaviours might be recorded using a structured system.

⬡ Structured observations

Structured observations involve various 'systems' to organise observations.

+ Structured observation is more objective and rigorous than unstructured observation thus it is less likely to be invalidated by such things as observer bias.

− It is more reductionist than unstructured observation such that the complexity of behaviour may be lost and important parts of it missed.

The two main ways to structure observations are:

1. Behavioural categories

In order to conduct systematic observations, behaviour must be operationalised. i.e. sorted into types known as **behavioural categories**, e.g. infant behaviour could include categories such as smiling, crying and sleeping.

Behavioural categories should

- be *objective*: clearly defined and include only directly observable behaviour.
- cover *all possible component behaviours* and avoid a 'waste basket' category.
- be *mutually exclusive*: a behaviour pattern belongs in one category only.

2. Sampling procedures

If there is too much data to record, observations may be sampled:

- **Event sampling** Counting the number of times a certain behaviour occurs, e.g. the number of times a person smiles in a 10-minute period.
- **Time sampling** Recording behaviours in a given time frame, e.g. noting what a target individual is doing every 30 seconds.

⬡ Example of a behavioural category system

Topál *et al.* (1998) used the Strange Situation technique (see page 41) to explore attachments between dogs and their owners. Two observers sampled ten behaviour categories (see left) every 10 seconds. The findings were that dogs, like people, were either securely or insecurely attached.

Apply it

1. In the study of attachment behaviour in dogs (above):
   a. Identify the sampling procedure used. (1 mark)
   b. Explain why the behaviours were videotaped. (1 mark)
   c. Explain why two observers recorded behaviours. (1 mark)
2. In each of the following observations state which sampling procedure would be most appropriate and explain how you would do it:
   a. Recording instances of aggressive behaviour in children playing in a school playground. (2 marks)
   b. Crying in human infants. (2 marks)

Suggested answers:

1. a. Time sampling. b. To enable the researchers to re-watch behaviour patterns and ensure that nothing was overlooked. c. In order to establish inter-observer reliability.
2. a. Time sampling as it would give a good impression of the frequency and nature of this relatively common behaviour.
   b. Event sampling because crying can be relatively infrequent and time sampling may miss it altogether.

Self-report techniques: Questionnaires and interviews

Questionnaires

A **questionnaire** is a set of questions designed to elicit information about a topic. They permit a researcher to discover directly what people think and feel, in contrast to observations which generally provide records of overt behaviour.

A structured interview

Questionnaires are always structured whereas an **interview** can be structured or unstructured. A **structured interview** has pre-determined questions, and is essentially a questionnaire that is delivered face-to-face (or by telephone) with no deviation from the original questions. It is conducted in real-time.

Unstructured interview

In an **unstructured interview**, the interviewer may begin with general aims and possibly a few predetermined questions but subsequent questions develop on the basis of the answers that are given.

Evaluation

Self-report techniques

+ Unlike methods that do not acknowledge cognitive processes, these techniques probe what people think and feel and allow them to describe experiences that would otherwise be inaccessible to researchers.

− People may lie or simply answer in a particular way in order to make a good impression (**social desirability bias**). Observations permit much more direct access to genuine behaviours.

− People sometimes simply don't know what they think or feel, so their answers may lack validity.

− The sample of people used may lack representativeness so the data collected cannot be generalised to an underlying population.

Questionnaire

+ Once a questionnaire has been designed and piloted, it can be distributed to large numbers of people relatively cheaply and quickly, enabling the researcher to collect plentiful data.

+ Respondents may feel more willing to reveal personal/confidential information than in interviews, which could make them feel more cautious.

+ The impersonal nature of a questionnaire may also reduce social desirability bias as compared to an interview.

− Questionnaires are only completed by literate people who are willing to spend time filling them in. This means that the sample may be biased.

Structured interview

+ Can be easily repeated because the questions are standardised. Participants' responses can be more easily quantified and compared.

− May be constructed according to the interviewer's pre-existing expectations and biases so that participants are 'strait-jacketed' into discussing only those things of importance to the interviewer and not to themselves.

Unstructured interview

+ More detailed, insightful and relevant information can be obtained because the interviewer tailors the questions to the participant's response.

− The necessity of using well-trained interviewers makes unstructured interviews more expensive to produce compared with structured interviews.

− As each interview is unique, it is not always possible to make comparisons between interviewees and make generalisations to others like them.

− A limitation of both structured and unstructured interviews is that the interviewer's expectations may influence the answers the interviewee gives (a form of investigator effect called **interviewer bias**). All interviewers have to be skilled to prevent interviewer bias as far as possible.

KEY TERMS

Interview
- A research method or technique that involves a face-to-face, 'real-time' interaction with another individual and results in the collection of data.

Interviewer bias
- The effect of an interviewer's expectations, communicated unconsciously, on a respondent's behaviour.

Questionnaire
- Data are collected through the use of written questions.

Social desirability bias
- A distortion in the way people answer questions – they tend to answer questions in such a way that presents themselves in a better light.

Structured interview
- Any interview in which the questions are decided in advance.

Unstructured interview
- The interview starts out with some general aims and possibly some questions, and lets the interviewee's answers guide subsequent questions.

Apply it

1. A group of students wishes to study mobile phone use in people aged 14–18. Why might it be preferable to:

   a. Conduct an unstructured interview rather than a questionnaire? (2 marks)

   b. Conduct a questionnaire rather than an unstructured interview? (2 marks)

Suggested answers:

1. a. Unstructured interviews may yield richer and more detailed information than a questionnaire because the respondents have more flexibility in what they choose to discuss.

   b. Questionnaires tend to be highly structured allowing the researcher to quantify responses and make comparisons between individuals, whereas unstructured interviews tend to yield answers unique to each interviewee.

KEY TERMS

Qualitative data
- Information in words that cannot be counted or quantified. Qualitative data can be turned into quantitative data by placing them in categories and counting frequency.

Quantitative data
- Information that represents how much or how long, or how many, etc. there are of something, i.e. a behaviour is measured in numbers or quantities.

Self-report design

Questionnaire construction

When writing questions there are three guiding principles:

1. **Clarity**. The respondent must be able to understand the questions. There should be no ambiguity, double negatives or double-barrelled questions.
2. **Avoidance of bias**. Biased (leading) questions encourage the respondent to give a particular answer. Respondents may to give answers that make them look more appealing, i.e. show **social desirability bias**.
3. **Planned analysis**. How the data will be analysed must be pre-planned.

Design of interviews

Recording the interview

Interviews may be audio recorded or video recorded for checking later.

Good interviewing skills

Interviewers need to put interviewees at their ease through:

- **Non-verbal communication** An interviewer's body language must communicate interest rather than indifference.
- **Active listening skills** An interviewer must listen with engagement attentively.

Questioning skills in an unstructured interview

A good interviewer memorises the questions, uses them flexibly and knows when and when not to speak.

Evaluation

Open questions

+ Respondents can give detailed information and expand on their answers.

+ Open questions can provide unexpected answers and new insights.

− Some respondents may be disadvantaged by having to express themselves verbally so important information is missed.

− Open questions produce **qualitative data** (discussed on page 100) which are more difficult to summarise because of the variety in responses.

Closed questions

+ Closed questions have a limited range of answers and produce **quantitative data** that can be analysed statistically.

− Data lack validity if questions limit how respondents can answer.

− Participants may select 'don't know' or have a preference to answer yes (an acquiescence bias) and therefore the data collected are not informative.

Apply it

1. A psychology student designed a questionnaire about attitudes to eating, including the two questions below:

   (1) Do you think dieting is a bad idea? (yes, undecided, no)

   (2) Explain your answer to question 1.

   For each question above:

   a. State whether it is an open or closed question. (1 mark)

   b. State whether the question would produce quantitative or qualitative data. (1 mark)

   c. Give one limitation of the question. (2 marks)

   d. Suggest how you could improve the question in order to justify your criticism. (2 marks)

Suggested answers:

1a. Closed

1b. Quantitative data (if the categories were assigned a numerical value)

1c. The terms used are open to interpretation, e.g. 'diet' and 'bad idea' can mean different things to different people so that their responses cannot be compared. (It is also a leading question that may encourage social desirability bias.)

1d. Define terms, e.g. 'dieting' becomes 'dieting in order to lose weight'.

2a. Open

2b. Qualitative data

2c. The respondent has no idea what length or depth of answer is required. It would be better to provide the respondent with some guidance about what is appropriate.

2d. Limit the response, e.g. 'In 100 words or less, please explain your answer to question 1', or 'Starting with the most important, list your top three reasons for your answer to question 1.'

Correlations

Correlation is a data analysis method for measuring the association between two, continuous co-variables, e.g. age and beauty. Correlations might be: positive: as age increases so does beauty, negative: as age increases beauty decreases, zero: there is no relationship between age and beauty.

 Scattergrams and correlation coefficients

Pairs of co-variable values can be plotted on a **scattergram** to show the relationship between them. A **correlation coefficient** indicates the direction and strength of the relationship and ranges from +1.00 to −1.00.

 Evaluation

Limitations: Difference between correlations and experiments

In experiments variables are manipulated so that causal conclusions can be drawn. In a correlation the variables are simply measured, therefore no conclusion can be made about cause and effect.

Limitations: Misinterpretation and intervening variables

Correlations may result from other **intervening variables**. See 'Apply it' below for an example.

 Strengths

Strengths: A means to an experimental end

Correlation can be used when experimental manipulation is unethical or impractical.

Strengths: A replicable, quantitative method

Correlational studies can be replicated so can be quantified and checked for reliability using statistical procedures.

KEY TERMS

Correlation
- The extent of an association between two variables (**co-variables**). They may not be linked at all (**zero correlation**), they may both increase together (**positive correlation**), or as one co-variable increases, the other decreases (**negative correlation**).

Correlation coefficient
- A number between −1 and +1 that tells us how closely the co-variables in a correlational analysis are associated.

Intervening variable
- A variable that comes between two other variables and can explain the association between them, e.g. a positive correlation between ice cream sales and violence may be explained by temperature, which causes increases in both.

Scattergram
- A graphical representation of the association (i.e. the correlation) between two sets of scores.

Apply it

Giuseppe Gelato always liked statistics at school and now that he has his own ice cream business he uses statistics to explain his ice cream sales. He found a correlation between his ice cream sales and aggressive crimes. Ice cream appears to cause people to behave more aggressively. The table below shows his data.

All data rounded to 1000s	Jan	Feb	Mar	Apr	May	Jun	Jul	Aug	Sep	Oct	Nov	Dec
Ice cream sales	10	8	7	21	32	56	130	141	84	32	11	6
Aggressive crimes	21	32	29	35	44	55	111	129	99	36	22	25

a. Sketch a scattergram of Giuseppe's data. Make sure to label the axes and have a title for the scattergram. (3 marks)
b. What can you conclude from the data and the scattergram? (2 marks)
c. What intervening variable might better explain the relationship between ice cream and aggression? (1 mark)
d. Describe how you would design a study to show Giuseppe that ice cream does (or does not) cause aggressive behaviour. (You need to operationalise your variables, decide on a suitable research design and sampling method, etc.) (4 marks)

Suggested answers

a.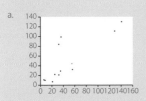

b. There is a positive relationship between ice cream sales and aggressive crimes.

c. The co-variables of ice cream sales and aggressive crimes may both be related to the intervening variable of temperature.

d. Recruit a random sample of similar adults and allocate them at random into two independent groups. Set up a laboratory-based test in which participants have the opportunity to give electric shocks (DV) to another person (a confederate of the experimenter). Give each member of the experimental group a controlled amount of ice cream (IV) to eat. Members of the control group receive no ice cream. Record the maximum severity of shock that each participant gives the confederate. Compare the two samples of scores to see whether, compared to controls, participants who have consumed ice-cream give higher intensity shocks.

KEY TERMS

Case study
- A detailed study of a single individual, institution or event. Case studies provide rich data but are hard to generalise from.

Content analysis
- A kind of observational study in which behaviour is observed indirectly in written or verbal material such as interviews, conversations, books, diaries or TV programmes.

Effect size
- A measure of the strength of the relationship between two variables.

Meta-analysis
- A researcher combines findings from similar studies and produces a statistic to represent the overall effect.

Review
- Combination of a number of studies into the same topic in order to reach a general conclusion about a particular phenomenon.

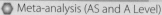

Other research methods

◯ Meta-analysis (AS and A Level)

Systematic review

Findings from carefully selected studies are collated and summarised to give an overview of knowledge in a particular area. An example is de Maat *et al.*'s **review** of psychotherapy studies.

Meta-analysis

In some reviews **meta-analysis** of quantitative data is used. An **effect size** statistic is the dependent variable and summarises overall trends, e.g. a meta-analysis of 53 studies of the cognitive interview (CI) technique (Köhnken *et al.*, 1999).

● Case study (A Level only)

A **case study** is a detailed study of a single individual, institution or event. An example is the case study of HM (page 26).

Content analysis (A Level only)

Content analysis is a form of indirect observation, in which the artefacts people produce, e.g. TV programmes, books, songs, paintings, are analysed.

◯ Evaluation of meta-analysis

Strengths: A greater sample size

Combining results from different studies increases sample size which can mean that findings can be generalised more widely.

Strengths: Clarification of the 'bigger picture'

Studies in a review may suggest contradictory results. Meta-analysis allows us to reach an overall conclusion by combining the different studies.

Limitations: A 'blunt instrument'?

Research designs in the studies selected may vary so they are not easily comparable. Combining them to calculate the effect size may obscure important differences thus meta-analytic conclusions are not always valid.

● Evaluation of a case study (A Level only)

Strengths: Depth of analysis

Case study data usually have a richness and depth that is not easily achieved using other methods.

Strengths: Good for studying rare cases

Case study is useful for investigating rare instances of events, e.g. brain damage. It would not be ethical to generate such conditions experimentally.

Strengths: Depth of analysis

The complex interaction of many factors can be studied, in contrast with experiments where many variables are controlled.

Limitations: Problems with establishing causality

Case studies are essentially observational so cause and effect is not easy to establish. There is often no control against which to make comparisons.

Limitations: Retrospective data

Case studies also often involve potentially unreliable recollection of past events.

● Evaluation of content analysis (A Level only)

Strengths: High ecological validity

Content analysis has high ecological validity because it is based on tangible evidence, such as recent newspapers.

Strengths: Reliability checking

When sources are in archival form, analysis can be replicated, giving us more confidence in the findings.

Limitations: Observer bias

Observer bias reduces the objectivity and validity of findings because different observers may interpret the data differently.

🐾 Apply it

1. Researchers reviewed studies on the effectiveness of antidepressants and found a difference depending on the severity of the depression. The effect size was 5% for mild depression, 12% for moderate depression and 16% for severe depression.

   What would you conclude from these findings? (2 marks)

2. Researchers wanted to investigate stereotypes presented in children's books (age stereotypes, gender stereotypes, etc.).

   How might you ensure that two researchers were using the behavioural categories in the same way? (2 marks)

Suggested answers:

1. The effect size increases with the severity of depression, suggesting that the more severe the depression, the more effective antidepressants are.

2. You would compare the two researchers' analyses to determine whether they were closely matched.

Mathematical skills
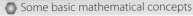 Some basic mathematical concepts

Fractions

A fraction is a part of a whole number such as ½ or ¾, e.g. if there were 120 participants in a study and 40 of them were in condition A, to calculate a fraction we divide 40 by 120 = 40/120 and simplify our fraction to 1/3.

Percentages

The word 'percent' means 'out of 100' (cent means 100). Therefore 5% essentially means 5 out of 100 or 5/100. 5/100 as a decimal = 0.05 because the first decimal place is out of 10 and the second is out of 100.

To change a fraction to a percentage, divide the numerator (the one on top) by the denominator (the one on the bottom), e.g. 19/36 = 0.5277777778. To make this into a percentage, multiply by 100 (move the decimal point two places to the right) to get 52.77777778%

Ratios

A ratio states how much there is of one thing compared to another thing.

Part-to-part ratios are used in betting. Odds are given as 4 to 1 (4:1) meaning that out of a total of 5 events you would be expected to lose four times and win once.

A part-to-whole ratio would be expressed as 4:5 meaning four losses out of five occurrences, and can easily be changed to a fraction, 4:5 is 4/5.

Ratios can be reduced to a lowest form in the same way that fractions are, so 10:15 would be 2:3 (both parts of the fraction have been divided by 5).

Estimate results

Estimates of result are useful because they can help you detect a mistake in more precise calculations.

The fraction 19/36 is fairly close to 18/36 which is the same as half (50%), therefore the estimate should be slightly more than half.

Example with big numbers: estimate the product of 185,363 times 46,208. Round up 173,362 to 200,000 and 46,000 to 50,000, then multiply 5 × 2 and add nine zeros – 10,000,000,000. The actual answer is smaller because both numbers were rounded up. It is 8,565,253,504.

Significant figures

In the example above it would look simpler to state the estimated answer at about eight billion (8,000,000,000). This answer is given to 1 significant figure.

However, rounding up is important. In the example, 8,565,253,504 should be rounded up to 9 billion (1 significant figure). Two significant figures would be 8,600,000,000.

The percentage 52.77777778% to two significant figures would be 53% (removing all but two figures and rounding up because the third figure is more than 5). This number to three significant figures would be 52.8%. If the number was 52.034267% then three significant figures would be 52.0%.

Order of magnitude

When dealing with very large numbers it is sometimes clearer to just give two significant figures and then say how many zeros there are. The convention for doing this for 8,600,000,000 is 8.6×10^9 where 9 represents how many places we have moved the decimal point. To convert 0.0045, write 4.5×10^{-3}.

Mathematical symbols

Mathematical symbols that you need to be able to use are in the table below.

= and ~	< and <<	> and >>	≤	∝
Equal and approximately equal	Less than and much less than	More than and much more than	Less than or equal to	Proportional to

Apply it

1. Represent 3/8 as a percentage. Give your answer to two significant figures. (2 marks)
2. A researcher wants to divide 4,426 by 42. Estimate what the result would be, explaining how you arrived at your answer. (2 marks)
3. Express 0.02 as a fraction. (1 mark)
4. Explain what the following expression means 'the number of girls < number of boys'. (1 mark)

Suggested answers:

1. 38% (3/8 = 0.375. then 0.375 × 100 rounded up)
2. 4000/40 = 100. Both figures have been rounded down before dividing.
3. 2/100 = 1/50
4. The number of girls is less than the number of boys.

KEY TERMS

Mean
- The arithmetic average of a data set. Takes the exact values of all the data into account.

Measures of central tendency
- Descriptive statistics that provide information about a 'typical' value for a data set.

Measures of dispersion
- Descriptive statistics that provide information about how spread out a set of data are.

Median
- The middle value of a data set when the items are placed in rank order.

Mode
- The most frequently occurring value or item in a data set.

Range
- The difference between the highest and lowest item in a data set. Usually 1 is added as a correction.

Standard deviation
- Shows the amount of variation in a data set. It assesses the spread of data around the mean.

Apply it

1. Calculate the mean, the median and the mode for the following data set. (3 marks)

    2, 3, 5, 6, 6, 8, 9, 12, 15, 21, 22

2. For the data set above which of the three measures of central tendency would be most suitable and why? (2 marks)

3. For the data set in question 1 explain what measure of dispersion would be most appropriate and explain why. (2 marks)

4. Calculate the ranges of the following two data sets. (2 marks)

    Data set A: 2 2 3 4 5 9 11 14 18 20 21 22 25

    Data set B: 2 5 8 9 9 10 11 12 14 15 16 20 28

Answers:

1. Mean = 9.91, median = 8, mode = 6

2. Median because the mean is being inflated by a few high scores.

3. Range, because it reflects the wide spread of scores.

4. A. 24, B. 27.

Measures of central tendency and dispersion

Levels of measurement

Nominal – Data consisting of frequency counts in named categories, e.g. number of fans supporting different football teams.

Ordinal – Rankings or ratings on a (usually numerical) scale. Intervals between each scale point are not necessarily equal.

Interval – Data are measured using units with equal intervals, e.g. temperature scales. The scale does not have a true (absolute) zero.

Ratio – There are equal intervals and a true zero, e.g. most physical measures.

Measures of central tendency

Measures of central tendency provide a typical value for a data set.

Mean, median, mode

The (arithmetic) **mean** is the sum of all the scores divided by the number of scores. Can only be used with ratio and interval level data.

The **median** is the central value in a set of data arranged in order of magnitude. Can be used with ratio, interval and ordinal data.

The **mode** is the most common value. With nominal data it is the category with the highest frequency count. With ratio, interval and ordinal data it is the number that occurs most frequently.

Measures of dispersion

Range

The **range** is the arithmetic distance between the top and bottom values in a set of data after adding 1, e.g.

3, 5, 8, 8, 9, 10, 12, 12, 13, 15 mean = 9.5; range = 13 (15 − 3 + 1)

Standard deviation

A **standard deviation** is a measure of how much scores in a data set differ from the mean. The calculated standard deviation for the set of numbers above is 3.69.

Evaluation of measures of central tendency

The mean

+ Most sensitive measure because calculating it uses all values in a data set.

− Sensitivity means it can be distorted by one (or a few) extreme values and thus misrepresent the data set.

− Cannot be used with nominal data nor does it make sense to use it with discrete values, as in averaging the number of dogs' legs.

The median

+ Useful when there are extreme scores as it is not affected by them. Appropriate for ordinal data and is easy to calculate.

− Not as 'sensitive' as the mean which uses all values in a data set.

The mode

+ Unaffected by extreme values.

+ The only method that can be used when the data are nominal.

− Not a useful way of describing data when there are multiple modes.

Evaluation of measures of dispersion

Range

+ Easy to calculate.

− Sensitive to distortion by extreme values.

− Fails to take account of the distribution of data, e.g. whether most numbers are closely grouped around the mean or spread out evenly.

Standard deviation

+ Is a precise measure because its calculation includes all the entire data set.

− May conceal some of the characteristics of the data set (e.g. extreme values).

Display of quantitative data and data distributions

 Display of quantitative data

Tables

Raw data can be set out in a table and/or summarised using measures of central tendency and dispersion. Summary tables are more helpful for interpreting findings.

Bar chart

The height of each bar represents the frequency of each item. **Bar charts** are suitable for data that are not continuous, for example categorical or nominal data. A space is left between each bar to indicate the lack of continuity.

Histogram

A **histogram** is similar to a bar chart except that the area within the bars is proportional to the frequencies represented. The vertical axis (frequency) starts at zero. The horizontal axis must be continuous. Categorical data are not suitable. There should be no gaps between the bars.

Scattergram

A **scattergram** is a kind of graph used when doing a correlational analysis (see page 95).

 Data distributions

Normal distribution

In large data sets the overall pattern of the data is called a distribution. The **normal distribution** is a bell-shaped curve. Many human characteristics are normally distributed, such as shoe sizes or intelligence.

- The mean, median and mode are at the exact mid-point.
- The distribution is symmetrical around this mid-point.
- The dispersion of scores or measurements either side of the mid-point is consistent and can be expressed in **standard deviations** (SD).

In normally distributed data, 68.26% of scores are contained within one SD above and below the mean. A total of 95.44% of scores lie within two SDs above or below the mean, so 2.28% of scores lie beyond them in each of the left and right tails.

Skewed distribution

A **positive skewed distribution** has a few atypically high scores. The mean is higher than the median and mode.

A **negative skewed distribution** has a few atypically low scores. The mean is lower than the median and mode.

KEY TERMS

Bar chart
- A graph used to represent the frequency of data; the categories on the x-axis have no fixed order and there is no true zero.

Histogram
- Type of frequency distribution in which the number of scores in each category of continuous data are represented by vertical columns. There is a true zero and no spaces between the bars.

Negative skewed distribution
- Most of the scores are bunched towards the right. The mode is to the right of the mean because the mean is affected by the extreme scores tailing off to the left.

Normal distribution
- A symmetrical bell-shaped frequency distribution. This distribution occurs when certain variables are measured, such as IQ or the life of a light bulb. Such 'events' are distributed in such a way that most of the scores are clustered close to the mid-point; the mean, median and mode are at the midpoint.

Positive skewed distribution
- Most of the scores are bunched towards the left. The mode is to the left of the mean because the mean is affected by the extreme scores tailing off to the right.

Scattergram
- A graphical representation of the association (i.e. the correlation) between two sets of scores.

Skewed distribution
- A distribution is skewed if one tail is longer than the other, signifying that there are a number of extreme values to one side or the other of the mid-point.

Apply it

1. Explain why the mean is always lower than the mode in a negative skew. (2 marks)
2. What kind of skew would you get if a test had a ceiling effect? (1 mark)

Suggested answers:

1. Calculation of the mean involves using all the scores in a data set so it will be drawn down by the few atypically low scores in a negatively skewed distribution. The mode is unaffected by extreme scores.
2. A ceiling effect occurs if a test is too easy for participants and most of them obtain high marks, therefore the skew would be negative (with a few low scores).

KEY TERMS

Primary data
- Information observed or collected first-hand.

Qualitative data
- Information in words that cannot be counted or quantified. Qualitative data can be turned into quantitative data by placing them in categories and counting frequency.

Quantitative data
- Information that represents how much or how long, or how many, etc. there are of something, i.e. a behaviour is measured in numbers or quantities.

Secondary data
- Information used in a research study that was collected by someone else or for a purpose other than the current one. For example, published data or data collected in the past.

Types of data

⚫ Quantitative data

Quantitative data are numerical measures of the variable(s) of interest, e.g.
- The **dependent variable** in an **experiment**.
- Answers to **closed questions** in questionnaires, e.g. age, attitude ratings.
- A tally of **behavioural categories** in an **observational** study.

⚫ Qualitative data

Qualitative data tends to be descriptive using words, meanings, pictures and so on, e.g. interviews yield qualitative textual data. They can often be converted into quantitative data by creating categories and counting frequencies.

Quantitative data	Qualitative data
Deals with numbers and measurable data	Deals with descriptions
Psychologists develop measures of psychological variables	Data that is observed not measured
Looking at averages and differences between groups	Observing people through the messages they produce and the way they act
	Concerns, thoughts, feelings and emotions
A psychology class	
24 students	Very enthusiastic about psychology
18 girls, 6 boys	Mixture of boys and girls
72% gained Grade A on mock exam	Hardworking students
10 plan to study psychology at university	School located in an innercity area

Apply it

1. On this page qualitative and quantitative descriptions are given of a hypothetical psychology class. Produce a similar table for one of the following:
   a. A television series. (6 marks)
   b. The town or city you live in. (6 marks)
   c. A major world event such as the Olympic Games. (6 marks)

2. In each of the following examples identify whether primary data or secondary data would be involved, or both. Explain your answers (2 marks each):
   a. Zimbardo's study of social roles (page 16).
   b. Study of HM (page 26).
   c. Schaffer and Emerson's study of infants (page 36).

Suggested answers:
Answers to 1. are debatable.
2 a. Primary data: direct observations of participants.
   b. Both. Direct observations of HM and examination of medical records.
   c. Both. Infants and mothers were observed directly and mothers were asked to recall infants' behaviour.

Evaluation of quantitative and qualitative data

Quantitative data

+ Quantitative data can be analysed using **descriptive statistics** and **statistical tests**. Conclusions are clear and can be checked for reliability.

− May be oversimplified, e.g. reducing complex attitudes to numbers on scales and so lack validity.

Qualitative data

+ Constitute rich, detailed information that can provide unexpected insights into thoughts and behaviour.

− Complexity of the data makes it more difficult to agree on the analysis.

⬡ Primary and secondary data

Both **primary** and **secondary data** may be quantitative and/or qualitative.

Primary data

Data that is collected first-hand using pre-planned methods such as experimentation, observation and self-report techniques.

Secondary data

Secondary data is information that was collected for a purpose other than the researcher's current one, e.g. government statistics about mental health. Correlation, review and meta-analytic studies often involve secondary data.

⚫ Evaluation of primary and secondary data

Primary data

+ The researcher has control over the data. The data collection can be designed so it fits the aims and hypothesis of the study.

− Primary data collection can be lengthy and expensive compared to secondary data collection in which data already exist.

Secondary data

+ It is simpler, quicker and cheaper to access existing data.

+ Such data may have been subjected to statistical testing and thus it is known whether it is significant.

− The data may not exactly fit the researcher's needs and may have gaps or inconsistencies that cannot be remedied, both of which threaten its validity.

Introduction to statistical testing

 Descriptive statistics and statistical tests

Descriptive statistics are used to summarise samples of data. **Statistical tests**, sometimes called 'inferential statistics', are applied to samples of data in order to make inferences about the populations from which they are drawn.

Two samples of data collected in an experiment will differ. A test can be applied to determine whether this difference is large enough to achieve **significance**, in other words, be statistically meaningful. If it is, the hypothesis being tested is supported.

The hypothesis can be directional (state the direction of the difference) or non-directional (state there will be a difference but not give its direction). A **one-tailed test** is applied to a directional hypothesis and a **two-tailed test** is applied to a non-directional hypothesis.

The **calculated value** in a test is compared to a **critical value** in a table of critical values. The table also gives a **probability (p)** value which is often 0.05. A test significant at this level indicates that the probability that we are claiming to have found an effect when we do not have one is 0.05 or 5%.

 The sign test

The **sign test** is a simple statistical procedure that can tell us whether the difference between two samples of data is significant.

- When to use the test – the sign test is used with paired or related data.
- How to do the test – indicate the difference between each pair of data with plus or minus, calculated value of S = total number of the least frequent sign.
- Look up critical value of S – need to know N and whether one-tailed test (directional hypothesis) or two-tailed test (non-directional hypothesis).
- Conclusion – if calculated value is less than or equal to critical value, the difference is significant.
- Probability level of 0.05 (5%) is commonly used.

KEY TERMS

Calculated value
- The value of a **test statistic** calculated for a particular data set.

Critical value
- In an inferential test the value of the test statistic that must be reached to show significance.

One-tailed test
- Form of test used with a directional hypothesis.

Probability (p)
- A numerical measure of the likelihood or chance that certain events will occur.

Sign test
- A statistical (inferential) test to determine the significance of a sample of related items of data.

Significance
- A statistical term indicating that the research findings are sufficiently strong to enable a researcher to reject the *null hypothesis* under test.

Statistical tests
- Procedures for drawing logical conclusions (inferences) about the population from which samples are drawn.

Test statistic
- A statistical test is used to calculate a numerical value. For each test this value has a specific name such as S for the sign test.

Two-tailed test
- Form of test used with a non-directional hypothesis.

Apply it

1. Do people's happiness scores improve after they go on holiday? To compare happiness ratings before and after a holiday, the sign test has been partially calculated in the following table.
   a. Use the table of critical values of S to decide whether there is a significant effect. (The hypothesis is directional.) (2 marks)
   b. What can be concluded about the effect of holidays on happiness ratings? (2 marks)

▼ *Table of results*

Participant	Happiness score before	Happiness score after	Difference (after-before)	Sign
1	6	7	1	+
2	3	4	1	+
3	4	6	2	+
4	8	6	−2	−
5	7	5	2	+
6	5	7	−2	−
7	7	5	2	+
8	5	8	3	+
9	4	7	3	+
10	8	5	−3	−
11	4	4	0	
12	8	9	1	+
13	6	7	1	+
14	5	6	1	+

▼ *Table of critical values*

Level of significance for a one-tailed test	0.05
Level of significance for a two-tailed test	0.10
N	
13	3

Answer:

a. $S = 3$. The critical value for $N = 13$ at $p = .05$ for a one-tailed test = 3. S must be equal to or less than this value for the test to be significant.

b. The test calculations show that there are more positive than negative changes in scores so holidays significantly improve happiness.

KEY TERMS

Peer review

- The practice of using independent experts to assess the quality and validity of scientific research and academic reports.

Apply it

1. A psychologist wishes to publish his research in a mainstream psychology journal.

   a. Explain why it is desirable for this research study to be peer reviewed before publication. (4 marks)

   b. The research paper is rejected for publication. Suggest **two** reasons why it may have been rejected. (4 marks)

Suggested answer:

a. Peer review is a form of quality control for research which should ensure that only well-designed, well-conducted, well-reported and worthwhile studies are made public. It helps to ensure that flawed or fraudulent research, with possibly damaging practical applications, does not proceed. Research that passes peer review may lead to more funding for the organisation concerned and raise its research status relative to similar organisations.

b. The paper may be rejected because the design of the study is not good enough to convincingly test the research question. This would mean that any findings obtained would be invalid and of no practical value. The paper may also have been rejected because it is not in line with already published research. Publishers may therefore be unwilling to publish it because it challenges the status quo and is therefore unlikely to b well-received.

Peer review in the scientific process

Peer review

Peer review (also called 'refereeing') is the assessment of scientific work by others who are experts in the same field (i.e. 'peers'). It is an essential part of the scientific process of building knowledge. Research plans and reports are shared openly amongst scientist so that their scientific quality can be judged. It is in everyone's interests that flawed or fraudulent research is avoided.

Usually there are a number of reviewers for each application/article/assessment. Their task is to report on the quality of the research and then their views are considered by a peer review panel.

The Parliamentary Office of Science and Technology (2002) suggests that peer review serves three main purposes:

1. **Allocation of research funding** Research is paid for by various government and charitable bodies. They require reviews to enable them to decide which research is likely to be worth funding.

2. **Publication of research in academic journals and books** via the peer review quality filter.

3. **Assessing the research rating of university departments** Future funding for university research departments depends on receiving good ratings from peer reviews.

Peer review and the Internet

The sheer volume and pace of information available on the Internet means that new solutions are needed in order to maintain the quality of information. Several online journals ask readers to rate articles. For example, on *Philica*, papers are ranked on the basis of peer reviews that can be read by anyone. On the Internet, however, 'peer' is coming to mean 'everyone' – a more egalitarian system but possibly at the cost of quality.

Evaluation

Strengths: A method of quality control

Peer review should ensure the quality of research so that flawed or fraudulent studies do not find their way into the public domain or get put into practice.

Limitations: Limited expertise

It isn't always possible to find an appropriate expert to review a research proposal or report. Poor research may therefore be passed because the reviewer didn't really understand it (Smith, 1999).

Limitations: Anonymity

Anonymity is usually practised so that reviewers can be honest and objective. However, this is not always achievable, especially in highly specialised and recognisable research. Some journals now favour open reviewing (where both author and reviewer know each other's identity).

Limitations: Publication bias

Journals tend to prefer to publish positive results, possibly because editors want research that has important implications in order to increase the standing of their journal. This results in a bias in published research that in turn leads to a misperception of the true facts.

Limitations: Preserving the status quo

Peer review results in a preference for research that accords with existing theory rather than dissenting or unconventional work. Science is generally resistant to large shifts in opinion. Change takes a long time and requires a 'revolution' in the way people think. Peer review may be one of the elements that slow change down.

Limitations: Cannot deal with already published research

Once a research study has been published, the results remain in the public view even if they have subsequently been shown to be fraudulent or the result of poor research practices. Therefore peer review does not ensure that all data we are exposed to are valid.

Psychology and the economy

The mission statement for the British Psychological Society is to be 'responsible for the development, promotion and application of psychology for the public good'. This relates to the economy of the country we live in. The 'economy' concerns the production, distribution and consumption of goods and services.

Economic psychology

Economic psychology is a blend of economics and psychology – seeking a better understanding of people's behaviour in their economic lives. The field is also referred to as 'behavioural economics' in which researchers investigate the effects of social, cognitive and emotional factors on economic decisions, chiefly with regard to rational (or irrational) decisions relating to economics.

Applying topics from your course

There are many topics covered in this book that can be applied to improving the economy of our country and world.

Social change

Research into understanding social influence has been used to improve behaviour, e.g. on page 22 a campaign to reduce drink driving was discussed where attitudes and behaviour was changed by making people aware of social norms. Such practices have the potential to bring about positive changes that will impact on the economy, however this approach is limited to tasks where behaviour is moderated by social criteria.

Improving eyewitness memory

The cognitive interview (page 33) is a technique based on psychological research that has improved the amount of accurate information collected from eyewitnesses. In fact the whole topic of eyewitness memory research is focused on improving crime detection. The implication for the economy is to be able to reduce expenses on wrongful arrests and to ensure that criminals are caught.

Attachment

Bowlby's theory and related research (page 43) on attachment continues to influence policies aimed at ensuring the healthy development of children so that they become productive members of society, thus improving world economy.

Mental health

The McCrone report (McCrone et al., 2008) commented on the use of drugs versus psychotherapies, saying that ' the number of people receiving medication provides a much greater economic gain than psychological therapies, which may produce similar benefits compared to medication but are far more expensive'. Evidence-based research on effective drug therapies is important in reducing costs and helping people return to work.

Biopsychology

Neuroscience offers the possibility of revolutionising our understanding of the human brain. An American government report suggested that this may have practical economic benefits in the area of 'smart' machines, i.e. machines that will think like humans (NIH, 2013). This does not mean building human-like robots but just money-saving intelligent machines to deal with, for example, questions on the telephone or recognise faces at airports.

Apply it

In 2008 Thaler and Sunstein published a book called *Nudge: Improving decisions about health, wealth and happiness* based on the research by Kahneman and others stating that human thinking is not rational. They reasoned that a kind of 'soft paternalism' could be used to nudge people into making better decisions (for themselves and for society) without taking away their freedom of choice. For example, sweets and junk food might be placed on supermarket shelves above eye level.

Suggest an individual and societal cost and benefit of product placement designed to discourage people from eating junk food. (4 marks)

Suggested points:

At an individual level, people may spend less on 'sweet treats' and other junk foods, leaving them more to spend on healthier options. They may consequently find it easier to control their weight and thus reduce their risk of tooth decay and obesity-related health problems such as hypertension and type II diabetes. At a societal level, the cost to the NHS in the UK of treating these increasingly widespread problems should decrease. The savings made could reduce the overall cost to the country of the health service or allow for more investment into prevention and treatment of other conditions, such as Alzheimer's Disease, which is currently on the increase.

Glossary

ABC model A cognitive approach to understanding mental disorder, focusing on the effect of irrational beliefs on emotions. Page 52

agentic state A person sees himself or herself as an agent for carrying out another person's wishes. Page 18

aim A statement of what the researcher(s) intend to find out in a research study. Page 81

anxiety An unpleasant emotional state that is often accompanied by increased heart rate and rapid breathing, i.e. physiological arousal. Page 32

attachment is an emotional bond between two people. It is a two-way process that endures over time. It leads to certain behaviours such as clinging and proximity-seeking, and serves the function of protecting an infant. Page 35

authoritarian personality A distinct personality pattern characterised by strict adherence to conventional values and a belief in absolute obedience or submission to authority. Page 19

autonomic nervous system (ANS) Governs the brain's involuntary activities (e.g. stress, heartbeat) and is self-regulating (i.e. autonomous). It is divided into the sympathetic branch (fight or flight) and the parasympathetic branch (rest and digest). Page 66

bar chart A graph used to represent the frequency of data; the categories on the x-axis have no fixed order and there is no true zero. Page 99

behavioural categories Dividing a target behaviour (such as stress or aggression) into a subset of specific and operationalised behaviours. Page 92

behaviourist People who believe that human behaviour can be explained in terms of conditioning, without the need to consider thoughts or feelings. Page 50

bias A systematic distortion. Page 88

biological approach Views humans as biological organisms and so provides biological explanations for all aspects of psychological functioning. Page 61

brain The part of the central nervous system that is responsible for coordinating sensation, intellectual and nervous activity. Page 66

brain plasticity The brain's ability to modify its own structure and function as a result of experience: developing new connections and discarding weaker ones. Page 73

Broca's area An area in the frontal lobe of the brain, usually in the left hemisphere, related to speech production. Page 70

calculated value The value of a test statistic calculated for a particular data set. Page 101

capacity This is a measure of how much can be held in memory. It is represented in terms of bits of information, such as number of digits. Page 24

caregiver Any person who is providing care for a child, such as a parent, grandparent, sibling, other family member, childminder and so on. Page 35

case study A research investigation that involves a detailed study of a single individual, institution or event. Case studies provide a rich record of human experience but are hard to generalise from. Page 96

central executive Monitors and coordinates all other mental functions in working memory. Page 27

central nervous system (CNS) Comprises the brain and spinal cord. It receives information from the senses and controls the body's responses. Page 66

circadian rhythm A pattern of behaviour that occurs or recurs approximately every 24 hours, and which is set and reset by environmental light levels. Page 75

classical conditioning Learning through association. A neutral stimulus is consistently paired with an unconditioned stimulus so that it eventually takes on the properties of this stimulus and is able to produce a conditioned response. Pages 39, 50, 58

coding (also 'encoding') The way information is changed so that it can be stored in memory. Information enters the brain via the senses (e.g. eyes and ears). It is then stored in various forms, such as visual codes (like a picture), acoustic codes (sounds) or semantic codes (the meaning of the experience). Page 24

cognitive Relates to mental processes such as perception, memory and reasoning. Page 60

cognitive-behaviour therapy (CBT) A combination of cognitive therapy (a way of changing maladaptive thoughts and beliefs) and behavioural therapy (a way of changing behaviour in response to these thoughts and beliefs). Page 53

cognitive interview A police technique for interviewing witnesses to a crime, which encourages them to recreate the original context of the crime in order to increase the accessibility of stored information. Because our memory is made up of a network of associations rather than of discrete events, memories are accessed using multiple retrieval strategies. Pages 33

cognitive neuroscience An area of psychology dedicated to the underlying neural bases of cognitive functions. Page 60

commitment The degree to which members of a minority are dedicated to a particular cause or activity. The greater the perceived commitment, the greater the influence. Page 21

compliance Occurs when an individual accepts influence because they hope to achieve a favourable reaction from those around them. An attitude or behaviour is adopted not because of its content, but because of the rewards or approval associated with its adoption. Page 14

computer model Refers to the process of using computer analogies as a representation of human cognition. Page 60

concordance rate A measure of genetic similarity. For example, if in 100 twin pairs, one twin of each pair has a phobic disorder and 40 of their co-twins also have that disorder, the concordance rate is 40%. Page 54

conditions of worth Conditions imposed on an individual's behaviour and development that are considered necessary to earn positive regard from significant others. Page 63

confederate An individual in a study who is not a real participant and has been instructed how to behave by the investigator. Page 83

conformity A form of social influence that results from exposure to the majority position and leads to compliance with that position. It is the tendency for people to adopt the behaviour, attitudes and values of other members of a reference group. Page 14

confounding variable A variable under study that is not the IV but which varies systematically with the IV. Changes in the dependent variable may be due to the confounding variable rather than the IV, and therefore the outcome is meaningless. To 'confound' means to cause confusion. Page 82

congruence If there is similarity between a person's ideal self and self-image, a state of congruence exists. A difference represents a state of incongruence. Page 63

consistency Minority influence is effective provided there is stability in the expressed position over time and agreement among different members of the minority. Page 21

contact comfort Physical contact with a caregiver that can provide physical and emotional comfort. For example, a crying baby held by its mother will calm down due to the feeling of safety physical contact provides. Page 38

content analysis A kind of observational study in which behaviour is observed indirectly in written or verbal material such as interviews, conversations, books, diaries or TV programmes. Page 96

continuity hypothesis The idea that emotionally secure infants go on to be emotionally secure, trusting and socially confident adults. Page 40

control Refers to the extent to which any variable is held constant or regulated by a researcher. Page 82

controlled observation A form of investigation in which behaviour is observed but under conditions where certain variables have been organised by the researcher. Page 91

correlation Determining the extent of an association between two variables; co-variables may not be linked at all (**zero correlation**), they may both increase together (**positive correlation**), or as one co-variable increases, the other decreases (**negative correlation**). Page 95

correlation coefficient A number between −1 and +1 that tells us how closely the co-variables in a correlational analysis are associated. Page 95

cost–benefit analysis A systematic approach to estimating the

negatives and positives of any research. Page 90

counterbalancing An experimental technique used to overcome order effects when using a repeated measures design. Counterbalancing ensures that each condition is tested first or second in equal amounts. Page 84

covert observations Observing people without their knowledge. Knowing that behaviour is being observed is likely to alter a participant's behaviour. Page 91

critical period A biologically determined period of time, during which certain characteristics can develop. Outside of this time window such development will not be possible. Pages 40

critical value In an inferential test the value of the test statistic that must be reached to show significance. Page 101

cues are things that serve as a reminder. They may meaningfully link to the material to be remembered or may not be meaningfully linked, such as environmental cues (a room) or cues related to your mental state (being sad or drunk). Page 30

cultural relativism The view that behaviour cannot be judged properly unless it is viewed in the context of the culture in which it originates. Page 47

cultural variations The ways that different groups of people vary in terms of their social practices, and the effects these practices have on development and behaviour. Page 42

debriefing A post-research interview designed to inform participants of the true nature of the study and to restore them to the state they were in at the start of the study. It may also be used to gain useful feedback about the procedures in the study. Debriefing is not an ethical issue; it is a means of dealing with ethical issues. Page 90

demand characteristics Cues that make participants unconsciously aware of the aims of a study or help participants work out what the researcher expects to find. They may become EVs or confounding variables. Page 87

dependent variable (DV) A measurable outcome of the action of the independent variable in an experiment. Page 81

depression A mood disorder where an individual feels sad and/or lacks

interest in their usual activities. Further characteristics include irrational negative thoughts, raised or lowered activity levels and difficulties with concentration, sleep and eating. Page 49

deprivation To be deprived is to lose something. In the context of child development deprivation refers to the loss of emotional care that is normally provided by a primary caregiver. Page 43

determinism Behaviour is determined by external or internal factors acting upon the individual. Page 64

deviation from ideal mental health Abnormality is defined in terms of mental *health*, behaviours that are associated with competence and happiness. Ideal mental health would include a positive attitude towards the self, resistance to stress and an accurate perception of reality. Page 48

deviation from social norms Abnormal behaviour is seen as a deviation from implicit rules about how one 'ought' to behave. Anything that violates these rules is considered abnormal. Page 47

directional hypothesis States the direction of the difference between two conditions. Page 83

dispositional Explanations of behaviours such as obedience emphasise them being caused by an individual's own personal characteristics rather than situational influences within the environment. Page 19

duration A measure of how long a memory lasts before it is no longer available. Page 24

effect size A measure of the strength of the relationship between two variables. Page 96

electroencephalogram (EEG) A method of recording changes in the electrical activity of the brain using electrodes attached to the scalp. Page 74

empiricism The belief that all knowledge is derived from sensory experience. It is generally characterised by the use of the scientific method in psychology. Page 57

endocrine system A network of glands throughout the body that manufacture and secrete chemical messengers known as hormones. Page 68

endogenous pacemakers Mechanisms within the body that govern the internal, biological bodily rhythms. Page 78

episodic buffer Receives input from many sources, temporarily stores this information, and then integrates it in order to construct a mental episode of what is being experienced. Working memory model An explanation of short-term memory, called 'working memory'. Based on four qualitatively different components, some with storage capacity. Page 27

episodic memory Personal memories of events, such as what you did yesterday or a teacher you liked. This kind of memory includes contextual details plus emotional tone. Page 28

ethical guidelines (code of conduct) A set of principles designed to help professionals behave honestly and with integrity. Page 90

ethical issues Questions of right and wrong. They arise in research where there are conflicting sets of values between researchers and participants concerning the goals, procedures or outcomes of a research study. Page 90

ethics committee A group of people within a research institution that must approve a study before it begins. Page 90

event sampling An observational technique in which a count is kept of the number of times a certain behaviour (event) occurs. Page 92

event-related potential (ERP) A technique that takes raw EEG data and uses it to investigate cognitive processing of a specific event. It achieves this by taking multiple readings and averaging them in order to filter out all brain activity that is not related to the appearance of the stimulus. Page 74

evolution Refers to the change over successive generations of the genetic make-up of a particular population. The central proposition of an evolutionary perspective is that the genotype of a population is changeable rather than fixed, and that this change is likely to be caused by the process of natural selection. Page 61

exogenous zeitgeber Environmental cue, such as light, that helps to regulate the biological clock in an organism. Page 78

experiment A research method where causal conclusions can be drawn because an independent variable has been deliberately manipulated to observe the causal effect on the dependent variable. Page 81

experimental design A set of procedures used to control the influence of factors such as participant variables in an experiment. Page 84

external validity The degree to which a research finding can be generalised: to other settings (ecological validity); to other groups of people (population validity); over time (historical validity). Page 82

externality Individuals who tend to believe that their behaviour and experience is caused by events outside their control. Page 20

extraneous variable (EV) In an experiment, any variable other than the independent variable that might potentially affect the dependent variable and thereby obscure the results. Page 81

eyewitness testimony The evidence provided in court by a person who witnessed a crime, with a view to identifying the perpetrator of the crime. Page 31

F scale Also known as the 'California F scale' or the 'Fascism scale', the F scale was developed in California in 1947 as a measure of authoritarian traits or tendencies. Page 19

failure to function adequately People are judged on their ability to go about daily life. If they can't do this and are also experiencing distress (or others are distressed by their behaviour) then it is considered a sign of abnormality. Page 48

field experiment An experiment conducted on the participant's 'home ground' and in which the IV is controlled by the experimenter. Page 85

fight-or-flight response A sequence of activity within the body that is triggered when the body prepares itself for defending or attacking (fight) or running away to safety (flight). This activity involves changes in the nervous system and the secretion of hormones that are necessary to sustain arousal. Page 69

flexibility A willingness to be flexible and to compromise when expressing a position. Page 21

flooding A form of behavioural therapy used to treat phobias and other anxiety disorders. A client is exposed to (or imagines) an extreme form of the threatening situation under relaxed conditions until the anxiety reaction is extinguished. Page 51

free will The ability to act at one's own discretion, i.e. to choose how to behave without being influenced by external forces. Page 63

functional magnetic resonance imaging (fMRI) A technique for measuring brain activity. It works by detecting changes in blood oxygenation and flow that indicate increased neural activity. Page 74

functional recovery Refers to the recovery of abilities and mental processes that have been compromised as a result of brain injury or disease. Page 73

GABA (gamma-aminobutyric acid) A neurotransmitter that regulates excitement in the nervous system, thus acting as a natural form of anxiety reducer. Page 55

gene A part of the chromosome of an organism that carries information in the form of DNA. Page 54

generalisation Applying the findings of a particular study to the population. Page 88

genotype The genetic make-up of an individual. The genotype is a collection of inherited genetic material that is passed from generation to generation. Page 61

hemispheric lateralisation Refers to the fact that some mental processes in the brain are mainly specialised to either the left or right hemisphere. For example, the left hemisphere is dominant for language and speech. Page 71

hierarchy of needs The motivational theory proposed by Abraham Maslow, often displayed as a pyramid. The most basic needs are at the bottom and higher needs at the top. Page 63

histogram Type of frequency distribution in which the number of scores in each category of continuous data are represented by vertical columns. There is a true zero and no spaces between the bars. Page 99

hormones The body's chemical messengers. They travel through the bloodstream, influencing many different processes including mood, the stress response and bonding between mother and newborn baby. Page 68

humanistic Refers to the belief that human beings are born with the desire to grow, create and love, and have the power to direct their own lives. Page 63

hypothesis A precise and testable statement about the assumed relationship between variables. Operationalisation is a key part of making the statement testable. Page 81

identification The extent to which an individual relates to a model or a group of people and feels that they are similar to them. Identification means that the individual is more likely to imitate the model's or the group's behaviour. Page 59

imitation The action of using someone or something as a model and copying their behaviour. Page 59

imprinting An innate readiness to develop a strong bond with the mother which takes place during a specific time in development, probably the first few hours after birth/hatching. If it doesn't happen at this time it probably will not happen. Page 38

independent groups design Participants are allocated to two (or more) groups representing different levels of the IV. Allocation is usually done using random techniques. Page 84

independent variable (IV) Some event that is directly manipulated by an experimenter in order to test its effect on another variable – the **dependent variable (DV)**. Page 81

informational social influence A form of influence, which is the result of a desire to be right – looking to others as a way of gaining evidence about reality. Page 14

infradian rhythms Rhythms that have a duration of over 24 hours, and may be weekly, monthly or even annually. Page 76

insecure-avoidant A type of attachment which describes those children who tend to *avoid* social interaction and intimacy with others. Page 41

insecure-resistant A type of attachment which describes those infants who both seek and reject intimacy and social interaction, i.e. resist. Page 41

Institutionalisation The effect of institutional care. The term can be applied widely to the effects of an institution but our concern focuses specifically on how time spent in an institution such as an orphanage can affect the development of children. The possible effects include social, mental and physical underdevelopment. Some of these effects may be irreversible. Page 44

inter-observer reliability The extent to which there is agreement between two or more observers involved in observations of a behaviour. Page 91

interactional synchrony When two people interact they tend to mirror what the other is doing in terms of their facial and body movements. This includes imitating emotions as well as behaviours. This is described as a synchrony – when two (or more) things move in the same pattern. Page 35

internal validity The degree to which an observed effect was due to the experimental manipulation rather than other factors such as confounding/extraneous variables. Page 82

internal working model A mental model of the world which enables individuals to predict and control their environment. In the case of attachment the model relates to a person's expectations about relationships. Pages 40, 45

Internalisation Occurs when an individual accepts influence because the content of the attitude or behaviour proposed is consistent with their own value system. Page 14

internality Individuals who tend to believe that they are responsible for their behaviour and experience rather than external forces. Page 20

intervening variable A variable that comes between two other variables, which is used to explain the association between those two variables. For example, if a positive correlation is found between ice cream sales and violence this may be explained by an intervening variable – heat – which causes the increase in ice cream sales and the increase in violence. Page 95

interview A research method or technique that involves a face-to-face, 'real-time' interaction with another individual and results in the collection of data. Page 93

interviewer bias The effect of an interviewer's expectations, communicated unconsciously, on a respondent's behaviour. Page 93

introspection The process by which a person gains knowledge about his or her own mental and emotional states as a result of the examination or observation of their conscious thoughts and feelings. Page 57

investigator effect (sometimes referred to as investigator or experimenter bias). Anything that an investigator does that has an effect on a participant's performance in a study other than what was intended. This includes direct effects (as a consequence of the investigator interacting with the participant) and indirect effects (as a consequence of the investigator designing the study). Investigator effects may act as confounding or extraneous variables. Page 87

laboratory experiment An experiment carried out in a controlled setting and in which the experimenter controls the IV. Page 85

leading question A question that, either by its form or content, suggests to the witness what answer is desired or leads him or her to the desired answer. Page 31

learning theory A group of explanations (classical and operant conditioning), which explain behaviour in terms of learning rather than any inborn tendencies or higher order thinking. Page 39

legitimate authority A person who is perceived to be in a position of social control within a situation. Page 18

localisation of function Refers to the belief that specific areas of the brain are associated with specific cognitive processes. Page 70

locus of control People differ in their beliefs about whether the outcomes of their actions are dependent on what they do (internal locus of control) or on events outside their personal control (external locus of control). Page 20

long-term memory (LTM) Memory for events that have happened in the past. This lasts anywhere from 2 minutes to 100 years. LTM has potentially unlimited duration and capacity and tends to be coded semantically. Page 24

matched pairs design Pairs of participants are matched in terms of key variables such as age and IQ. One member of each pair is allocated to one of the conditions under test and the second person is allocated to the other condition. Page 84

mean The arithmetic average of a data set. Takes the exact values of all the data into account. Page 98

measure of central tendency A descriptive statistic that provides information about a 'typical' value for a data set. Page 98

measure of dispersion A descriptive statistic that provides information about how spread out a set of data are. Page 98

median The middle value of a data set when the items are placed in rank order. Page 98

meta-analysis A researcher looks at the findings from a number of different studies and produces a statistic to represent the overall effect. Page 96

107

minority influence A form of social influence where members of the majority group change their beliefs or behaviours as a result of their exposure to a persuasive minority. Page 21

misleading information Supplying information that may lead a witness' memory for a crime to be altered. Page 31

mode The most frequently occurring value or item in a data set. Page 98

modelling A form of learning where individuals learn a particular behaviour by observing another individual performing that behaviour. Page 59

monotropy (monotropic) The idea that the one relationship that the infant has with his/her primary attachment figure is of special significance in emotional development. Page 40

motor cortex A region of the brain responsible for the generation of voluntary motor movements. Page 70

motor neurons Form synapses with muscles and control their contractions. Page 67

multi-store model An explanation of memory based on three separate memory stores, and how information is transferred between these stores. Page 26

natural experiment A research method in which change in the IV and its effects on a DV occur fortuitously. In a true experiment, the IV can be manipulated and random allocation of participants to conditions by the experimenter occurs but, as this is not possible here, causal conclusions must be tentative. Page 86

naturalistic observation An observation carried out in an everyday setting, in which the investigator does not interfere in any way but merely observes the behaviour(s) in question. Page 91

nature Behaviour is seen to be a product of innate (biological or genetic) factors. Page 64

negative correlation Describes a correlation where, as one co-variable increases, the other decreases. Page 95

negative skewed distribution Most of the scores are bunched towards the right. The mode is to the right of the mean because the mean is affected by the extreme scores tailing off to the left. Page 99

negative triad A cognitive approach to understanding depression, focusing on how negative expectations (schema) about the self, world and future lead to depression. Page 52

neurochemistry The study of chemical and neural processes associated with the nervous system. Page 61

neurotransmitter Chemical substances that play an important part in the workings of the nervous system by transmitting nerve impulses across a synapse. Pages 54, 67

non-directional hypothesis States that there is a difference between two conditions without stating the direction of the difference. Page 83

non-participant observation The observer is separate from the people being observed. Page 91

normal distribution A symmetrical bell-shaped frequency distribution. This distribution occurs when certain variables are measured, such as IQ or the life of a light bulb. Such 'events' are distributed in such a way that most of the scores are clustered close to the mid-point; the mean, median and mode are at the mid-point. Page 99

normative social influence A form of influence whereby an individual conforms with the expectations of the majority in order to gain approval or to avoid social disapproval. Page 14

nurture Behaviour is a product of environmental influences. Page 64

obedience to authority Obedience refers to a type of social influence whereby somebody acts in response to a direct order from a figure with perceived authority. There is also the implication that the person receiving the order is made to respond in a way that they would not otherwise have done without the order. Page 17

observer bias Observers' expectations affect what they see or hear. This reduces the validity of the observations. Page 91

obsessive compulsive disorder (OCD) An anxiety disorder where anxiety arises from both obsessions (persistent thoughts) and compulsions (behaviours that are repeated over and over again). Compulsions are a response to obsessions and the person believes the compulsions will reduce anxiety. Page 49

one-tailed test Form of test used with a directional hypothesis. Page 10

operant conditioning Learning through reinforcement or punishment. If a behaviour is followed by a desirable consequence then that behaviour is more likely to occur again in the future. Pages 39, 50, 58

operationalise Ensuring that variables are in a form that can be easily tested. A concept such as 'educational attainment' needs to be specified more clearly if we are going to investigate it. For example it might be operationalised as 'GCSE grade in Maths'. Page 81

opportunity sample A sample of participants produced by selecting people who are most easily available at the time of the study. Page 88

order effect In a repeated measures design, an extraneous variable arising from the order in which conditions are presented, e.g. a practice effect or fatigue effect. Page 84

overt observation Observational studies where participants are aware that their behaviour is being studied. Page 91

participant observation Observations made by someone who is also participating in the activity being observed, which may affect their objectivity. Page 91

peer review The practice of using independent experts to assess the quality and validity of scientific research and academic reports. Page 102

peripheral nervous system The part of the nervous system that is outside the brain and spinal cord. Page 66

phenotype The observable characteristics of an individual. This is a consequence of the interaction of the genotype with the environment. Page 61

phobias A group of mental disorders characterised by high levels of anxiety in response to a particular stimulus or group of stimuli. The anxiety interferes with normal living. Page 49

phonological loop Codes speech sounds in working memory, typically involving maintenance rehearsal (repeating the words over and over again). This is why this component of working memory is referred to as a 'loop'. Page 27

pilot study A small-scale trial run of a study to test any aspects of the design, with a view to making improvements. Page 83

pituitary gland The 'master gland', whose primary function is to influence the release of hormones from other glands. Page 68

population The group of people that has the characteristics the researcher is interested in and from which a sample is drawn. The group of people about whom generalisations can be made. Page 88

positive correlation Refers to the instance, in a correlation, of covariables both increasing together. Page 95

positive skewed distribution Most of the scores are bunched towards the left. The mode is to the left of the mean because the mean is affected by the extreme scores tailing off to the right. Page 99

post-event discussion A conversation between co-witnesses or an interviewer and an eyewitness after a crime has taken place which may contaminate a witness' memory for the event. Page 31

post-mortem examinations Ways of examining the brains of people who have shown particular psychological abnormalities prior to their death in an attempt to establish the possible neurobiological cause for this behaviour. Page 74

presumptive consent A method of dealing with lack of informed consent or deception, by asking a group of people who are similar to the participants whether they would agree to take part in a study. If this group of people consents to the procedures in the proposed study, it is presumed that the real participants would also have agreed. Page 90

primary data Information observed or collected directly from first-hand experience. Page 100

priming Automatic enhanced recognition of specific stimuli, e.g. exposure to word 'yellow' makes it more likely a person would say 'banana' when asked to name a fruit Page 28.

proactive interference (PI) Past learning interferes with current attempts to learn something. Page 29

probability (p) A numerical measure of the likelihood or chance that certain events will occur. Page 101

procedural memory Memory for how to do things, for example riding a bicycle or learning how to read. Such memories are automatic as the result of repeated practice. Page 28

psychodynamic Refers to any theory that emphasises change and development in the individual, particularly those theories where 'drive' is a central concept in

development. The best known psychodynamic theory is Freudian psychoanalysis. Page 62

qualitative data Information in words that cannot be counted or quantified. Qualitative data can be turned into quantitative data by placing them in categories and counting frequency. Pages 94, 100

quantitative data Information that represents how much or how long, or how many, etc. there are of something, i.e. a behaviour is measured in numbers or quantities. Pages 94, 100

quasi-experiments Studies that are 'almost' experiments. They are similar to natural experiments but can be pre-planned. Lack of manipulation of the IV and of random allocation means that causal conclusions can only tentatively be drawn. Page 86

questionnaire Data are collected through the use of written questions. Page 93

random allocation Allocating participants to experimental groups or conditions using random techniques. Page 84

random sample A sample of participants produced by using a random technique such that every member of the target population being tested has an equal chance of being selected. Page 88

range The difference between the highest and lowest item in a data set. Usually 1 is added as a correction. Page 98

reciprocity Responding to the action of another with a similar action, where the actions of one partner elicit a response from the other partner. The responses are not necessarily similar as in interactional synchrony. Page 35

reinforcement A term used in psychology to refer to anything that strengthens a response and increases the likelihood that it will occur again in the future. Page 58

relay neurons The most common type of neuron in the CNS. They allow sensory and motor neurons to communicate with each other. Page 67

repeated measures design Each participant takes part in every condition under test, i.e. each level of the IV. Page 84

retrieval failure occurs due to the absence of cues. An explanation for forgetting based on the idea that the issue relates to being able to retrieve a memory that is there (available) but not accessible.

Retrieval depends on using cues. Page 30

retroactive interference (RI) Current attempts to learn something interfere with past learning. Page 29

review A consideration of a number of studies that have investigated the same topic in order to reach a general conclusion about a particular hypothesis. Page 96

right-wing authoritarianism A cluster of personality variables (conventionalism, authority submission and authoritarian aggression) that are associated with a 'right-wing' attitude to life. Page 19

sampling The selection of participants from the target population intended to produce a representative group from that population. Page 88

scattergram A graphical representation of the association (i.e. the correlation) between two sets of scores. Page 95

schema A cognitive framework that helps organise and interpret information in the brain. A schema helps an individual to make sense of new information. Pages 52, 60

science A systematic approach to creating knowledge. The method used to gain scientific knowledge is referred to as the scientific method. Page 64

scientific method The use of investigative methods that are objective, systematic and replicable, and the formulation, testing and modification of hypotheses based on these methods. Page 57

secondary data Information used in a research study that was collected by someone else or for a purpose other than the current one. For example published data or data collected, in the past. Page 100

secure attachment This is a strong and contented attachment of an infant to their caregiver, which develops as a result of sensitive responding by the caregiver to the infant's needs. Securely attached infants are comfortable with social interaction and intimacy. Secure attachment is related to healthy subsequent cognitive and emotional development. Page 41

self Our sense of personal identity, used synonymously with the terms 'self-image' and 'self-concept'. Page 63

self-actualisation A term used in different ways. Rogers used it as the drive to realise one's true potential. Maslow used it to describe the final stage of his hierarchy of needs. Page 63

semantic memory Shared memories for facts and knowledge. These memories may be concrete, such as knowing that ice is made of water, or abstract, such as mathematical knowledge. Page 28

sensory neurons Carry nerve impulses from sensory receptors to the spinal cord and the brain. Page 67

sensory register This is the information at the senses – information collected by your eyes, ears, nose, fingers and so on. Information is retained for a very brief period by the sensory registers. We are only able to hold accurate images of sensory information momentarily (less than half a second). The capacity of sensory memory is very large, such as all the cells on the retina of the eye. The method of coding depends on the sense organ involved, e.g. visual for the eyes or acoustic for the ears. Page 26

short-term memory (STM) Your memory for immediate events. STMs are measured in seconds and minutes rather than hours and days, i.e. a short duration. They disappear unless they are rehearsed. STM also has a limited capacity of about four items or chunks and tends to be coded acoustically. This type of memory is sometimes referred to as working memory. Page 24

sign test A statistical (inferential) test to determine the significance of a sample of related items of data. Page 101

significance A statistical term indicating that the research findings are sufficiently strong to enable a researcher to reject the null hypothesis under test. Page 101

skewed distribution A distribution is skewed if one tail is longer than the other, signifying that there are a number of extreme values to one side or the other of the mid-point. Page 99

sleep–wake cycle Alternating states of sleep and waking that are dependent on the 24-hour circadian cycle. Page 75

social change This occurs when a society or section of society adopts a new belief or way of behaving which then becomes widely accepted as the norm. Page 22

social desirability bias A distortion in the way people answer questions – they tend to answer questions in such a way that presents themselves in a better light. Page 93

social norms interventions These attempt to correct misperceptions of the normative behaviour of peers in an attempt to change the risky behaviour of a target population. Page 22

social releaser A social behaviour or characteristic that elicits caregiving and leads to attachment. Page 40

social roles are the behaviours expected of an individual who occupies a given social position or status, conformity to. Page 16

social support The perception that an individual has assistance available from other people, and that they are part of a supportive network, and resistance to social influence. Page 20

somatic nervous system The part of the peripheral nervous system responsible for carrying sensory and motor information to and from the central nervous system. Page 66

somatosensory cortex A region of the brain that processes input from sensory receptors in the body that are sensitive to touch. Page 70

spinal cord A bundle of nerve fibres enclosed within the spinal column and which connects nearly all parts of the body with the brain. Page 66

split-brain research Research that studies individuals who have been subjected to the surgical separation of the two hemispheres of the brain as a result of severing the corpus callosum. Page 71

standard deviation Shows the amount of variation in a data set. It assesses the spread of data around the mean. Page 98

standardised procedures A set of procedures that are the same for all participants in order to be able to repeat the study. This includes standardised instructions – the instructions given to participants to tell them how to perform the task. Page 81

statistical infrequency Abnormality is defined as those behaviours that are extremely rare, i.e. any behaviour that is found in very few people is regarded as abnormal. Page 47

statistical tests Procedures for drawing logical conclusions (inferences) about the population from which samples are drawn. Page 101

Strange Situation A controlled observation designed to test attachment security. Page 41

stranger anxiety The distress shown by an infant when approached or held by someone who is unfamiliar. Page 36

stratified sample A sample of participants produced by identifying subgroups according to their frequency in the population. Participants are then selected randomly from the subgroups. Page 88

structured interview Any interview in which the questions are decided in advance. Page 93

structured observation A researcher uses various systems to organise observations, such as behavioural categories and sampling procedures. Page 92

synapse The conjunction of the end of the axon of one neuron and the dendrite or cell body of another. Page 67

synaptic transmission The process by which a nerve impulse passes across the synaptic cleft from one neuron (the presynaptic neuron) to another (the postsynaptic neuron). Page 67

systematic desensitisation A form of behavioural therapy used to treat phobias and other anxiety disorders. A client is gradually exposed to (or imagines) the threatening situation under relaxed conditions until the anxiety reaction is extinguished. Page 51

systematic sample A sample obtained by selecting every nth person (where n is any number). This can be a random sample if the first person is selected using a random method; you then select every nth person after that. Page 88

test statistic A statistical test is used to calculate a numerical value. For each test this value has a specific name such as S for the sign test. Page 101

time sampling An observational technique in which the observer records behaviours in a given time frame, e.g. noting what a target individual is doing every 15 seconds or 20 seconds or 1 minute. The observer may select one or more behavioural categories to tick at this time interval. Page 92

two-process model A theory that explains the two processes that lead to the development of phobias – they begin through classical conditioning and are maintained through operant conditioning. Page 50

two-tailed test Form of test used with a non-directional hypothesis. Page 101

ultradian rhythms Cycles that last less than 24 hours, such as the cycle of sleep stages that occur throughout the night. Page 75

unstructured interview The interview starts out with some general aims and possibly some questions, and lets the interviewee's answers guide subsequent questions. Page 93

validity Refers to whether an observed effect is a genuine one. Page 82

vicarious reinforcement Learning that is not a result of direct reinforcement of behaviour, but through observing someone else being reinforced for that behaviour. Page 59

visuo-spatial sketchpad Codes visual information in terms of separate objects as well as the arrangement of these objects in one's visual field. Page 27

volunteer sample A sample of participants that relies solely on volunteers to make up the sample. Also called a self-selected sample. Page 88

weapon focus The anxiety experienced when the presence of a weapon distracts attention from other features of the event. This reduces the accuracy of identification of the perpetrator. Page 32

Wernicke's area An area in the temporal lobe of the brain important in the comprehension of language. Page 70

working memory model An explanation of the memory used when working on a task. Each store is qualitatively different. Page 27

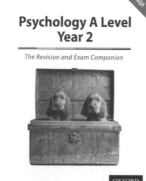